JOHN BIRMINGHAM tells stories for a living. For doing so he has been paid by the *Sydney Morning Herald*, the *Age*, the *Australian*, *Penthouse*, *Playboy*, *Rolling Stone*, *HQ*, *Inside Sport* and the *Independent Monthly*. He has also been published, but not paid, by the *Long Bay Prison News*. Some of his stories have won prizes including the George Munster prize for Freelance Story of the Year and the Carlton United Sports Writing Prize. John's earlier works are *He Died with a Felafel in His Hand* (now a feature film starring Noah Taylor), *The Tasmanian Babes Fiasco*, *How to be a Man*, *The Search for Savage Henry*, *Leviathan*, and the second *Quarterly Essay*, 'Appeasing Jakarta'. He lives at the beach with his wife, baby daughter and two cats. He is not looking for any more flatmates.

Off One's Tits ILL-CONSIDERED

RANTS AND RAVES FROM A GRACELESS

OAF NAMED John Birmingham

VINTAGE

A Vintage Book
Published by
Random House Australia Pty Ltd
20 Alfred Street, Milsons Point, NSW 2061
http://www.randomhouse.com.au

Sydney   New York   Toronto
London   Auckland   Johannesburg

First published in Australia by Vintage in 2002

National Library of Australia
Cataloguing-in-Publication Entry

Birmingham, John, 1964–.
Off one's tits.

ISBN 1 74051 128 X.

1. Political corruption – Australia. 2. Australia – Social life and customs.
3. Australia – Social conditions. I. Title.

919.4

Cover photograph by Geoff Lung
Cover and internal design by Gayna Murphy, Greendot Design
Typeset in Garamond by Midland Typesetters, Maryborough, Victoria
Printed and bound by Griffin Press, Netley, South Australia

10 9 8 7 6 5 4 3 2 1

For Brian Toohey.
Who gave me a hundred bucks
and a lot of ideas above my station.

And for Ipswich.
Nobody ever escapes their home town.

CONTENTS

Beer

White wine spritzer

Tequila slammer

Two-fisted whiskey

Jolt Cola

Bong water

Beer

'PILES OF WARM CRUSTY BREAD ROLLS ARRIVED BUT THE ONE OR TWO EAGER JUVENILES WHO REACHED FOR THEM WERE QUICKLY SMACKED BACK INTO LINE. A BIG TRAP FOR YOUNG PLAYERS. SAVE SPACE FOR THE MEAT.'

PIG NIGHT OUT

It is a truth universally acknowledged that a pack of hefty blokes in possession of a good appetite must be in want of a pork fest. Unconscionably protracted in the planning, painfully abridged in the execution, our night of the suckling pig drew together such a team of these greedy yahoos that its like will ne'er be seen again.

The Night of the Pig was a mission from God, should she exist. A magnificent obsession. Out there with mad Cap'n Ahab's hunt for the great white whale or the Man of La Mancha's crazed charges against enemy windmills.

And Don Quixote de la Mancha is no gratuitous classical reference cast like a cultured pearl before you beery swine. Well, actually, it is. But it segues really nicely into a consideration of Don Quixote's House of the Suckling Pig, the centre of the pork-loving universe. Familiar to generations of Sydney movie-goers through its cheap, scratchy, Whitlam-era cinema ads, The Don caught my eye when some pompous twit of a food critic swanned through to nickle and dime the joint to death. As if I give a fuck about the lack of radicchio and tiramisu—whatever the hell they are. For me, the kicker from that review was the clear impression that these guys could supply you with more pork than you could possibly eat.

Oh baby, I salivated quietly, racking gut cramps here I come.

My original plan called for twelve good men and true to repair to the The Don's place to stuff themselves insensible on hot, salty pork while drinking so much Mexican beer that someone would accidentally get a tattoo and join the merchant navy. And with but one exception every red-blooded son of Anzac I approached felt as I did, to the universal horror of their girlfriends and heart surgeons, whose eyes bulged at the thought of them gorging on pork until they could gorge no more. Their neediness was even a little scary. One, a lawyer for a multinational arms conglomerate, suggested hiring a private room where we could eat naked whilst dusky serving wenches scurried hither and yon with tape measures to track the expansion of our waistlines: first to enlarge himself by 20 per cent to win. As word spread through the city hopeful pig brothers appeared from all corners wanting a piece of the action. One even flew up from Melbourne, avowing that he wouldn't be happy until his fingertips turned grey from restricted blood circulation due to the massive quantities of hog fat congealing in his bloodstream. Sadly we were to be undone by our own appetites.

Meeting in the Century Tavern above Hungry Jack's on George Street, we discovered that despite brave words to the contrary the women in our lives had not organised some counter pig night (or Teste-Fest '98 as one dubbed it). A picnic at Shakespeare in the Park had been mooted at one point. Or a Jane Austen video binge. But despite the tantalising prospect of organising five or six bloke-free hours together at that stupid, interminable *Cloud Street* play, nothing transpired. After copious hits off the Tooheys Old taps we all agreed this had something to do with girls not being good at sums.

While these weighty deliberations took place, yon editor and photographer inspected the facilities. A couple of thin tweedy-looking college boys—looked like a good fuck and some pork crackling might be the end of them—they were escorted through the voluminous kitchens by Manuel, who's been with the restaurant for about three hundred years. They were introduced to our own specially selected porker, procured from a secret alpine breeding station, the source of The Don's succulent white meat for three decades. All around them other little piggies lay happily marinating in their trays or slowly roasting in the ovens, a process which can take up to six hours. Manuel became very excited by the prospect of another magazine review. His only other brush with fame was a cover story in something like *Pig Breeders Monthly* a long time ago. The details are a little hazy due to many schooners of Tooheys Old warring with the San Miguels I switched to on arrival; the chewy overbite of a cold San Mig being the only possible consort to such a repast.

With the team finally in place at the bar, our sixteen big men blocked all access to and from the body of the restaurant, drawing worried glances from the wait staff and other diners. The Don's place presented a little like the flagship outlet of an upmarket 'Alamo-theme' restaurant chain; lots of weathered oak and brick and, in the bar, what looked like a couple of wooden cannon bookends untainted by the merest hint of irony. It was the perfect site for an all male meat fest, but I gotta say we didn't understand all the couples who kept arriving for what were obviously to be romantic dinners. The presence of those few Asian tourists still standing after the regional financial meltdown had sent their tinpot economies back to wholesaling sacks of guano and betel nuts was understandable. They were here by mistake. But surely the locals should know better. Maybe it had something to do with excellent dating facilities; specifically, The Don's dance floor on which riotously tipsy thick-waisted hipsters punished the macarena while Zorro's great-grandson tickled the synth with all the dexterity which his famous forebear deployed in carving his mark into the chests of California's avaricious landowners.

Waiters who hovered with offers of garlic prawns were dismissed to the kitchens with stern orders to start bringing the carcasses and to keep bringing them until our corrupt and bloated bodies lay groaning on the floor, covered in a thick greasy sheen of glistening lard and faintly creaking as the monstrous volume of meat pressed against straining ribs and taut belly skin.

I don't think they knew what they were dealing with.

Piles of warm crusty bread rolls arrived but the one or two eager juveniles who reached for them were quickly smacked back into line. A big trap for young players. Save space for the meat. The first pig which arrived was laid on the table and I do not exaggerate when I say that its bones had been sucked clean before the somewhat superfluous vegetables arrived two minutes later. It was around about this point that Manuel, who had previously been the very picture of a genial host, became worried. 'More pig! More pig!' we cried. More plates arrived and were cleaned off with ferociously efficient despatch. 'Ha ha,' laughed Manuel nervously. 'We normally get romantic couple in here. They don't eat so much.'

'More pig! More pig!' we cried.

The waiters eyed each other anxiously and began to back away from the table. The horrible truth began to dawn on me. A special alpine breeding station. Six-hour cooking time. A restaurant full of diners all tucking into their meals while we denuded the bar. They were short of pig. Or, more likely, they had enough pig for a normal night but this was most assuredly not a normal night.

'All joking aside Manuel,' muttered Robbie, 'where's the rest of the pig, man?'

They were sweating by now. We suggested they might care to scrape the plates of the other diners whose eyes had proven too big for their bellies. I don't know whether they did this but we were about to do it ourselves when a few more plates turned up. And let me just say that this was magnificent pig. The best any of us had ever tasted. So keen was Adam Spencer for a few more scraps of its golden goodness that he and Barnes picked clean the skull of the first beast Manuel had laid before us. Eyeballs and all.

But there just wasn't enough, dammit!

As we spilled out onto George Street a raucous argument broke out over whether we should head back to the Century to drown our sorrows and fill the empty spaces in our pig-loving hearts with Tooheys Old. Or whether we should go to Hungry Jack's first.

I think you all know which option we chose.

BACHELORHOOD

There was a time when, like all men, I dreamed James Bond dreams of bachelorhood. Dreams of black dinner jackets and dry martinis; of high-rise apartments with sunken lounge pits and Olympic-sized hot tubs in which frolicked an endless parade of giddy blonde soap actresses. A designer vision of lone wolf nirvana.

The wolf's den sat in the centre of this vision. The perfect batch pad of the imagination, a lotus trap for the hundreds of doe-eyed bimbos who would find the lure of its lava lamps and deep shag pile carpets completely irresistible. I imagined wining and dining them out on the terrazzo. Dizzying them with my masterful command of half a dozen regional cooking styles. Plying them with obscure little numbers from my collection of vintage champagnes. Wondering how long it would take to get them out of that low-cut Versace cocktail dress and into my evil clutches.

And all in heroic defiance of the fact that for most

blokes being a bachelor means sitting at home alone, watching *Star Trek* reruns and late night infomercials as a big dollop of chilli con carne and sour cream lands on your unwashed Homer Simpson tee shirt. You scoop it up with a spoon, look at the stain and wonder, 'Hmmm, how long is that gonna take to wear out?'

Sadly, young men—i.e. the only men possessed of the physical stamina needed to really do the bachelor life justice—are generally always short of both the cash and, more importantly, the social graces needed to bring off the act with any style. I am reminded of a guileless young country lad who, having unexpectedly tumbled some daughter of the landed gentry into his bedroll, was taken aback to discover she had morphed into a sexually carnivorous hellcat demanding he 'talk dirty' to her. Thirty seconds of hot, still embarrassed silence ensued before he could bring himself to cough, 'Uh . . . price of greasy wool was really shit this year.'

Is it any wonder that the average bachelor tends to spend a lot more time with other bachelors than with women? In other words, with his natural competitors rather than his natural prey. Because, while prey they may be, prats they are not. Like twitchy gazelles sniffing the danger wafting from a pack of mangy, pot-bellied old cougars, smart women approach the bachelor's lair with ears pricked, nostrils flared and getaway routes planned well in advance. This wariness is even more pronounced when advancing on a group of males sharing the same house, cave or hollowed-out tree stump. Not counting our mothers, the last bachelor house I shared in, we had only three women visit in eighteen months. And perhaps put off by the half-chewed Big Mac steadfastly refusing to decompose atop the TV set throughout those eighteen months, none ever made a return visit.

Some men, sensing the ineffectiveness of traditional bachelor role models, attempted to subvert the paradigm. Hence, throughout the eighties and early nineties we were subjected to snags. Not the delicious crumbed variety available from any butcher at about two dollars a kilo. The other sort. The ones we don't like to talk about anymore because it's a bit embarrassing for all concerned. The sensitive, lumpy jumper-loving back rub specialists, who turned away from their brothers, moved out on their own and started inviting the womenfolk around for home-cooked dinners, only to present them with an earthen mug of hideous, non-alcoholic beetroot wine and couple of home-baked roughage muffins, with no sugar or chocolate or anything, only love to hold together a handful of rolled oats and shrubbery. No, we won't talk about them.

Well, maybe a bit. Because for all of their smiley-faced vacuousness the snags got one thing right. Lone wolves have to operate on their own. When I realised this I moved out of the beer boy party house scene and made for the beach. Checked out the seaside villages up and down the east coast. Figured I might settle into one as a sort of lone wolf writer in residence. My house would be on a headland with a wooden deck out the front and a white beach curving into the sea mist like a scimitar lying in the morning sun. I'd be up early, running along the beach and returning to a breakfast of fruit salad and black coffee, prepared by Miko, my enigmatic and beautiful Japanese house maid. There would be rumours about us in town. I'd probably hit the typewriter at eleven o'clock. You would hear my old black Underwood start up like sporadic gunfire in a bad neighbourhood. Later I'd walk comfortably through the town's covert but vigorous Latin quarter where the night roared to tequila-fuelled bar fights, vendettas and card games, where handcarts, stray dogs and snake sellers wound their way through Russian transvestites, Mexican sailors and drunken two-fisted warrior poets on the lookout for cheap whores and broken hearts. I would have the rich, heady hash cake of bachelorhood and I would eat it too.

Sadly, things didn't turn out that way. For starters Nambucca Heads had no Latin quarter at all. And then the bloody TV networks just had to run all three *Star Trek* series on separate nights. And some evil bastard set up a delivery service which brought both beer and pizza right to your banana lounge. And the laundromat was just a bit too far away to get my Homer Simpson tee shirt washed every month. And . . . well, you can guess the rest.

No martinis. No soap stars. No hot tubs or dinner jackets.

But at least I hear that next month the pizza place is offering two supremes for the price of one. Maybe I could get a few mates over.

PADDO THE BRAVE

This is how men give birth. They roar like bears. They think with their blood. Muscles bunched, eyes rolling, lips drawn back from canine fangs, they rear up and smash their knobbled bloody heads together. Bones crunch on bones. Flesh bruises, muscles tear and steam rises from their backs. They run in packs. They snarl. They pile one atop the other in cold, sucking cauldrons of mud. Beads of blood fall through the creeping dark to lay upon the grass like poison dewdrops. Rivulets of warm snot pour from the nose unheeded as they snorkel great draughts of frigid air into the lungs. They gasp. They pant. They charge into the breach once more. And what do they receive in return for their pains, but yet more pain to fill the empty spaces in their hearts.

Before all this, before the pain, there was an absence in a traveller's heart. Danny Maher, his name was, and for three years he wandered over most of Europe and the Middle East, then back to England, and across the grey

Atlantic to America. It's not unusual, during such a long haul, to hunger for familiar cuisine, to miss the sounds of home, or the company of old friends. However, as Danny Maher dragged his backpack around the northern hemisphere he felt the lack of all these things, but perhaps most of all—and don't laugh now—Danny Maher missed rugby bloody union. He missed it so much that within days of landing in Sydney he was nursing a melancholy beer in Kitty O'Shea's on Oxford Street, wishing he'd made it all the way back to his home town of Canberra where he could easily whip up a crowd of old mates for a trundle around the paddock.

Aiding and abetting these late night meditations in a fug of beer breath and cigarette smoke were the hulking brothers Cahill; Paul and DJ Cay-hill that is. Prop and halfback to Maher's fullback. Their giant meaty soldiers' paws turned schooners into middies while Maher's smaller fingers remembered the deep crenelated feel of the stitching seam along a fifteen-ounce leather ball. The reek of smoke and sweat seeped deeper into their clothes as another working week annihilated itself in the roaring maw of Friday night. Watching them from across the bar you may not have seen a group of men struggling with their creative mission. Chances are, I guess, you'd have glanced over and seen nothing more than a bunch of pisspots up way past their bedtime. But you'd have been wrong.

These big, coarse, Army guys and their friend, a much more refined-looking computer guy, were laying plans which would change the lives of other Army guys and computer guys . . . generally for the better. As the greasy plastic bank notes in their wallets steadily vanished into the till behind the bar and frightening quantities of beer came back in exchange, they meandered from maudlin talk of how good it would be to have a run with the lads back in Canberra to increasingly excited talk of how great it would be to establish their own team, here, in Sydney, where they could play competition football every weekend. DJ knew plenty of guys up at Victoria Barracks who'd be keen as, he reckoned. And he figured, sure, the Army would let them use the Barracks' historic field as a home ground. After all, the Army just loved to see a lot of big, boofy blokes running around kicking seven kinds of hell out of each other. It was like their *raison d'être*.

Naturally enough, nothing came of all this. Not at first anyway. At first, this team was just a twitch of drunken longing in an Irish pub. It was a scattered tribe of men, many of whom didn't even know each other yet, and some of whom had never held a football in their lives. It was a vague sense of dissatisfaction with a roll of fat around the gut of an infotech consultant in Burwood. It was a chance move to the big smoke by a young man who feared he was not that young anymore. It was an Army captain with a second love—a love almost as strong, he'll tell you carefully, as that which he has for his wife. A love which keeps him scratching around in his spare time, looking for fifteen men to put onto a field, and losing sleep about not being able to. This team was promises, broken and fulfilled. It was a first chance and a last. And it was nearly stillborn.

There were supposed to be forty of them on that first day at the University of Western Sydney. The day before the game at UWS-Nepean this had ebbed away to eighteen. And then there were ten. When an amateur rugby team takes the field at least fifteen men are supposed to run out together. But because it is a violent game which often inspires violent passions, the fifteen who run on are generally not the same fifteen who drag their sorry, beat-up carcasses off the field eighty minutes later. More men wait in the wings to replace the fallen. In theory anyway. On Saturday April 11 that comfortable assumption ran headfirst into the uncomfortable realities of launching a new team from the dubious base of beery, late night enthusiasm.

A few days after another drinking session, where they decided they really would put a team together, four of the would-be pioneers, including Maher and the future club captain Andy Muscat, had fronted up at the ARU Death Star and assured the Union that they could put forty, hard-charging sons of Anzac onto the field. No problemo. (And how many did you actually have? I asked Maher later. More like the four sitting in front of them, he grinned somewhat ruefully.) They were holding a lot of promissory notes which never paid off. Fellas who said they had six mates, ten mates, whatever. All dying for a game. Fellas who'd been dead set legends when they played schoolboy rugby for Australia, mate.

'We went recruiting every Friday night,' said Maher. 'We see some guy in the pub, he looks like a prop, so we'd front him. We'd front complete strangers. The bouncer from the Coogee Bay Hotel, this huge dreadlocked gridiron player from the US. He ran on for one game, but he couldn't afford to get injured so he didn't come back. There were six English guys drinking with a friend at a pub. I dragged every single one of them down to the game. They'd never played before but jeez we needed them.'

Drinking with his girlfriend, John Dillon, the team's talented lock-cum-breakaway-cum-second rower, discovered a Croatian builder who must have stood ten, maybe eleven foot in his socks and tried desperately to lure him into the front row. A couple of Army guys pursued a work mate, Larry Moon, who, like Godot and Mr Snuffle-upagus, was always rumoured to be coming along any moment now. Moon had never even seen a game of rugby, and when he appeared in the dressing room in the sixth week of the season and his new team mates asked him where he wanted to play he turned his trusting, bovine eyes up to them and answered simply, 'Goalkeeper'. Not every press-ganging effort went so badly astray. Three weeks into the season Allen Smyth, a blocky-looking Dubliner, checking out a rugby international on the teev with a big crowd at Bridie O'Reilly's, found himself nailed at the bar by a couple of gimlet-eyed fanatics who said they knew he'd played before, they were trying to get a team together and they were desperately short of players. How about it? Inside his dark, well-cut suit Smyth was a believer. He had played schoolboy and club rugby in Ireland and had been threatening for years to go back to the game. The sedentary, long lunch lifestyle of an IT consultant was thickening his waist and dulling his spirit and he found the lure of an easy run with a 'sixth grade sub-district' club completely irresistible. It was, he thought, the lowest form of organised rugby you could play.

It was a pity that Paddington took three weeks to stumble across Smyth bending his elbow in the faux Gaelic surrounds of Bridie O'Reilly's. They could have used him on April 11, although playing that Saturday with a full, well-drilled squad would have been a hell of a thing anyway. The temperature climbed above thirty hours before kick-off. The ground was a barren, hard-baked slab of misery out in the deepest western reaches of the city; so hard, in fact, that you couldn't get your studs into the ground. There was no water, no showers, no facilities, nothing. The field was perfectly mown but dead. There were splinters instead of grass and everybody spent Monday morning picking slivers of wood out of them-selves. Compounding the frightful playing conditions and Paddington's lack of manpower was the shocking state of those few who actually had put in an appearance.

Unfortunately the Union had scheduled the team's first match for the morning after DJ Cahill's bucks party; a non-negotiable binge-a-rama of savage intensity. Six of the ten Paddington players were suffering a karmic backlash of Pol Pot proportions from that ghastly episode. At noon, brother Paul, who had slipped the keys into his own front door after sunrise that morning, swung around to raise DJ and an unsuspecting, itinerant relative called Brendan from their filthy bedclothes. They motored down the Hume Highway, vomiting and dry-retching from the windows, stopping only to buy mouth guards, which

Brendan called 'gum shields', and to place within their possession two longnecks of VB, without which their Irish
cousin refused to continue. They dry-heaved crossing the
road into the ground, walking onto the ground, and eventually all over the ground.

Captain Andy Muscat was still vomiting prodigiously at
one o'clock, two hours before kick-off. Biting down on the
rising bile and nausea he drove through the pain to find
dozens of opposing players jogging up and down the field
in bright, clean jumpers, looking very well-drilled, very
efficient and not at all as sick as scabrous dogs. His own
players you could have counted on a butcher's left hand.
Was Larry the goalkeeper coming? he asked. Nope. Well,
has everyone here played before? Nuh. Hmmm, could we
have been any less prepared if we'd tried? Probably not.

Danny Maher shuttled between his nine sore and sorry-
looking charges, the referee who didn't want to let them
play and the Union poobah who had driven all the way out
to this shit hole just to see how this new team would
perform. After fifteen long minutes when it became
obvious that Paddo's full complement of players was already
there, sitting around with their heads in their hands, Maher
conceded they'd have to forfeit if the ref wouldn't let them
onto the ground. The ref, to his surprise, said okay. Maher
thought, great! Then, Oh God! As he realised what he was
asking of his new team mates. 'I turned around, sure they'd
say no, and asked you want to play with ten? Everyone
looked at each other, said yeah, and jumped to their feet.'

John Dillon thinks he may have been the only one
without a ruinous hangover, having missed the bucks night.

He could only stare incredulously as the rough-headed clutch of men gathered in a circle, a very small circle, for Captain Muscat's prematch speech. Muscat, still green in the gills, said, Look this doesn't bother me at all, I've played in plenty of games with less than ten players. So let's get out there and do our best. Dillon sort of looked at him and thought, Well I don't know where you've played mate . . .

They played five in the forwards, five in the backs, and DJ barrelled over the students' line for a try within the first three minutes. The boys couldn't believe it, and with good reason. That was the last game this season they saw the far side of anyone's try line. UWS had just under thirty players but they were all young and soft and they played an ill-advised, profitless style of football. The vomiting, knot-gutted monsters from Paddo played as tight as they could, given the circumstances, kept the ball locked up in the forwards at the centre of the field and ran the blindside as a matter of faith. And although there were theoretically ten of them lurching around the raw scar tissue of that oval, their effective strength was often below that as one player or another was taken down by cramp or the dry heaves or the blind, unbending forces of natural attrition. Leaning in to a scrum feed one Cahill brother was poleaxed by the other. He was playing loose head prop, says DJ, massaging his jaw. The two halves of the scrum had met, and just as I bent down to feed he reached across with his open arm to grab the other prop and smashed me clean across the jaw. My own brother, my own team mate.

Paul smiles. Even if I'd seen you there, I woulda done it anyway.

Danny Maher was decapitated by a wild tackle he doesn't remember to this day. He was concussed, knocked blind and shortly thereafter he zoned in on a winger who was making a break wide. Maher had him covered for about twenty metres but his radar was shot and like a malfunctioning Sidewinder he just careened on into the crowd and the bushes behind them, a crazy guy, drenched in his own blood, running full tilt the wrong way because he forgot not to. At the end of the game he had no grass stains on him at all, just a painful mass of cuts, scrapes and livid bruises as though he'd played on bitumen not greensward. He had no skin on his knees, no skin on his forearms, his head was split open and leaking its own bright juices like an overripe rockmelon. Like his team mates, he was bristling with splinters. Yes, all things considered, this was much better than travelling through Europe.

The students threw a barbecue for them after the match. Snags and free beers on the road by the oval because they had no club house and the University enforced an eccentric rule that you couldn't sell beer on campus but you could give it away by the tanker load. The students had won but Paddo were probably the happier team. They had led through most of the game, ten seedy old bastards against thirty young braves. Exhaustion and the press of numbers eroded their defences in the dying stanzas of the match, allowing the youngsters to steal three late tries. But Damian 'DJ' Cahill remembers being well pleased with their efforts and thinking that, gee these boys weren't very good, and if this was the standard of the comp they were going to have a very good season. Didn't turn out that way though.

The very next week Paddington had their clock cleaned by premiers, Liverpool: a rampaging barbarian horde from the outer wastelands; enormous beer bellies, really worrying haircuts, and giant hamhock fists which they swung with gay abandon and a sort of bloodthirsty mirth. (I fret sometimes that these are the people John Howard is referring to when he starts bleating about Mainstream Australia.) 64-nil our lads went down. The first of a long series of hammerings, mostly around the fifty zip mark, but once climbing to 91-nil against a tight, well-drilled pack of Maoris on the Manly Peninsula. Eight, nine, ten weeks rolled by without one Paddington player setting foot on the right side of the goal line. Their scrums fell like wheat before the threshing machines. Their leaky defence ruptured and let through torrents of try-scorers. Injury lists grew; broken collar bones, twisted knees, torn hamstrings, ripped cartilage and crushed fingers. Danny Maher himself was forced to hobble out with the water most weekends after ripping his groin from its moorings in that very first match at UWS.

Much of this was to be expected, of course. A new team, under-strength, formed from a grab bag of no-talent strangers and drunken Irish relatives can't expect too much. What wasn't expected, though, was the curious way that Paddington grew stronger with each horrible drubbing. It's not reflected in the team's score sheets. They're pretty much uniformly dreadful. But something happened the second time they played Liverpool. They were thrashed by exactly the same margin as in their first match: 64-nil. But where they had simply curled up and died under the onslaught in April, they were cheered from the bleak and muddy field by the same ugly brutes in June.

'It was a game we went into with some apprehension,' nodded Allen Smyth under the arched walkways at Victoria Barracks. He was dressed in a business suit for the team's Wednesday night training run. Having damaged his wrist, he'd found himself unable to stay away and so turned up anyhow, just to watch. 'They gave us a hiding at the start of the season,' he said. 'But the apprehension went in the first few minutes. We had to get stuck in or we were going to be on the wrong end of seventy, eighty points again. And I think for the first time this season the team played together, cohesively, with a bit of aggression and pride that'd been sadly lacking.'

They played short-handed again, cut down to thirteen men by injury in the first few minutes. But where Liverpool had swarmed all over them in their first encounter, this time the premiers spent long periods trapped in their own half. They went scoreless for nearly half an hour during one passage of play. Their heavier, more experienced pack butted itself uselessly against the heads of Paddington's stand-in front row. And most of their second-half points came against the run of play, off charge-downs and an intercept. Although their victory roar was just as loud, they must have known that this time they benefited more from luck than superior firepower and skill.

'There comes a point,' said Smyth, 'if you think a team's going to put thirty, forty points on you that you drop your head and wonder what the hell am I doing here, this happens every week. But it just didn't happen that way. We said, no more. They're not that good. We've got some talent. We've got a good side. Let's go at them. A couple of key players got fired up. They fired up the guy beside them. It's amazing how quickly a team gets engulfed.'

When that happens even the dim prospect of victory in the future seems enough compensation for the conspicuous lack of one so far. John Dillon, who played in Canberra with Maher and who says his playing days are fast running out, recalls taking a game off the top team some years ago. It was unexpected. It was grand. And that day, he knows, will come for Paddington too. I still dream about that day, says Maher. There was no way we should have won. We came off, guys were shaking. One guy reversed into a tree, he was shaking so much.

That's why they come back in greater numbers each week. Because that day is coming soon. These guys just will not give up. They're out every weekend no matter what. They roar like bears. They think with their blood. They smash their knobbled heads together. They run in packs. They snarl. They pile one atop the other in the mud. They gasp. They pant. They charge into the breach once more. And that is how men give birth.

MAD DOGS AND COUNTRY MEN

Brian looked up from the cabin of his tractor at ten to five in the afternoon and saw the hail storm which was coming to eat his ripening wheat crop alive. A strange incandescence seemed to precede it. *Oh*, he thought, *this is different*, as he turned the machine around to make a run for it. The first stones struck the cabin roof as he neared the paddock gate, and then hail was bouncing off the bonnet like marbles and Brian Gainsford couldn't see across the one-lane road.

If you were fool enough to drive west on that road, into the black heart of the thing, and you made it through to the other side, you may have come across Brian's cousin, Mick, on the way home from Cowra. Mick Cusack was coming out of clean sky and could see something like a giant black hammer hanging over his town. His wife, Mary, was under it. She had watched it come in from the west, building in three incredibly dark layers, suffused at the lowest level with that same strange light which Brian had noticed. As a child,

Mary had known apple farmers to launch phosphorous rockets into such clouds; the heat and sound were supposed to disrupt the formation of ice; women and children prayed. Neither did much good, she said.

Elsewhere in town, Mark Munro, a general duties manager at a cotton farm, was having trouble with the Missus when the hailstorm broke. She wanted to put the car safely inside the garage, but Munro already had 300 bottles of home-brew in there and didn't think much of moving them outside. The car, he insisted, would have to take its chances by the side of the house.

Willie Kellermeyer was on his way home from school as the stones started bouncing around him. He ran for the swimming-pool complex, which sits across from the oval where his cricket team had been flogged the previous week and where he'd open the batting this Saturday. If he cared to stick his head into the storm, he could watch the wicket turn white inside a few minutes.

The storm caused a lot of fear in Narromine. Thousands of hectares of wheat surrounding the town had already been drenched by heavy, unseasonal rain in the previous weeks. If that didn't break with a hot, dry stretch, the black smut would soon creep through those fields, ruining the year's harvest. While magic rockets may not go skyward with the same frequency and faith as in Mary Cusack's day, farmers' prayers probably do. But when the heavens over Narromine turned black and green instead of a hard, steady blue, it must have seemed to the devout that they had a spiteful God on their hands this year.

It wasn't so. When Mick Cusack hit the 60 zone outside

town, his Falcon started to fishtail. White stuff was every-where and it looked like a real hurting had been put down on Narromine, but when Mick picked up one of the stones, he found they were disc-shaped and harmless. Falling to pieces in the palm of his hand, he realised they weren't the sort of thing that busts wheat heads or tears down orchards. The town, as so often before, had passed through the trouble and survived in much better shape than anyone really expected.

Narromine village was proclaimed on 20 March 1885—the name coming from two Aboriginal words meaning 'place of honey'. The town sits on the border between the hills which roll back east for hundreds of kilometres and the plains which just go on and on, getting flatter and hotter, in time becoming the Never Never.

White civilisation took root ten years before the procla-mation with the district's earliest recorded cricket match between married and single men at Timbrebongie. Such matches were an important part of the district's social fabric. It wasn't unusual for outlying bush men to go for two or three years without coming into town. Even for those living closer in, a game of cricket might provide the only chance for human contact in a month or more. One of the early landowners, George McKilop at Buddah, was so passionate about the game that sundowners who wandered into his property looking for work were asked whether they could bowl. If so, they soon found them-selves earning their keep by rolling the arm over to keep George's eye in.

Cricket is still taken very seriously in the bush, much more so than in the city. It isn't unusual for a bush cricketer to drive hundreds or even thousands of kilometres for a game. 'Bush league' has generally been levied as a term of mild abuse, but were it not for bush cricket, Australian Test teams would have had to get by without the likes of Don Bradman, Doug Walters and Richie Benaud.

Brian Gainsford, as chair of the NSW Country Cricket Association, is charged with ensuring the bush remains a fertile seeding ground for Australian cricket. His grandparents got to Narromine just in time for the great rural Depression of the 1890s. Walter and Margaret Gainsford arrived in a covered wagon with no money, several children and an unknown number of chickens and cows. They worked for years to finally get a return on their property, Yarran Farm, in 1901. In 1902, a plague of rabbits ate all the fodder and their stock starved to death.

They hung on, though, and by the early 1920s, the Gainsford name had become prominent in the district. In 1922 the clans Gainsford, Elrington, Crawford, Jones and Coram formed the Backwater Cricket Club, the name derived from a small nearby waterway. Matches were played in the grounds of Yarran Farm on an ant-bed pitch with a kerosene tin as a wicket. Brian's father, Ken, a good right-hand bat and, like most of his brood, a wicketkeeper, was in the original team and you can still meet him every Saturday the team plays at the oval across the street from his house. Since he took to the field 71 years ago, a Gainsford has always played for Backwater.

Recently, times have been leaner for both the club and

the town. Brian, youngest son of Ken, grandson of Walter, has seen 47 seasons in Narromine. For 33 of them he has played for Backwater when the wheat fields weren't calling. He kept wicket for Country against the West Indies in '75 and took three catches. His son David now plays with Manly in Sydney and daughter Melinda sprints for Australia at the Olympics. There are nine Gainsford boys in Brian's generation, but only four on the land.

'In our day,' he says, 'all the boys stayed on the land. The opportunity was good. But now they see the droughts and floods and mice plagues, the poor returns and so on and they don't want to stay. The costs of farming are different from the old days. Your margins get eaten and, for a lot of the young ones, there's no choice but to move on.'

Some towns die of it. They don't go down like a modern *Marie Celeste*, with plates laid out for dinner and the TV set jammed on white noise. The vital energy of a place just leaks into the grey, lifeless dust at the edge of town. People's faces grow older, the train stops running and, gradually, the sound of children disappears.

Government policies of regionalisation which are supposed to help sometimes don't. Agri-centres like Dubbo, just up the road from Narromine, score the federal and state lolly, start to grow and often suck the life out of little hamlets by the gravitational pull of their money and power. Narromine itself has done well out of the deal. It has increasingly been seen as a pleasant satellite of Dubbo—a nice place to live outside the big smoke but close enough for work. The edge of town rings nowadays to the clash of hammers and nails as new house frames go up. There are almost no empty shops in the main street and, most telling of all, blacks and whites smile and greet each other as they pass by.

The farmers are less dependent on nature's mercy due to a large, privately owned irrigation scheme that runs off the nearby Macquarie River. A diverse range of crops have grown up around the scheme so that someone is always harvesting, planting, or spending money in town. And that's enough in these times. To stop is to die in the Outback—just ask Burke and Wills.

Across a broader stage, however, the regional process has posed problems for Brian and the Country Cricket Association as they guard against slipping standards. 'The level of the game isn't very good in some of these small places,' he says. 'And if you have a young fellow with a bit of talent, he's not going to get on if the cricket is just an excuse to drink beer and run around a park on the weekend.'

They take things more seriously in Narromine, as evidenced by the effort to play against neighbouring Trangie in conditions that would have found most Test players throwing a massive tantie and *simply refusing* to come out of their dressing room.

On the morning of the match, an ugly blue-black wall of cloud briefly built up behind the Narromine Hotel before slipping around to the south to leave the day with a high, vaulted ceiling of uniform grey. A strong sou'wester bent the trees and whipped red dust devils along the streets around Dundas Park. The ground, which had seen more water than most rice paddies, was a deep, spongy green; it was so thick that only a ground stroke of rare brutality would make it all the way to the fence.

The first players arrived as heavy black smears of rain reached down ten kilometres to kiss the far side of town. Leaves raced across the ground, and the first spiky drops of cold rain splattered the windows of the players' cars herded under some trees. There was no question of abandoning the game. Some of the blokes had driven 50 kilometres for this. And as Trangie was catching the worst of an outlying storm right now, what was the point in going back?

From the first over, the batsmen were fending off balls that struck the pitch, stopped and seemed to alter their trajectory in fits and starts. Mark Munro, cotton hand, mad-keen home-brewer and opening bat, had real trouble with the weird, unbalanced physics and chased any half-decent ball the same way a child might pursue a Christmas beetle with a stick.

At the other end, young Willie Kellèrmeyer sent one ball steaming to the deep with a beautiful hook shot, but swatted the next like an ineffectual girl. He and Munro soon unveiled a collection of strokes seemingly inspired by a fondness for pirate movies and the early broad-sword epics of Arnold Schwarzenegger. Senior players gathered around the cars mumbled about 'kicks in the bot' and 'toes in the date'.

The saving of the two adventurers was the Trangie fielding, which seemed to be inspired by a fondness for the early work of Larry, Moe and Curly. Many, many catches were wrestled manfully to earth. To be fair, Trangie were short some players, so juniors from the morning competition had to make up the numbers. The team sported a variety of caps and pants of different lengths. They ranged in age from mid-forties to a boy of maybe ten or twelve in grey, knee-length shorts who had to work third man at both ends. Even so, Munro insisted on pushing his good fortune heavily into overdraft and he was eventually caught—more by the law of averages than any fielder. Kellermeyer may have been owed money by his partner so keen was he to follow him. On 22, he unrolled a big ugly golf swing and hurried away from a set of stumps which had been scattered further and wider than the twelve tribes of Israel.

Thus Captain Sharkey and Gainsford were thrown together. The rhythm of the innings wound back and the shots became pleasant to watch, the willow drawn back on a spring and held until the ball reluctantly left the pitch and presented itself for dispatch. The sound of the shots was healthier, less hollow. Elbows were straight and heads kept down. Gainsford was a yin-yang study in balance: bat between slightly bowed legs, the tip not lifted very far, the ball running quickly across the ground when hit.

The two farmers never settled into their game, though. While they punched, glanced and trotted between the wickets, a great brown cocoon of cloud wrapped itself around the town, turning the sky into a mottled surrealist work. The light turned a sick yellow and, in the space of an over, the obscene-looking cloud morphed into a red giant. It looked violent. When the sky split open, everyone ran for it.

'We shouldn't really be playing at our age,' said Mick Cusack. 'Gaino's 47, I'm 41, Tim won't see 30 again. Apart from Munro, the rest are teenagers and schoolboys. But we've got to hang in for Backwater. In two or three years, this will be a great team again.'

On the Sunday evening, after the match, with Trangie blown off the field by the storm, Mick sits at the head of his table. The leavings of his family's Sunday roast stretch out before him. He'd taken a junior team to a match a few hundred kilometres down the track—driving there and back in one day. His arms are burnt and the paler skin inside one bicep is marred by a lurid, ball-shaped bruise. He drinks coffee and draws on a smoke as he slowly turns over the idea that the next Backwater premiership would be won by children, not men.

Mick, cousin of Brian, president of Backwater, opening bowler and wool agent, is in his fourth season with the club. He played grade cricket for Randwick as a younger man, but had his greatest days with Baulkham Hills. 'I still follow that club,' he says. 'It was the first club I took 50 wickets for. I played there for ten years and we took two premierships. But,' he smiles softly, 'those days are gone. That was when I could play cricket.'

Backwater last won the premiership in 1989, but since then the great wheel has turned and the fields of Narromine have been a barren place. 'We're rebuilding,' says Mick. 'But it's difficult. Being the farmers' team, we're always losing blokes to harvest or planting, or just losing blokes outright. We've got a couple of good fellas playing now, but they'll be leaving Narromine for good soon.'

This echoes cousin Brian's lament that out of nine Gainsford boys, only four will stay on the land. Maybe there'll be a day when no Gainsford will take the field for Backwater; maybe after 71 years that day was coming soon. It lent urgency to the notion that the old men had to pass something on. Mick edges towards this as he speaks uncertainly about the feeling of standing with a cricket ball in his hand: the rough seam, the smooth glazed leather, the curiously satisfying weight of the orb as he tosses it from one hand to the other.

On these western plains, which Mick loves, a man could stand under a big cathedral sky and feel himself at the centre of something—lines of history, or the breathing of Gondwanaland. Sidney Nolan may have caught it in his Ned Kelly paintings: alien landscapes peopled by those strange, disturbing figures, filling up the hollow places of your Australian heart, creating a sense of place in the middle of nothing.

This language doesn't come easily to Mick, though. He's not used to talking about himself and stares at the tip of his cigarette while doing so. He speaks about his playing days in a slightly dismissive tone, and underlies it with a sort of reverence for circumstance, which has let him do something he loves for all of his life.

'When a dozen blokes are in the middle, and one runs in and bowls and . . . maybe you knock him over then, maybe he takes 200 off you . . .' Mick shrugs. 'Well . . . you know.' It *means* something, and maybe that's all you need to know right there.

Mick has a knowledge beyond words, certainly beyond the trophies that take pride of place on the mantelpiece in his dining room. There are many there, but only two, he says, which mean anything. One is for Best Aggregate Bowling, which he'd carried off as a 40-year-old. The other is for Sportsman Of The Year, which his wife explains he received not just for his bowling figures, 'but for putting in time with the kids and that sort of thing.'

'You do it for the love of the game,' he says. 'You pass it on. It's a hell of a thrill to play for Backwater with my own son. Next year, I'd like to toss him the ball and say, "Right, you, open the attack. I'll go first change".'

He smiles and draws on his cigarette. 'I guess I'll have to play one more season.'

JURY DUTY

The quality of mercy is not strained, as the big guy once mused. It droppeth as the gentle rain from heaven. Sometimes, however, the drops are amber and sparkling and brewed by Castlemaine Perkins. Perhaps I should explain.

A long time ago, when I was scratching around trying to make a living as a baby writer, I found a summons to jury duty in my mail box. My budget ran to about five bucks a day at that time, and as jury duty paid upwards of twenty or thirty dollars a day I was in like Flynn. The other little Easter egg I soon discovered was that jury duty was catered. You were entitled to a free lunch and tea breaks and in Queensland, or at least in Ipswich, the jury also received a fresh carton of beer. Every day.

I sat as chairman on my first two juries because I'd been reading a book in the foyer of the court and my fellow jurors thought this marked me down as a man of extravagant intelligence and worldliness. This was Pauline Hanson's electorate, remember.

And I guess that partly explains what happened in the third jury I sat on. Let me give you the condensed version. Young black guy, let's call him Leo, a solid citizen, is at the footy with his old man. They buy a six-pack but only drink two or three cans. Leaving the grounds, the old guy spots a muddy, discarded jacket on the ground and suggests wrapping the sixer in it, to keep the tubes nice and frosty. So his son does. Next thing he knows there's a lot of racist abuse flying around and some rugby player accusing him of stealing the jacket. Leo tries to give the jacket back and a young constable intervenes. The cop just wants everyone to chill out and be happy but the victim wants Leo charged.

So a few months later we're all sitting in court to sort this mess out. And the thing is, I can tell the judge and the prosecutor and the defence lawyer and even the constable called to give evidence think the whole thing is a crock. I've been watching these guys for three weeks and they cannot believe they're wasting their time on this. The prosecutor isn't even trying to claim Leo stole the jacket. It's agreed some other actual villain did that. But Leo was the one with carriage of the goods so there we were. The evidence takes about one hour to hear and the prosecutor runs dead with his case.

Cut to the jury room.

I'm sitting there thinking the gravy train has come to a halt. We're not even going to score a free lunch out of this. I didn't want to be chair of this jury, because it's close to hard work and I figured the case was a simple acquittal, so I flicked the job to a guy I'd been a little hard on earlier. He thanks me and says to the room, 'Well, I reckon the black bastard done it. They don't understand nothing about property rights you know. What do you all reckon?'

And then it's like I'm sitting there in some antipodean Klan meeting and everyone is bayin' for a lynchin'. Everyone except myself and this old guy I'll call Artie. Well, old Artie, he'd seen off Rommel in the northern desert, lost a lot of good mates in the fight against racism and fascism, and he was having none of it.

But there was nothing we could do to argue the majority around. They had their blood up and they wanted to string up poor old Leo by his thumbs. Reasoned argument quickly degenerated to unreasoning bitterness. Some ugly things were said, feelings hurt, and by the time lunch arrived the old jury room was the site of a minor civil war. It was also home to a couple of increasingly irascible drunks, as Artie and I polished off the beer from the previous day, then started in on the fresh batch.

By four in the afternoon we were six sheets to the wind, full of piss and bad manners and the other jurors could hardly look at us. They just wanted to convict and depart. Just after a worried clerk stuck his head in to say it was getting late and to ask if we needed anything, Artie and I drunkenly announced that lateness be damned, we were never going to convict this guy. If need be we'd just sit there drinking free beer from this day to the ending of the world.

And you know, they voted to acquit less than a minute later.

Justice may be blind, but occasionally it helps if she's also blind drunk.

DRUNKY BOSS

What to do when you discover your boss is a boozer? Break out the generic Coles brand Spumante and celebrate, my friend, because you have just fallen arse backwards into a pot of gold. I'm not thinking of anything so gauche as blackmail here. Oh no. Perish the thought. We want to help our bibulous little fascist. We want to help him to locate that half bottle of brandivino hidden deep behind the curling stacks of redundant A4 photocopy paper. We want him to stumble across that mouldy bladder of fiery Turkish burgundy we snuck through customs five or six years ago. And we want him sneaking away to the toilets every fifteen minutes or so to fish a sixer out of the cistern.

We want that old bastard so blasted that he is incapable of bringing the hammer down on our dizzy noggins when we are similarly indisposed. Even better, we want him conspiring with us against the gimlet-eyed legions of the uptight in upper management; those smug self-righteous yahoos with their complimentary bar fridge and executive relaxo-lounge.

Oh, we know what goes on upstairs, don't we JB, we want him thinking; bitterly, if possible. We know what those shameless hypocrites on the top floor are up to, running their toes through deep executive shag pile carpets while imported slavebabes from the third world top up their mai tais and slippery nipples—while we lumpenproles down here in steerage are flogged senseless if we so much as look up from our workstations and lick the small, salty beads of sweat from our lips . . . salty like the rim of a diamond crisp, icy cold margarita. Mmmmm, margarita . . .

Hey boss, fancy a trip to the pub for lunch?

Yes my friends, be not dismayed or embarrassed to discover your overlord is often as drunk as Lord, for a righteous path has been laid before you—so long as you care not for your future with this company. I have worked for rum-sodden inebriates more than once and can vouch for the admirable qualities they bring to any hierarchical disorganisation: ineptitude, laziness and procrastination in all matters save those of a spirituous nature. Unable to discipline themselves, they are incapable of disciplining their so-called employees, especially when those employees are possibly the only people still talking to, drinking with or even breathing the same noxious miasma of stale cigarette smoke and boxed riesling fumes as our wretched alcoholic superior.

So be not afraid of your boss's substance abuse problems. With understanding and ruthless exploitation they are but the first steps on the happy staircase to successfully realising your own full-blown meltdown. And all at the expense of the despotic corporate greedheads who would otherwise reduce you to their personal wage slave monkey butler.

Cheers.

GENIUS AT WORK

To every generation is born a genius, your Michelange-
los, your Shakespeares, your Britney Spears. But sadly,
home-baked Australian genii have been a little thin on the
ground, at least in the world of literature.

Oh, sure, your pointyheaded types might sport a bookish
woody for Patrick White and his so-called Nobel prize. But
did any of Patrick White's characters face certain death by
plummeting over a massive Antarctic ice cliff in a shot-to-
hell hovercraft while being pursued by a bunch of murderous British SAS guys, only to whip out some bodacious
James Bond-style moves leading to a heavy ass-whoopin' for
aforesaid SAS guys? Did any of White's so-called novels ever
feature attacks by pods of murderous killer whales, inter-
galactic OK Corral shoot-outs in the New York Public
Library or secret weapons built out of lost Aztec relics so
powerful they could blow a third of the Earth's planetary
mass into orbit around Jupiter? Well, did they?

If the answer is a solid uh . . . no, as you and I but

know it is, Patrick White can hand over his propeller beanie of genius to the one author of world stature our so-called literary community has ever produced. That author's name is Matthew Reilly. Reilly first burst through the flimsy plywood door of literature like a heavily-armed and badly drug-affected special forces renegade with a self-published gem called *Contest*. Reilly, like the best writers, is unafraid to address the timeless verities of the human condition, such as the little-known verity that every hundred years a champion is chosen from among us to do battle against a pack of bloodthirsty space gorillas, shapeshifters, biomechanical attack pooches and alligator chicks. The sole survivor is declared the most kickarse species of the century. Through an error in talent-spotting procedures, we don't get represented by Arnie or Jean-Claude. Instead, a radiologist, Dr Stephen Swain, single dad of eight-year-old Holly, is left with little more than a Bic lighter to save his hide and his daughter. Can he do it? Is the human race the most kickarse race in the Milky Way? Need you ask?

For once, the publishing industry was on the ball and recognised in *Contest* the arrival of a rare talent. Pan Macmillan signed up *Ice Station*, the work which would establish Reilly in airport bookstores worldwide. *Ice Station* presents as a hyper-accelerated sci-fi shooter, with Lieutenant Shane M. Schofield (aka Scarecrow, because of the two vertical scars that slash through his eyes) leading a marine recon team into a lethal crossfire at an Antarctic research station. Foreign special forces teams, all of them chock full of violent nuts, battle to reach the possible crash site of an alien spacecraft.

The genius of this work is its unrelenting pace. The hovercraft scenario takes place over several pages in *Ice Station*. Picture this. You're being pursued across the ice by half a dozen or so SAS hovercraft. Your only ally is a hopeless doofus of a scientist. You plunge over a huge cliff? Violent death below. Violent death above. You're falling, falling. Are you going to live? These are the big questions Reilly asks on every second page. I mean that. Every second page. Sometimes twice in one paragraph. I don't think Patrick White asked the hovercraft question once in *Voss*.

Thankfully, White is dead now and so valuable shelf space in megabarn bookmarts can be more fruitfully given over to Reilly's most recent release, *Temple*, a state-of-the-art thriller with competing teams of ruthless killers and stumbling heroes in different centuries, searching for a lost artefact with which to blow up the world.

You know you are in the presence of a major new talent in the opening pages when a pack of postmodern SS goons invades a monastery and shoots everybody in the head.

Modern Australian literature has many failings. Specifically, it's very, very boring. Matt Reilly, genius, has addressed the issue of what to put in between the interesting bits—and there can be only one reward. Five big cheeseburgers.

A BRIEF APPRECIATION OF THE HIGHEST FORM OF LITERATURE: THE TECHNO-THRILLER

Oh. My. God. Ohmygod! Ohmygod! Ohmygod! An explosive new adventure by Eric L. Harry has snuck into airport book stores and nobody told me. I can only imagine that this oversight has something to do with the world media being distracted by the drawn-out American presidential election and the arrival on tour of Brian Lara's blonde girlfriend. Because there can be no other excuse for this appalling neglect of the greatest writer of military thrillers since William Shakespeare knocked up *Henry V*.

Harry's broad canvas masterpiece, *Invasion*, encompasses nearly six hundred pages of eye gougin', missile firin', tank bustin' close quarter combat between a two million strong Chinese invasion force and the desperate fag end of what's left of the American military after a decade of treasonous neglect and appeasement by the usual cabal of left-wing vegetarians who control high executive office nowadays.

This baby has everything: Chinese armoured divisions hunkered down in the car parks of McDonalds and KFC joints all over Texas; righteously crazy Green Beret maniacs sneaking around the car parks of McDonalds and KFC joints all over Texas knocking off Chinese guys with a fat catalogue of James Bond-style weaponry; fat Bubbas with hunting rifles doing their bit for Ol' Glory; fat Bubbas without hunting rifles getting their throats slit and their tongues used as neck ties by ticked-off Chinese guys in reprisal; and the daughter of the American president kicking a whole heap of Chinese butt . . .

Say what? That's right. Eric L. Harry is an equal opportunity guy, and with things gone so pear-shaped you can't even get no decent bucket o' devilled chicken wings in Texas no more on account of all the main battle tanks the Chinese have got cluttering up the local drive-through, women have been dragooned into the infantry. The central role of Stephanie Roberts, daughter of President Bill Roberts, does lead to a fair amount of emotional character development which might have been better focussed on black budget weapons development, but for once, I'll ignore the shortcoming. Harry is such a good writer you don't even notice that a couple of Chinese regiments have gone begging for an ass-chewin' while the Prez and his kid workshop their relationship.

What is it that makes Harry such a read? Is it his way with gunshot wounds of all kinds? His exciting anecdotes about modern trench warfare? Or is it, as I suspect, that Harry, like many modern literary prodigies, has put in some solid grunt time with the Marines. He wisely eschewed the effete surrounds of Malcolm Bradbury's writing classes for an altogether more valuable series of lessons in hand to hand combat and small unit infantry tactics. Perhaps if we just abolished the Literature Board and packed our so-called authors off for a summer of hijinks and bastardisation with the 3rd Battalion RAR we might finally see a few more Bookers flying home on Qantas.

Or maybe not. Because first we'd have to go mano a mano with the old boys of the finest writing school in the English speaking world, the British SAS. One wonders how any terrorists actually get a good seeing to in the old Dart nowadays, with so many graduates of the Regiment's killing house abandoning their MP5s for a laptop and a three book deal. Chris Ryan, the handsome, highly-trained commando and bestselling author of *Tenth Man Down*, *Zero Option* and now *The Hit List*, is a testament to the cultural efficacy of a few years spent in hyper-violent, deniable black ops on behalf of HM Government. For the price of a few child care centres the Brits get both a lethal instrument of foreign policy and an A-grade spinner of ripping yarns. *The Hit List* manages to combine dozens of interesting ways of taking out Serbian secret police guys, with cameos by Salman Rushdie, Madonna and former press baron Robert Maxwell. Indeed Maxwell is kind enough to light the story fuse, getting himself necked by Her Majesty's Secret Service in the opening pages.

While a mere pretender like Rushdie is never likely to threaten Ryan's hold over next year's Booker, his old army bud Andy McNab just might. Another retired SAS type, McNab has moved into the emerging field of cyber-thrillers with *Firewall*, the story of Nick Stone, a former

SAS guy turned freelance kidnapper who runs afoul of the Russian Mafia. It's beyond me why Stone didn't just front up at Random House with a manuscript if he was a bit short of the folding stuff. But lucky for us he didn't, because then we'd have been denied one of the best opening paragraphs it's been my pleasure to read. I won't spoil the fun for you, just be assured that McNab's foray into the virtual world doesn't mean we're going to miss out on any sticky business. What we do get is four hundred pages of Nick Stone settling up with Russian crims and secret agents in a manner that should encourage John Howard to boost the budget of our own special forces, if he really cares about the arts.

By way of contrast I was prepared to be underwhelmed by Stephen Coonts' contribution to the genre. After all, his name is sort of funny, for a techno-thriller author. Not at all like your virile, no-nonsense Larry Bonds or Andy McNabs. And it sounds a lot like Dean Koontz, who is perhaps—no, who is without a doubt—the worst writer ever to defile the shelves of an airport bookstore. The cover of Coonts' four hundred page shooter looks like it was painted in watercolours by a prison inmate. And there's no mandatory glossary of really cool military terms. Or list of characters to separate the eight or nine dozen plot lines for the slower readers. And the title, *Cuba*? It's a little underdone, don't you think? Why not *Death Smoked A Cuban!* Or something like that. But I do the old Coonts a disservice.

On reading his bio while searching fruitlessly for tactical maps I discovered the dude was a naval aviator who flew combat missions over the 'nam. 'All righty then!' I thought. That's more like it! Screw your literary awards and fawning critics. Give me a bit of time on the flight stick and maybe a few cruel-looking scars from a spot of unarmed combat, or maybe five years in a bamboo cage eating rats for your country. That's when I know I'm dealing with a quality author.

Unlike a lot of other ex-military types who take to riding a word processor instead of a gunship, the versatile Coonts is happy working across the services. In *Cuba* we get aircraft carriers, stealth bombers, marine recon squads, even a couple of CIA guys spooking about with garrottes and big, silenced hand cannons. Guys get eaten by sharks, jump off ICBMs in launch phase and chase after a warehouse of bioweapons which have gone missing, presumed stolen by the villainous Vargas, head of Cuba's secret police. When Fidel Castro turns up his smelly old toes from cancer the race is on between a cast of lantern-jawed warriors and a despicable crew of Latino vermino who plan to cook off a bunch of super-viruses all over the American south. Of course, nowadays there's a law against gross ethnic carica-tures, even in airport novels, so there's a few stand-up guys on the Cuban side too. However, there was more than enough blood, villainy and time-critical shenanigans to make me ashamed I had ever doubted Mr C.

Dale Brown never actually got to kill anyone when he was driving bombers for the USAF, so he's not nearly as good an author as Coonts. But his title-picking prowess and cover art could teach the former naval aviator a thing or two. Brown writes about bombers, and not much else, but you'd have to admit that bombers are pretty cool anyway. In *Battle Born*, a secret bunch of military guys sort of steal a lot of stealth bombers and intervene in a war between a united Korea and China. There's about ten pages of love interest which a true aficionado could have done without. But once you've established that the competent but horny female bomber commander and her spunky but unruly lead pilot have bumped uglies with the usual, pointless emotional disruption, the icky girl scenes are pretty easy to skip and you lose nothing.

You'll want to skip them, too, because they get in the way of dozens of whizbang pages about a new weapon which disintegrates stuff with a big ball of plasma. When I first read about this baby I thought, 'Whoah! Dale Brown might never have killed anyone like a proper author, but he sure can imagine it real good.' Fitting the plasma missiles to the semi-stolen stealth bombers, the rowdy but determined mavericks of the 111th Bombardment Wing kick some serious Chinese butt, which, as all techno-thriller fans will know, is the easiest and most satisfying sort of butt a determined but unmanageable maverick can kick. A great book, worth five cheeseburgers, although Brown will want to cut back on the icky stuff next time. Love interest is something a daring but irascible bomber pilot has for his plasma missile, not his female commander.

Of course if the love interest is between two female commanders, that's different. Thus if there is a weak point in the works of SM Stirling I've yet to find it. You've got your girl-on-girl raunch. You've got your parallel Earths. You've got more girl-on-girl raunch. And you've got your gratuitous violence, your exciting gizmos, your totally villainous villains and your timeless moral questions, like whether our man Stirling could pack in a little more girl-on-girl raunch.

Short answer? You bet he could!

There's always room for one more ultraviolent, genetically enhanced überbabe in the non-stop girly pillow fight to the death which is the SM Stirling Draka trilogy. Now that's what I call real feminism, Germaine. Numbering four novels and one curious, fan-created spin-off, this is one of the great trilogies of the modern era. It began with *Marching through Georgia*, a numbingly violent and minutely detailed account of a steroid-boosted gun fest which kicks off when a company of Draka paratroops go the biff with what seems like a whole Nazi Army Group. Turns out the Nazis are just a piss poor bunch of master race wannabes compared with the Draka and they get their tightly clenched butts righteously kicked clear out to Wednesday.

I guess you'll be needing a little backstory around about now. In the Draka series, the antique trailer trash who lost the American civil war got exiled to Africa instead of hanging around to invent fried chicken and discussion topics for Jerry Springer. They style themselves as the Draka, after Sir Francis Drake, who they thought was really cool, and their turn-ons are good food, horse riding and enslaving the world. Stirling doesn't seem to think that's such a bad deal though. On the one hand the Draka are cruel masters, and if you cross 'em, they'll impale you, pants down, on a big sharpened stick with lots of splinters. On the other hand, they're all blonde and kind of cute and the chicks put out like bandits. Of course, if they decide to put out with you, and you even think of knocking them back, it's pants down and stand over there by the big stick, buddy, I'll be with you in a minute.

The fourth book in the trilogy, *Drakon*, is a slight departure, with one of these voracious strumpets called Gwen Ingolfsson falling through a wormhole to fetch up on our Earth, the one with KFC and Springer and her nemesis, a fat, hairy New York detective named Henry Carmaggio. Gwen wastes a bunch of dudes. Races off a few more, including Henry's girlfriend, and generally makes a nuisance of herself trying to impale the whole planet on a big pointy stick. It's hard to fault Stirling's work in this series. I suppose he could have packed in a little more bloodshed and lesbianism, but there comes a point, believe it or not, when just like with fried chicken and Jerry Springer, a guy can't take no more. Five cheeseburgers with fries and a pallet of Coke for Mr Stirling.

Another guy doing Doctor Greer's work for her is James Cobb. The author of chick-driven techno-thriller, *Choosers of the Slain*, Cobb pays the rent cranking out the sort of books this so-called feminist should be working on instead of bitching and moaning and trying to take away all of our cool guy stuff. Imagine if little girls had a hero like Captain Amanda Lee Garret to read about, rather than the rantings of some bitter and wizened old feral cat. They'd grow up worrying a lot less about equal pay and a lot more about electronic silhouettes of Chinese missile boats.

Amanda Lee G, you see, is the commander of the stealth destroyer USS *Cunningham*, who is forever finding herself in the geopolitical drawing room with a bunch of dead bodies draped over the furniture and some guilty Ivan in need of a first class ass-whoopin'. In *Choosers of the Slain*, some top shelf whoopage is doled out to the Argentine military, who are an acceptable stand-in if you can't lay hands on any likely looking Nazis or expansionist Chinese types. (The latter get all the whoopin' they can take from Commander Amanda in the sequel, *Storm Dragon*.)

It's kind of disconcerting following the adventures of a destroyer captain who keeps in shape with jazz ballet and who is inclined to come over all teary and pre-menstrual when one of her crew gets iced. But then she wastes so many Argies by deploying the awesome power of a fully operational death star all over their pathetic navy as it tries to steal Antarctica that you've got to cut her some slack. If only she'd go out on a date with Christine, her spunky Intelligence Chief, instead of mooning over Vince, that dopey helicopter pilot, all the time. A minor quibble, and nowhere near serious enough to deny her five cheesy big ones hot off the griddle.

White wine spritzer 'WE

ARE NOT NEARLY SO SCARED OF
WOMEN STEALING INTO OUR CLUBS,
OUR REGIMENT, OUR MANAGING
DIRECTOR'S CHAIR AS WE ARE OF THEM
CREEPING QUIETLY THROUGH THE
BARBED WIRE ENTANGLEMENTS WHICH
GUARD OUR SHIVERING HEARTS.'

VEGAN SWINE! THE BACKLASH STARTS HERE

I know of no spectacle so ridiculous as the vegetarian populace in one of their periodic fits of morality. We seem to be suffering through one of these dire intervals at the moment, brought on by a Ms Jane Salmon's recent declaration that thinking women find vegetarian men infinitely more attractive than the carnivore norm.

In barbecued pig's ear, wench.

Face facts, babe, real chicks dig guys with cars, scars and bacon breath. I'll admit, your younger, less confident, less worldly women are attracted to the safety zone of painfully shy and sensitive shoe-gazing floppy-haired boys. But women who like men like them to behave as men, and no self-respecting man ever actually wants to eat a vegetable. But like flowers, conversation and clean underpants, they may sometimes be a necessary evil, a small token of your willingness to abide by the rules early in the hunt. And I'll admit that vegetables—like bottled water when it's frozen into cubes and plopped into a glass of whiskey—even have their uses. Mashed potatoes, for instance, can be moulded into an excellent dam for holding excess gravy, and what tray of meaty bar snacks is complete without a peanut, which is a close cousin if not an actual member of the vegetable race. Everything in moderation though.

Oh, there's been some overripe moralising around the town since you opened your mouth, Ms Salmon. Letters to the editor, questions in the House, brother set against brother. And for what? Have you forgotten that awful time in the 1980s, then thought of as the New Romantic period but, thanks to science, now revealed as The Great Confusion. A time when 'boys' came back into prominence. Not the hardy, cricket playing, Turkish trench attacking lads of yesteryear. More your foppish, pointy boot and scarf clad refugees from the romantic novels of the early nineteenth century.

Did you ever actually date any of the weirdos from Men Opposed to Patriarchy, Salmon?

That's right my friends. They called themselves Mop. They were an early '90s campus phenomenon and a wetter, limper, greyer bunch of gender rebels you could not have hoped to find. They published a newsletter called *Wet Patch*, and they were all vegetarians, or pretending to be. Their sort always are. They're still around and you can still spot them a mile off. They prefer cats over dogs. They're always coming on with this mock sensitive fooferol at dinner parties ('Oh yes, I cried all the way through *How to Make an American Quilt*. It was such a passionate film'). They affect a certain nonchalance in gay nightclubs, where they take their significant others to demonstrate their incredibly relaxed attitudes, where their chicks won't be disturbed by having to rub up hard against meat-eating straight men, and where—may the Devil take their souls—they insist on dancing. Even though as hetero-sexual white men they have no rhythm whatsoever and are thus an embarrassment to us all.

Try as they might to deny it, however, gender is destiny. I knew a couple of these extremists who were confronted by the age-old dilemma. Two guys. One babe. I was there with them while they tried to work it out. Two more reasonable, empathetic, caring and sharing types you'd never meet. One of them even had a vegan cat, fed it nothing but brown rice and legume gruel (I used to slip it a bit of meat-lover's pizza and chocolate milk every now and then, the poor little bugger). Anyway, these guys tied themselves into a Gordian knot of PC high-mindedness over which of them was going to get the girl. You could tell, from the tension behind the reasonable words and constant reassuring arm touching, that they just wanted to beat seven bells out of each other. And they should have too. Should have stepped outside and settled it like men, rather than deciding, according to their customs, that they would offer the girl a chance to go out with them both and make up her own mind.

Between you and me, Salmon, I don't think the sisters are going to thank you for encouraging these guys, for harking back to an age when the time-honoured acces-sories of manly virtue like fist fighting and sausage eating were out, and depressive introspection, poetry and holding hands were in. Because luckily, unlike you it seems, most women were not fooled for a minute. While these two jokers were workshopping their love triangle I grabbed their wench, took her out for a mixed grill and a couple of schooners, and introduced her to the delights of a man with a belly full of red meat and cold beer and whole lotta lovin' to give.

THE VALERIES

For a long time I was the sole male member of an all girl surf crew. The Valeries, I called them. As in Ride of the Valeries . . . sort of a lame Wagnerian reference. Our home break was Bondi, not the greatest surfing beach in the world. But ours. Dude, we had that place wired. From the narrow, sucking channel which surged out along the rocks by the kiddies wading pool at the northern end of Bondi—or Paris end, as we like to think of it—through the great arc of the bay, the shifting, treacherous rips which divided the surf into convenient zones—here family friendly, there hungry and wild—all the way down to the freight train rip at the southern end of the beach, yuppie turf, the home of Hugo's and Bondi Tratt and Jones the Grocer, downstairs from young Packer's place.

Riding bodyboards, or shark biscuits as they're known to shortboarders, we tended to farm the break in the centre of the beach. Before the volleyball stadium reworked the fluid dynamics of the whole bay, there were a couple of paired rips there, strong enough to kill the occasional drunken backpacker, but a personal gift from the Great Pumpkin himself for anyone on a board needing to drill through a seven-wave set of Bondi's notoriously unpleasant close-outs. Some of the finest days of my life have spooled away out there, threading between heaving green mountains of water, dialling into rare, surging walls, and once, only once, slipping quietly into the green room, an intimate, swirling tube which peeled left for what felt like two or three months, ribboning around my entire world with a deep, sucking roar.

The Valeries are take-charge babes, lawyers one and all. I have seen them haul themselves out through serried lines of Godzilla waves which robbed me of my manhood. I have watched them smashed by Thor's own hammer, manifest in the world as a rogue wave, a cruel outsider which rolled in through the mouth of the bay like a baby tsunami, sucking everyone up its black face, then pitching them through the air, backwards, arms and legs flailing, half a second before tonnes of cold sea water fell in on them. I have watched sunsets of painful beauty with them, from atop snaking blue ridges; seen the sun rise over the slumbering apartments on Ben Buckler, rendering even the ugliest Whitlam era rent slab into something wonderful for just a moment. I have surfed with them in sessions of such ridiculous duration that afterwards I have felt as though I was hallucinating through my skin.

And, God help me, I have travelled with them.

A couple of years ago two magazine editors hired a

witch to place a hex on me. We won't go into details. I was never able to ascertain the specifics of the curse, but I suspect a lot of chicken blood was spilled to lay a heavy burden on my surfing trips with the überbabes of the Valeries.

Over four or five years we have never once had a successful excursion from our home break. Not even next door, to Tamarama, the home of the shark biscuit. Not on the other side of the world, in Sardinia, where I had been promised a few little nuggets spat up by giant North African storms.

Our first expedition, north to adventure, with Wagner's 'Ride' as the Coppola-inspired soundtrack, was mauled by a malign confluence of poor weather and the herpes virus. The Mexican Valeries, those who grew up south of the Rio Grande—or the Tweed River as you may you know it—were unprepared for the brutal, machine-like steam press of tropical humidity, and spent their first night in Brisvegas spread-eagled on the floor, gasping obscenities it would defile my keyboard to type. The sunshine broke, but not the heat or humidity, and our week at Noosa was marked by vicious, contrary swells and stormwater run-off which turned the surf red, a disturbing phenomenon, as the water itself was already blood-warm. Bluebottles and football-sized jellyfish flew through the air, hurled by breaking waves, as we tried to paddle out. The final ignominy was delivered by my mate Pete, a guest for the weekend, who waited until every Valerie had supped from the spring water bottle before scratching his head and saying, 'Hmmm, perhaps I shouldn't have drunk from that bottle. I've had a cold sore tingle for the past couple of hours.'

My mate Pete fell vertically down the face of a fifteen foot Godzilla wave at Whale Beach. It was considered a fitting end for him.

The next time we tried for a surf in the deep north, at Palm Beach, I tore off my big toenail in an accident at the Qantas Club on the way up. The sand in my flippers which operated like a cheese grater on the exposed nerves made it a tad difficult to generate the required acceleration. Perhaps normal folk would have taken the message by now. But there is a curious trick the surf will play on those fool enough to challenge it. The break always looks better just over there. And so, a few days before New Year's Eve 2000 we saddled up for Blueys Beach, a stretch of coastline as dear to the Dreaming of surf nazis as was Valhalla to the Valkyrie.

We struggled through the holiday traffic jams, which delayed us so much we had no time to check out the Big Ayers Rock at Leyland Brothers' World. Put that bitter disappointment to one side. And geared down to deal the next. Our luxurious beachfront yurt was, in reality, a swampy, mosquito-infested back street dive. The sort of cinder block bunker favoured by serial killers who like to keep to themselves. The barbecue was non-functional, the beds were prison surplus, the cane furniture draped in old horse blankets to hide some deeply disturbing organic stains. The TV did not work, and while the accumulated foot odour of twenty years' worth of holidaymakers was fascinating, it was not that great a substitute. Luckily, the oven exploded some time after midnight and we had an excuse to leave.

The surf, of course, was blown out by the foul weather.

Next year, I'm thinking maybe we'll just road trip it down Campbell Parade to Jamie's end of the beach.

WHEN A MAN REALISES
HE'S BAD

The thing is, most guys labour under the delusion that they are basically good when in fact we are basically bad, programmed for mischief and evil from our very first days. When a man understands this he comes to freedom. I came to freedom on Christmas Eve at the foot of a rumpled bed in a huge, decaying old Queenslander. It was explosively hot in that dark little bedroom and a young woman lay just in front of me, close enough to reach out and touch had I felt like it—which I didn't. She had drawn herself up into a tight foetal ball and I stood back with my hands in my pockets, regarding her long, shuddering sobs and cries with a sort of wry, empowered detachment. I thought I loved her, you understand, and it felt good to see her this way.

She'd done me wrong, this girl, put a real hurting on me. I'd never known anything like it and don't suppose I ever will again. At that moment I was enjoying the fiction of breaking up with her. Really, quietly, getting off on it,

even though she'd actually put a bullet into our relationship a long time beforehand. A weak little thing, it had
twitched and thrashed about on the floor and neither of us
had had the sense to finish it off until now. I'd pushed my
way into her room—perversely hoping to catch her with
someone—tossed a poorly-wrapped Christmas present at
her and started in on an hour or so of carefully crafted
emotional torture.

I had intended to say my piece and escape with some
dignity after a few minutes. But as she curled into a bundle
of woe at the foot of the bed something weird happened. I
started to feel good. Started to walk with the King, as they
say. I was behaving badly and really enjoying it. Truth be
known, it was giving me a bit of a woody. I felt stronger
than I had in weeks, not just inside, but outwardly, as
though my profile had somehow pressed hard into the
room. Such a change from the timid spectre I had presented to the world the past few weeks. Such a pity nobody
was there to see it and applaud.

I guess I should explain. You'll be wanting all the details.

When I met her I thought she was Irish. She had these
green eyes. And piles of dark, wine-coloured hair. She wore
cheesecloth and hung rubber bats from her bedroom ceiling.
Kept a skull with a candle melted on top by her bed. We first
kissed under a dinner table while Guns n' Roses screamed
out of a really old, cheap Sanyo and two of our friends tried
to sleep off three helpings of her awesome lasagna. She was
beautiful. After we went to bed for the first time we had
cheese and pepper on crackers for breakfast. She taught me
how to drink Tequila slammers, how to listen to the Pixies'

'Surfer Rosa', and how to move safely through a room where everyone has recently risen from the dead. I cooked chicken curries, used her toothbrush and made a bucket bong from which we pulled a thousand cones. It didn't last very long and when it was over I fled interstate.

But back to this performance on our last morning. I've forgotten exactly what I said to affect her so badly. It was probably just a lot of bitter bullshit anyway. Hardly worth repeating. I do remember being taken with the sound of the word 'dog' though. I have a really vivid, digital memory of lashing her with the phrase 'you treated me like a dog' maybe six or seven times over the course of an hour. Really whipped into her with it. And she cringed and curled up, just like a dog on the end of a chain. It's kind of shameful to think about it now.

Fact was, however, I'd always been a bit of a prick. Selfish, more than anything else. And lazy too, I guess. Most guys are when you get past our publicity. The acid bath of this relationship simply stripped me back to basics. Still, it was kind of surprising. I'd always known a few cads or bounders; just never considered myself amongst them. Never considered myself a brother of Scotty, the champion deflowerer of naive schoolgirls. Never thought I could match it with Harry, an obsessive collector of women, cross-matched by alphabetical and geographical reference. He started with Anya from Amsterdam and was joining the dots on his way to Zoe from Zimbabwe. Even had a database on his computer to keep track of progress. And I never really put myself on the same team as Robbo, a full disclosure man whose enormous sexual appetite seemed to be driven mostly by a need to entertain his mates over drinks. Robbo it was who knocked up his high school maths teacher. Robbo it was who bedded a novice nun. And Robbo it was who liked to demonstrate his remarkable control by getting naked, cradling a bowl of milk in his lap and drinking up every last drop . . . but not with his mouth. Now there was a guy who knew he was bad. A man who had come to freedom. He once told me about how he'd been rogering some poor blonde thing, motoring away, making her head bang into the wall with every thrust. He was drunk. Spastic drunk. Sweating and spinning out and giggling to himself as this girl's head banged into the wall again and again.

—bang bang bang bang bang—

It seemed to go on for hours. He was starting to tire. Starting to get muscle cramp. And still nothing had happened. An incredibly hot ball of tension had built up in his groin but it just wouldn't burst. He gritted his teeth and clenched his buttocks and pumped even harder.

—bang bang bang—

And then a geyser let loose. Bursting. Gushing. Surging. Rushing. On and on and on and on. And on. He was beer-bleary and brain-fogged with sex but he knew there was something wrong. He withdrew and clambered unsteadily to his knees. His condom was growing. It was the size of a football and still growing. He had time for a confused and drunken grunt of 'Huh?' before the engorged rubber launched itself across the room on a high-powered stream of urine. Good old Robbo. Nearly sprained his ankle running to tell the lads about that one.

Funny thing was, though, nobody thought the worse of him for it. Not even the unfortunate blonde on the receiving end. He had a way of telling the story, you see. Had this raffish charm working for him. Even women seemed to think it was pretty funny and I think it was basically down to his complete lack of shame. A really weird sort of innocence informed his whole routine. It wasn't so much a psychopathic disconnection from the consequences of his actions as much as a full-blooded celebration of them. He understood, down in his meat, that bastards are just guys being natural about things, which is why babes dig them so much.

A lot of guys get themselves all torn up over this. Especially sensitive undergrads on their first swing through Simone de Beauvoir. I saw one of these guys recently at this Egyptian restaurant. It was a pretty cool place, had really great food, but it also had this belly dancer. And I hate that belly dancer shit. Just hate it, you know. There isn't a white man alive feels comfortable in the presence of a belly dancer. Anyway there's about half a dozen of us there, all late twenties, all established couples. So there is zero sexual tension, it's a dead issue. All we want is a feed and to be left alone by the belly dancer.

Sitting at the table next to us is this young white male. And he's got a date with this incredibly horny-looking Arab girl. A real seven veils character, but only sixteen years old. One of those girls who can actually give you chest pains because your heart constricts when you first see her and you realise you'll never even say hello. And this poor bastard had a date with her. He wasn't good-looking. Had no charisma. Had nothing going for him really. Except a pair of stainless steel cojones. He'd done the one thing that no other man had done on this particular night—he'd asked her for a date. Got past her awful, intimidating beauty and put the question. At first I thought, 'Good on you pal', because I'm not even jealous. It's not an issue.

But after a while I realise it's just not going to happen. She wasn't very impressed with this middle eastern restaurant. That was his first mistake, operating on her territory. He should have taken her out to a dance or a pub, hooked into a bit of surf and turf. But he's tried to make her comfortable, tried to do the multiculturally correct thing, and now all these fried donkey dicks and roasted grasshoppers are turning up and he's just losing it. After ten minutes they run out of small talk. And then the belly dancer sees him. And these belly dancers are cruel women, you know. They can smell fear. And she flies over and starts giving it to him, the belly dance thing, and he's hopelessly embarrassed. He's sitting there burning up. His girl goes off to the toilet. He can feel every eye in the place watching him. The whole fucking joint knows. I'm sitting there feeling for this kid. It was like a bond, you know. A brother was hurting. And I'm thinking if only there was some way I could do the Vulcan mind meld. Like reach over and grab his carotid or something, effect a direct transfer of power, pour out all my hard-won knowledge, years of bitter frustration and fucking it up until I got it right. I wanted to give it all to him. But I couldn't of course. We finished eating and we left. I kept looking back as we walked up the street. I was praying that she would lead him from the place, take him in hand, take him home and do incredible middle eastern sex things to him. But I know that just didn't happen. I know he probably dives into shops to avoid meeting her gaze on the street now.

I used to be the same way before I was bad. I went through a phase of tying myself into a tangled ganglion of neuroses over these completely marginal issues. Like, should I pay for dinner? Do you kiss on the cheek or just brush the lips to establish your credentials as a non-date-rapist? Is it acceptable to start a fist fight with a guy who gives your date some lip on the way to the restaurant? What form of words are appropriate when grabbing a handful of breast? And upon arising from the dinner table with an erection, does policy really require an enlightened man to shuffle around like a half-folded flick knife? You get the idea? I don't lose a lot of sleep over these things now. I woke up on an interstate train a few weeks back with a massive erection—sometimes known as a Travelling Horn or The Hummer—stood up, stretched and turned around to find a whole carriage load of schoolgirls and their attendant nuns agog at this indiscretion. A long time ago I guess I would have turned grey and dived back into my seat. But now I simply scratched my engorged member, nodded to the head penguin and strolled off towards the bar car. Because I'm bad.

There was some hard road travelled before I got to that point, and I'll tell you about it, I promise. But I've got to say, I didn't start out completely innocent. None of us do. It's true that I came to freedom on that Christmas Eve a few years back. But I'd been nudging my way there over the years anyway. For instance, had I not ripped off a church poor box once, desperate for beer money with which I planned to get a good mate's girlfriend drunk and horizontal? Had I not invented a completely fictional younger sister only to kill her off in an equally fictional but nonetheless gigantic service station explosion on the Nullabor Plain so that I could sob to a sensitive young lady that I didn't want to spend the night alone? Yes, it all comes back to me now. We've all got it in us. It's just that we usually need some catalyst to bring out our best.

And mine was this girl, curled up in front of me.

A few days after the scene at the end of the bed I drove down to Byron Bay for a week-long recuperative cone-fest with a good mate. He'd always been a little sceptical about the girl but he knew the way of things. We talked it out on the way down. Three or fours hours of solid road work. It's a crock that guys don't know how to express themselves. It's just they only ever do it around other guys. I remember spending a morning on the roof of a friend's flat in St Kilda, helping him move and paint some heavy furniture. There were three of us up there. All men. All friends from years before in Queensland. It was grey and cold and a mean-spirited wind was howling up from Bass Strait, making it a bit of an endurance test staying outside for that long. But we were all good talkers and stay out we did, getting into the physical labour and the harsh weather and telling our favourite stories about women. Not conquest stories. Real ones. About women who'd had the measure of us. Howard, a pallid, night-stalking rock legend in thin, black, stovepipe jeans told us about Hillary, a corporate lawyer who'd run a skewer through his soul by marrying a chubby accountant and moving out to the burbs. Evan, an improbably strong, heavy-set graphic designer, confessed to self-loathing at his seduction of an overweight, part-time nurse whom he couldn't bring himself to leave because of a crushing case of guilt. And me? I recounted my hopeless pursuit of the lovely Joanne, which came to an end the day she suggested we go away on a holiday and I couldn't unlock my jaw to reply because of a black fear which welled up inside my chest, a fear of eventually, inevitably, losing her. It's kind of a pity that women never get to see that shit—it might give them pause to think. But then again, maybe not. Men implicitly understand these failings in each other. Women just think they're pathetic.

Anyway, Dave and I were headed down to Byron a few days after Christmas. We had a big bag of smoke in the back of the car and a house rented just outside town with a bunch of babes we knew. We weren't fixing to hit on these babes. They were old friends who were just too fast and too smart for the likes of us. Dave simply figured I should hang out with some women who weren't going to gut me at the first opportunity. He'd come out of a bad scene a year or so back himself, a real Medusa scenario— you know, head full of snakes—so he'd been there. And I was one tender puppy on that road trip. The sense of power which had filled my bones at the foot of the bed back in Brisbane had turned cold and sour about fifteen minutes after I'd pimp-rolled out the front door. Dave was a hardy, barrel-chested sort of character, but he understood. We talked about guy stuff for the first hour or so:

sport, politics, drugs. He broached the topic of women shortly after we'd stopped for a chocolate-covered banana in northern NSW. Asked how the girl was going.

'The big splitteroo,' I shrugged and then fell quiet, because you don't want to spill your guts.

Dave nodded and eased into a telling of his twelve months with Medusa. He'd had to fight off the attentions of three or four other guys to get to her and he was kind of bemused now that he'd even bothered. Kept smiling to himself as he told stories about her. She was European, a Pole or something like that, second generation, and poor old Dave had turned himself inside out trying to cater to her ethnic whims. He dragged himself around an endless series of folk festivals and family outings and tried to ignore the increasingly complex and arbitrary little psycho-dramas by which she spiced up their relationship. It took a secret attack on his flat—after he'd dipped out of a visit to a Polish film night—before Dave, standing amid the rubble of upturned tables and slashed cushions, realised he might have made a mistake chasing this particular babushka. He ditched the flat, moved way across town, and didn't go out for six months.

It made me feel a little better. The girl on the bed hadn't cut up my clothes or anything, only my feelings. And of course I gave back as good as I got. And in a weird kind of way, I enjoyed it. I remember careening around my house a few days after the Christmas Eve scene. I remember this moment of absolute clarity. Like Colonel Kurtz at the end of *Apocalypse Now*. Martin Sheen has arrived, all fucked up and confused and ready to do him in, and this bald-headed lunatic is just sitting there mumbling good-natured shit like, 'Are you an assassin, Willard?', and trying to explain the pure crystalline nature of horror, and how finally comprehending it had been like being shot through the head with a diamond. Or something like that. In my confused state it made perfect sense. I remember stalking the house slapping my own forehead at the purity of the experience I'd just gone through with this girl. She had fucked me up. Totally and irrevocably. There were no half measures or weasel words. For a very short time I had loved her. And now I didn't. There it is.

I rang her that afternoon. I felt like I was in the eye of a storm, or maybe experiencing one of those moments of clarity that only madmen and drunks really know about. Looking back now I'm still amazed at my absolute calm as her phone rang. I had to get to her before it passed, as I knew it would. She was surprised to hear my voice, as you can imagine. I didn't stay on long. I told her I had to say this now while I still could. She waited nervously.

'Thanks,' I said. 'Thanks for everything.'

And hung up, come to freedom.

SCARY CHIX

I came late to the knowledge. It's a pity really. I guess, like most of these things, I blame the Christian Brothers. They flogged the fear into me. There was a girls school across the street from ours, our sister school I guess you'd call it; a mysterious place peopled by strange, exotic creatures. We'd been separated from them at age ten and that segregation was enforced with traditional Irish brutality. My first memory of high school is of three boys being hauled before an assembly of 300 and energetically flogged for dallying on St Mary's side of the road after school. It's no wonder that fear was a cold, subterranean stream running beneath the surface of any exchange with those remote would-be women. It is a wonder, however, that I came so late to the knowledge of what fear means.

Just a few years ago I could stare you in the face and deny it. I remember doing just that at some roaring, drunken affair, a book launch I think, for Helen Razer and Mikey Robbins at the North Bondi RSL. Some of the wonderbabes from *Australian Women's Forum* were there—throwing down the free booze, lending a little flash/trash cachet to the evening. I'd fallen into conversation with the then editor, an attractive, intelligent big-haired type who was trying to convince me that men were scared of her. Not scared in the way of trembling before her insanely violent editorial temper tantrums. For these were non-existent. She had a laid-back vibe with the blue pencil. But just scared. Scared of her looks, her smarts, her money, her success, her life. We were, my brothers and I, unmanned at the prospect.

I wouldn't have it, of course. I was younger then and did not understand. Yes, I agreed, some of these guys, your older guys, they hadn't coped well with the feminist revolution. But what did you expect? Gratitude? Give me a break. Crazy old witches wanted to kick down the gates of our kingdom, snuff out the divine right of guys, bring the hammer down on all the really cool stuff we'd been sacking away for thousands of years. Guys don't go directly from king of the world to tame, domesticated überwench accessory without a few adjustment problems.

It's a generational thing, I gesticulated, beer flying everywhere. Those guys who'd grown up after the Liberation had come to terms with it, but you couldn't expect the old guys to cope. Have a little sympathy. The temple had come down around their ears. Just ignore their cries and get on with it. They'll die out eventually.

No, she argued. You don't understand. It's you guys, you young, enlightened, post-Lib men. You are the problem.

I didn't believe her. But now I do.

The response of Neanderthal man to the modern femme is hearty bluster and buffoonery. It is mostly guileless and benign, for all of its offensiveness, and may best be contemplated in the likes of John Herron or John Howard condescending to the likes of Lowitja O'Donoghue as 'my dear lady . . .' When carried off with antique grace it can be forgiven, even endearing, like an invite to a young woman to take an ironic spot of lunch at the Melbourne Club with her grandfather. When directly propagating exploitation, coercion and long-discredited power relationships, Neanderthal man retains a capacity to do some appalling damage. But as Justice Bollen discovered after contemplating the acceptability of a little rougher than usual handling in the marriage bed, he runs the risk of massive retaliation.

The younger, wiser man, for whom there is no generational excuse, turns instead to subterfuge, to the sham camouflage of the sensitive new ager or to whatever devious mutation of that Trojan Horse of the gender war might currently hold sway. These are the young high-flying law firm partners who would cringe at naked discrimination. They know only too well the productivity benefits of hiring young female lawyers out to prove themselves to the upper ranks of the profession's bloated, mediocre men. They know too that their own progression into those ranks will not likely be upset by most of those women, whose careers will be aborted by their desire for children within ten years of leaving law school. In conversations with them, the smartest men will be earnest, sincere and entirely treacherous. They will never hand over the keys to the kingdom. These men are all of the creative directors, the chiefs of staff, the internet gurus, political fixers, chief accountants, heads of department, kings of share housing and much-loved cult authors who know that we need only be half as good to fly twice as high.

They are the disappointing objects of my big-haired *Forum* friend's drunken diatribe. We were all of us cowards, she insisted. Be we dotcom millionaire or post-grunge playwright, we had been judged and found wanting by the second sex. And the thing is, you know, she's right. What a long, hesitant course I took coming to this knowledge, more by chance than design. Once again I can blame, or maybe thank, the Christian Brothers for this. Having been denied any normal sort of friendship with women as a teenager, I sought them out as a young man. Now approaching middle age I found myself surrounded by them: forbiddingly intelligent, attractive women, witty, forthright, driven and alone in the world.

For years in my twenties, I paid no heed when my fan-tastically accomplished and desirable girlie friends would lay it on thick about the dearth of 'good men'. Having endured some long dry spells without the lovin' of a good woman I figured they were simply wandering the same desert and in time its barren passages would fall behind them too. Later, as it became more perplexing, I put their lonesomeness down to the huge number of gay men in Sydney, and later still, and more absurdly, to the slight sta-tistical imbalance favouring the number of women in any given population. I wasn't alone. The media was awake to the problem and ever ready to cash in.

As I travelled more often on publicity tours I began to think it less curious when, late at night, over the dying beers of the day, women I hardly knew would ask if I had a secret stash of guys I could parcel out to their incomprehensibly single female friends. Something was afoot. In other bars, over many more beers, this time with my secret stash of available guys, I'd broach the subject of why they'd never made any serious attempts on our mutual friends, the überbabes. Through a stream of drunken, barely articulate responses came a moral certainty. They were scared of them and of what they would demand.

It seemed that, for all of our pretence at pashmina-soft sensitivity, we are essentially the same old barbarian horde guy, fighting like a dog to maintain a righteous lock on the biggest, juiciest bones. Women might have changed some these last thirty years but men haven't. The sad clowns of the men's movement are simply the exceptions who proved the rule. While they donned loincloths and face paint and promised to sleep on the wet spot, legions of regular guys wised up enough to pay a little lip service to the idea of an equal partnership between the sexes. But every survey of household labour shows us still kicking back while our babes do the hard yards. And far from being feminised, the public sphere has instead become a realm of super-exploitation where women either toil in low pay, low status McJobs, or flog themselves witless in professional roles trying to prove themselves worthy of entry to a boys club they can never hope to join.

Perhaps in time the market will force its own resolution,

at least for highly-skilled women. Over the long arc, companies that understand what a valuable resource they have in their desperate female crew and respond accordingly will grab a competitive advantage over their old, steam-driven corporate rivals. But what I'm wondering is whether it'll make a damn bit of difference to the private lives of those women whose careers might conceivably benefit. For deep beneath the cover story of equal opportunity and the post-feminist man, our traitor's hearts beat with a weak fluttering arrhythmia. The hearts of frightened sheep. We are not nearly so scared of women stealing into our clubs, our regiment, our managing director's chair as we are of them creeping quietly through the barbed wire entanglements which guard our shivering hearts. Because there they will find the truth, that we are afeared of them.

There is a passage from de Beauvoir I've always loved: that for man, Woman is the vertigo of ruin. It is through her that the young man learns of felicity and suffering, of vice, virtue, lust, renunciation, devotion and tyranny, that he learns to know himself. She is also, half a century later, an intruder raking in the hearts of men for the secrets we have hidden there, the truth of our duplicity and fearfulness. We do not love her as our equal. We fear her as an invader.

We have no answers for her demands; that if we are to be her one true love we may have to put aside our childish prerogatives, that we should yield some of our desires and dreams to hers, and that we must abandon the conceit that the world is all about us.

Thus the curse of a young, beautiful woman—that she

will terrify mortal men—may in time be visited on any woman strong enough to seek us in our lair. For who stands before us there? Virago of battles past and inward greatness, confident, knowing, our equal in all things save those in which she is our better? Or is it just the vertigo of ruin, the envoy of hard change and an end to an eon of inherited comfort, privilege and autonomy. She stands alluring and ominous, and most men looking on her do not see their salvation but their doom. Most men are fools.

WOMEN'S WEIGHT-LIFTING

Why are people so unkind? What is it that makes them smirk and snort and shake their heads when told you are off to the women's weight-lifting? Forty-eight kilogram class. It's almost as though they think you're off to an old-fashioned circus freak show, with the bearded lady twirling a couple of dwarves over her shaggy bonce. Although I guess I can forgive a bit of smirkage, having watched the light division of the men's weight-lifting, with those nuggety little guys flexing musculature which doesn't even look human—more like the remnant stumps of pterodactyl wings growing from their chest and backs.

The weight-lifting boofmeisters seem to have been awake to the burlesque potential of the first ever women's Olympic event and so laid on the feminine makeover with a trowel. Due to the growing popularity of women's weight-lifting, a boofmeister told the audience at Darling Harbour, an increasing number of enthusiastic female spectators were being drawn to the sport and thus the world weight-lifting federation had proclaimed this day 'The Day of Women in Weight-lifting'. To celebrate, a number of very 'special ladies' behind the sport's ascent to Olympus were introduced and thanked before a bemused audience. Some more special ladies, the competitors, were introduced and presented with a single flower by powerfully connected blazer-clad boofmeisters. After which the same barrel-chested poobahs moved slowly through the venue, with bunches of flowers in ham hock fists, seeking out other special ladies in the audience—or really, any ladies in the audience—to similarly menace with a 'floral gesture'.

The special ladies on stage, the track-suited pioneers, seemed small inside their team clobber, but a medal prospect like American Tara Nott, I was assured, could snap twice her body weight into the air above her ponytail. Or to bring it home, she could pick up your hefty, beer-gutted correspondent and carry him out of the venue like a cheap tin trophy. And if he weren't such a happily domesticated chap, that idea might be kind of exciting, especially as Tara had the ol' red, white and blue painted onto her teeth, giving her something of a comely barbarian air when she strained at the clean and jerk.

Twelve small women made up this first contingent of Olympians. No lusty, sheep-tossing Aussie wenches amongst them, more's the pity, but the boofmeisters had rounded up an apostle's dozen from the US, Indonesia, Japan, PNG, France, Myanmar, Brazil, Bulgaria, and Italy, the last a senorita with a name to die for in the weight-lifting world: Giganti.

Dika Toua, a sixteen-year-old student from Port Moresby, was given the honour of being the first woman to step up for glory, and the import of the moment must have robbed her of strength or, more likely, technique, as she fluffed the big moment on the first attempt, only to return within two minutes and snatch aloft 45 kilos with such alacrity she seemed to surprise even herself. When she slammed the bar down it was as an afterthought and the weights bounced back, threatening to smack her in the shins for her forgetfulness. The bright, white, beautiful grin which split her face, however, spoke of a carefree, joyous sartori, an intoxicated being-in-the-moment that will forever separate those who watch from those who do.

The much-anticipated freak show failed to materialise. As one special lady after another emerged from the warm-up room to the sort of hog-stomping rock anthems or mock epic torch songs favoured by high-end lap-dancing clubs, they revealed themselves, sans trackies, as magnificently sculpted athletes, without the weird, prosthetic-like supplementary muscle slabs of their male counterparts. There was much to enjoy, and maybe a little to fear, in the intense Grace Jones stare of French woman Sabrina Richard, as she whipped 70 kilograms over her head like it was an old straw hat. The Indonesians, Indriyani and Rumbewas, were so little troubled by throwing around even greater weights that they could probably find an easy dollar tossing irksome militia out of West Timor, although Rumbewas' odd, double-jointed elbows did bend back alarmingly whenever holding the bar high. And the crowd favourite, American Robin Goad, provided as much entertainment approaching the podium as she did heaving her loads skyward. She burst out of the big blue doors to the back stage area, storming along, full of angry pills, yelling to herself, flapping her arms, yelping as she grabbed the bar, grunting and roaring like a bear as she hoisted it high. Goad, in appearance the archetypal girl-next-door, didn't just attack the bar, she opened a big can of whoop-ass on it, shaking her fists, shouting threats and imprecations, whipping up the audience along with her. With Goad on stage you couldn't but help jumping to your feet and hollering stuff like, 'Yo! Kick its ass girlfriend!'

'Twas not to be, though. The former Soviet Bloc still has a lock on this sport, partly from hauling their tractors out of sucking mud pits for so long, and partly because of their well-developed pharmaceutical industry. While the American's histrionics furnished the sizzle, a quiet Bulgarian named Izabela Dragneva walked off with the gold through the simple expedient of launching the equivalent of three well-fed sportswriters into the ether. Unfortunately it turned out she was chock full o' roids at the time. So maybe the hefty chicks don't have that far to go before they're the equal of their male counterparts.

Tequila slammer 'I MEAN, WHAT IS IT WITH YOU PEOPLE? YOU DON'T LIKE QUALITY ENTERTAINMENT? OR IS IT JUST THAT YOU SPELL QUALITY WITH A "K"?'

SATAN'S MOBILE

'I rang customer service.'

I had lost my first mobile phone, the Brick. I had loved the Brick. It was ugly. You could club a man to death with it, but it had served me well. Luckily—and I write that with some irony—I had insurance. I spent a day gathering paperwork, visiting cops, filling in forms. That done, I tried to find the Optus shop in the city to lodge my claim. There had been one in the mall, but when I got there, the shopfront was bare. I rang customer service, who directed me to some geek outfit on the other side of town. An electronics place. A long hot walk, but I don't mind a trundle, so I set off. Unfortunately, when I arrived the geeks just gave me the blank, dead look of the deeply disinterested and said they could not help. (They did try to sell me a $1200 Nokia though. Enterprising little geeks.)

I rang customer service. Try this other place, they said. Back across the city I trekked. To some no-name outfit behind a train station who ignored me and talked amongst themselves for an hour until they realised I wasn't going away. They took my details, said they'd send the claim on.

They lied.

A week later I rang customer service to see if my paperwork had been processed. They had no paperwork. I lost another day providing them with some. Finally, weeks after the Brick disappeared, I received a call: I could pick up a replacement . . . after paying an excess. $150. Oh, I said, a slight flicker of nervous energy twitching my eyelid. That's a surprise. There'd been no mention of that before. But I figured, okay. Chill out. You can't encourage people to go losing their mobiles. There has to be some incentive to look after them.

So, after a few unexpected delays, I had a new digital phone. I was excited. I'd heard good things about digital. How much better it was, how much clearer, more secure. Sadly, I was not to experience these delights myself. The phone they 'gave' me for $150 was not actually a mobile phone. It was just a piece of crap, cunningly disguised as a mobile phone.

I turned it on. Nothing. Nada. The big goose egg. Okay. It was lunch time. All the phone guys might be at Pizza Hut. I waited another hour. Still no connection. I rang customer service. They said they'd take care of it, try again later. I did. No connection.

I rang customer service. I don't want to bore you with the details (and they are very, very boring, believe me), but I dealt with another six or seven, maybe even eight phone reps. Or to put it another way. I rang customer service again. And again. And again. And again. And again. And, well, you get the drift. Some were confident. Some were confused. Some even had the decency to be embarrassed. But none could make my phone work. Around midnight a science guy decided one of the phone reps, probably the confused one, had 'deleted' my account. I was an Uncustomer.

Another day shot to hell. Next morning, a Saturday, I did not ring customer service. I cabbed directly over to the Optus Death Star in North Sydney, a $25 fare, and we sat at a computer and made everything beautiful. We actually got the thing up and working. I nearly cried.

I probably should have.

You see, I'd noticed the keypad seemed a little 'sticky'. Not sticky as in I'd just spilled a glass of Coke on it, but sticky as in sometimes you had to press it three or four times to get a response, and other times you'd press a key and it stayed pressed, beeping away like a demented insect. I asked the science guy if this was normal and he came over all shifty and wouldn't look me in the eye and said yeah, new phones are like that. You have to wear them in. Like jeans. O-k-a-y, I thought. You succeeded where others failed. I'll trust you.

What a fool I was. By the afternoon, the 'sticky' keys were stuck. Completely. The phone, now connected to the network, was useless.

I rang customer service.

Take the phone to our repair place at the end of the universe, they said. You'll have it back in a few days.

At about the three-week mark I rang customer service

again, to discuss this 'few days' business. They told me it was waiting in dispatch. Oh thank God, I thought, I'll pick it up tomorrow. But I didn't. That took another two weeks.

And when I got it, it worked fine! For two days. Then it was a useless piece of crap in the shape of a telephone again. Man, I almost wept when those keys stuck. I can't even begin to make you understand the black waves of despair and rage which boiled up inside me. But I won't be ringing customer service this time. No, I'm calling the Vatican, or maybe even *A Current Affair*. Because I know now that I am in possession of Satan's Own Mobile Phone.

FICKLE MUSH-HEADS

Late on Whacking Day, Springfield Mayor Diamond Joe Quimby's stretch limousine glides to a halt outside Homer's place, where a huge crowd has gathered. The future President of the United States alights and some flat-headed killer in an off-the-rack suit appears beside him with a briefcase full of pre-whacked snakes. B-e-a-u-t-i-f-u-l, thinks Quimby and, taking a handful, he waves them at the crowd. 'Look everyone, dead snakes.' But something has happened and the people of Springfield, previously mad with a brain fever for killing these critters, turn on Quimby like he's some sort of monster. Outraged, he hits back. Says he's had it with them, they're nothing but a bunch of fickle mush-heads.

Truer words were never spoke.

I mean, what is it with you people? You don't like quality entertainment? Or is it just that you spell quality with a 'K'? You lap up *World's Worst Drivers VI* and ignore *Drop the Dead Donkey*. Somebody broadcasts yet another hour of blooper reels, commercials and a Daddo sibling and there's no holding you back. I'm stunned. Incredulous. I'm like, sweet mother of God, do people meters only go to families who all sleep in the same room and play banjo with their toes? Or is it just that sitting in front of the box with flat, lifeless eyes and slack jaws waiting to see who can hang the longest tendril of drool is your idea of a home entertainment system?

It's not, you say? Oh. Well, allow me to retort!

Exhibit One. *The Larry Sanders Show*. The least watched best show of the summer. You think *Frontline* is dark? A little unfair on Ray? Well this show is evil. E-e-e-e-e-v-i-l, I tells ya! Television does not get any blacker, more malevolent and funnier than this. That's right— funny. It's satire, people. I can't believe that some of you think it's all for real and get pissed that the guests are only on for a few minutes. You want to watch the cancerous heart of network politics and mass media narcissism laid open by experts? You want to see David Duchovny confess an unhealthy obsession for an egomaniacal talk show host? You want to watch Rip Torn play one of the most complex, engaging villains since Shakespeare was a boy? Then watch Larry. I'm begging you. Before Ten bin it forever and run endless loops of cut and paste Benny Hill specials instead.

Exhibit Two. *Homicide—Life on the Street*. No, it isn't set on beautiful Sydney harbour. No, you will not get to whip yourself into a lather of adolescent expectation over the prospects of Maggie and PJ rubbing their pink bits together. And no, there is not a chance in hell of a guest appearance by anybody from Summer Bay. So I guess you won't be watching, will you? I mean, it's only the best cop show in the world. Buried by Seven on two separate nights in the ratings dead zone. Because you cretinous oafs wouldn't know great acting, tight scripting and top class character-based drama if it jumped up and bit you on the arse.

Exhibit Three. The new *Blankety Blanks*. And this is what happens. This is the result of letting network goons play you for fools. I can't . . . it's just that . . . oh forget it.

I don't know why I bother. You make me sick. Just go away.

THE DECLINE OF THE
STRIP CLUB

It's a disgrace I tell you. A gold-plated, five star cluster-fuck of world class quality. Long after the last Olympic turista has departed they'll still be shaking their heads, muttering sadly if we're lucky, angrily if we're not. As Shakespeare had Mountjoy put it when Agincourt went horribly pear-shaped for the French, 'Shame upon unutterable shame'. Or something like that.

What sort of a joint puts itself about as a global city of the new millennium when it can't even throw together a decent red light district? So low has Sydney fallen in the annals of naughtiness that we've had to import a jumbo load of foreign trollops to service the needs of our Olympic visitors. I ask you, is this the sort of message we want to send to the world? That we can't even organise a fuck in our own brothels?

Time was when Sydney could stand proudly beside Newark, New Jersey, as one of the most corrupt cities in all of Christendom. But a New Puritanism has laid a heavy

hand on the sex industry. The last time I entered a house
of ill-repute may well be the last time I enter a house of ill-
repute, at least in Sydney. The Pink Pussycat I think it was,
or maybe the Love Machine. It's a big ask to remember
through the thirty Scotch barrier. I had repaired there with
my agent, Miss Annette, to discuss some minor financial
embarrassment to the interests of JB Pty Ltd in the People's
Republic of Burma, or Myanmar or whatever those greedy,
two-timing motherfuckers in the SLORC junta call their
godforsaken fourth world shit hole now . . . Anyway, long
story short, we needed a quiet drink in the relaxed atmosphere of a sophisticated gentleman's retreat for our business
meeting, and a little girl/girl raunch on stage wouldn't have
gone astray either.

Well, you can imagine our distress when the promised
hard liquor and live sex turned out to be entirely illusory.
It transpired that our booze, which certainly cost as much
as a schooner of Maker's Mark, were a couple of fizzy low
rent faux pisstakes on the concept of a Clayton's drink. The
barkeep explained that with the imprisonment of a large
number of former business associates in the Police Service,
it had become untenable to run an unlicensed bar. I was
astounded. I had been given exactly the same pathetic
excuse at another strip club across the road just ten
minutes previously. I thought that to lose your influence
with corrupt licensing branch detectives once might be
considered bad luck. But twice just looked like very bad
management.

My surly disposition was not improved by the disgraceful travesty playing itself out on stage. A friendly young

miss was attempting to throw her hips into a mock provocative routine which suffered from one fundamental flaw. She wouldn't take her clothes off. Now, I don't know about you but when I hand over a big wad of the folding stuff to see someone grossly exploited in a perpetuation of long-discredited sexual power relationships I want to see some actual exploitation. Not this farrago of a tired old belly dance shuffle. The distraught incredulity on the faces of our fellow patrons testified to their own distress.

It was an outrage I tells ya. I well remember my first visit to the Cross, possibly to this very same establishment, when the obscene blandishments of the spruikers had not proved to be so fanciful. For six bucks I got to drink watered down whiskey and watch some hatchet-faced junkie drag a lost mental case onto the stage and fuck him with the assistance of a big tub of chicken fat. Now that's what I call world class! The whole scene was so horribly confronting that three Indian men in the row behind me tripped over each other trying to flee from the joint. In between acts, which included a number of top notch novelty performers such as the snake lady and a Thai girl who could fanny pop a ping pong ball clear across the room, broken down old prostitutes with eyes of glass and hearts like tape recorders would circulate amongst the patrons asking, somewhat misleadingly, if anybody wanted a lady. God only knows where they planned to find one, but at least they made the offer.

No more though. I can only shudder to think of what Juan Antonio and his fellow committee members will make of the embarrassing charade being touted as Sydney's adult entertainment district. Imagine the headlines when they want to nip into a marital aids store to pick up a little something for the significant other only to be asked to pay a cover charge. Quelle horreur.

We shall be an international laughing stock. Mark my words.

WHY I WILL NOT BE
WRITING FOR YOU

Memo To: Campbell, D, editor of *Semper*
From: Birmingham, J
Re: Newcastle Youngsters Festival

You vicious bastard! I cannot believe you worthless punks are still chasing me over that damned phonecard bill! It was years ago, for Christ's sake. I'm a respected author now goddamn it. You simply cannot pull these undergraduate stunts with me anymore. My cruel and ambitious agent Miss Annette will no doubt be in contact to discuss both the bill and the removal of your nuts and their imminent transformation into a fetching if somewhat hairy little purse.

Yes, I will admit that technically I may have used the office plastic as a bartercard at the Purple Parrot's long-lost and much lamented house of whoopee, but if you check your predecessor's files I'm sure that somewhere down the back of the cabinet, maybe even on the ground somewhere nearby, you will find a full authorisation, signed in my own dried nasal blood on the back of the spare electoral enrolment form I borrowed from my fellow alumnus Mr Mike Kaiser.

You could, if you wish, follow through on your stated intention to hand over all the material to the Federal Police task force investigating the Reith phonecard imbroglio. But do we really want to bicker and argue about who killed who? Hmm, David? You might be interested to know that my people had you tagged from the very moment you stepped out of the Vice-Chancellor's stretch limo in Newcastle, and while I might not have cut such an intimidating figure, passed out as I was in a pool of my own urine at the rear of the Festival Club, that does not mean your own indiscretions (as well as those of that woolly-headed cretin you insist on travelling with) were not noticed, photographed and distributed widely amongst my operatives.

Your pathetic little gambit in sending the Angry Poet after me when he was unmanned by severe alcohol poisoning on Sunday night was a cruel abuse of the poor man. Did you really imagine that being bitchslapped by the Poet was likely to put the frighteners on me? He was just lucky that I was so stoned on chocolate space cake I didn't realise I'd been smacked until about twenty-five minutes later, by which time he had slunk off into the night, howling like a wounded dog, clutching that handful of Union food vouchers you'd bribed him with, you nasty little crim. What will happen when the poor old Poet tries to cash those babies in? A bunch of your goons are gonna fall on him and gang fuck him into submission like they did with that poor publications officer. You make me want to wretch. To think that the high office of *Semper* has fallen into the sticky fingers of such as you.

And I don't care what so-called photographic evidence you think you have. To quote Diamond Joe Quimby, 'That could be anyone's ass!'

I spent my five days in Newcastle giving a number of comparatively very well-attended talks on a series of industry panels with other highly regarded mainstream Australians. You claim to be able to produce at least half a dozen people who suffered mild to middling psychotic reactions after being 'forced' by my good self to sample a number of hashish-laden confectionery products. Well excuse me, David, but how the hell do you 'force' people to gobble down handfuls of crumbling hallucinogenic Anzac cookies? Those people were greedy pigs! And what's more they were, by their own admission, completely fucked on illegal drugs. I can't believe you would be so naive as to imagine that they would survive more than three minutes of cross-examination by my high-priced legal rottweilers.

And as for your intention of dragging the Festival organisers into your sordid little schemes, I can only pray that you leave the poor youngsters out of it. They're a good bunch of kiddies, trying to put on a show with very little support, and they've done a bang-up job three years running without any help from you. You can lay money on the barrel that if they ask for my advice about your stupid idea of floating the whole Electrofringe Festival on Nasdaq and using the profit to leverage a forced entry into the US college dorm porn cam market I will be telling them to keep the folding stuff safely in their pocket. You losers are in enough financial trouble already without dragging down a posse of innocent dupes from brave little Newcastle. (Hah, didn't think anybody would take the Union Treasurer's wild accusations seriously, did you, David? Well, welcome to Mike Munro hell, my friend. When the invoice for that jet and all of those Mexican hookers you chartered over the Olympic fortnight finally hits the press you will be dead meat on a stick, buddy. Every tabloid jackal in the country will be gnawing on your penis as a novelty tapas item by nightfall.)

You might have noticed that the jacarandas came out early this year. Ask not for whom the purple flower blooms . . . Very, very soon now you'll be pitched out of *Semper*'s velvet-lined jacuzzi and onto the street and then you'll be in my world, little man. I don't think you and the woolly-headed one really want to go back to pushing dicky to pay for your electrolysis, do you? So if you have half a brain you'll forget about the phonecard bill. Blame it on young Reith or something. Come on board for the big win. Those pinheads in the AFP will believe anything. And you can forget about coming the heavy with me. It didn't work for Mike Kaiser and he is so far out of your league you'd have to consider it a privilege to eat a scraping of his dick cheese on a Ritz cracker.

So no, David, there will be no gratis report from Newcastle. You were there. If you had managed to drag yourself out of the trough of the men's urinal where my sources tell me you passed out, covered in your own sick, in the early hours of the weekend, you might have had a shot at explaining away your massive expenses claim. But c'est la vie, motherfucker. And good luck finding a job.

[This piece was published by David Campbell in *Semper*, the University of Queensland student mag, after many months of pestering JB to write a charity piece for his old alma mater.]

MR BROWN GOES TO THE
RACES

This week's Montgomery Burns Award for Outstanding Achievement in the Field of Excellence goes to Greens Senator Bob Brown for his foray into the online gambling fiasco. At no point did this teddy bears' picnic become more disconnected from the world of real things than at the moment when Brown compared licensing net betting to setting up state-sponsored heroin farms.

Well, you know, Bob, maybe heroin farms aren't such a bad idea. They'd plug a gushing leak in our balance of payments and prop up a very ordinary-looking budget—assuming the Feds didn't want to cut anyone else in for a piece of the action. And you'd have to figure that John Howard's government-issue smack would have a nice, creamy consistency totally lacking in your average foil of street heroin.

But I doubt Senator Brown would be interested. For a supposedly progressive guy he's got a really censorious, judgmental streak to his character. It makes for an interesting combination, what with his legislative nincompoopery and general political boneheadeness. I don't have a clue why he was so keen to roll over and give it up for the racing industry while simultaneously trying to deep-six the nascent net gambling export sector. But there he was, in the heat of battle with Richard Alston, pulling on the armour and saddling up his trusty burro for a tilt at a very odd windmill.

'I'm really very much against online gambling on such things as poker machines,' he told the ABC after the Government released its curiously sophisticated online gambling policy.

Net betting was creating a whole heap o' trouble, according to Brown, 'So I think we have to separate them from the racing industry which is a big employer region-ally and has got a long history in the country, otherwise we would be setting up plenty of heroin farms to create new jobs.'

I would never have taken Bob for a fan of the gee-gees. But I guess there's no figuring a guy who'd like to protect one of the most endemically corrupt industries in Australia while he shitcans our last great hope to snip armies of gullible foreigners for a fat wad of the folding stuff.

Of all the players in what's erroneously referred to as an internet gambling policy debate only Brown had the stand-up cojones to provide a genuinely startling moment of comedy relief. Kate Lundy, the ALP's Information Tech-nology shadow minister, phoned in a predictable perform-ance, rote-slamming the Government whilst cunningly shifting her own position to constantly obscure the massive sucking vacuum which science has proven exists at the exact same coordinates you would expect to find Labor Party policy. The Democrats' Natasha Stott Despoja came over commendably gimlet-eyed and libertarian, opposing the legislation because she didn't think it was feasible or desirable to hassle anybody about anything. And the Government got to put themselves about as the sort of arch conservatives who'd make a Taliban mosque full of Buddha-hating mullahs look like a bunch of bootie train conductors.

If there was any surprise beyond Senator Brown's fondness for the nags it was that the Government lost a rolled gold opportunity to spin their One Nation demographic a yarn about how they had a cunning plan to protect chronically addicted local gamblers, whilst also taking off a global market of rich, dopey ethnics. Surely they could have retailed an image of decent Aussie punters corralled safely behind the Coalition's digital picket fence while our rapacious bookies looted the world of its spare pounds, greenbacks, Deutschmarks and zlotys.

Maybe it's just that, having decided to authorise the likes of Kerry Packer to grab up the world's punters by the ankle and give 'em a damn good shakedown, Alston and crew were somewhat less than keen to boast of their new-found pirate sensibilities, seeing as how their dumbarse moratorium aborted a multibillion dollar export sector in the first months of its life.

I meant what what I said before when I described the Coalition's plan to scam the outside world at online black-jack as sophisticated. Politically it is. (Technically, of course, it's a dead dog.) But it's hardly bragworthy material when you realise that while they've been cooking up this brilliant scheme, the number of global internet casinos has doubled, 54 other governments have legalised internet gaming, and the United States has realised there is a quid to be made. I think our chance to soak the world on this one has well and truly gone.

Perhaps the Ayatollah of the Communications Department might consider putting aside his cat-o'-nine-tails for a minute and thinking about the payday we've just missed. After all, there is one other great moneymaker online which we haven't really exploited yet. Nooky.com.

IT'S RAINING COPS

David Weldon noticed the young girl as he tried to escape, hurrying through the park as cops charged past him. She was alone, moving towards the gate like him. She wore black jeans and a tee shirt and she had short, dark hair. A cop drew level with her and let one go—a round house punch to her face which knocked her off her feet. He kept moving but pivoted to see the effect. It was a good hit. 'He smiled,' said Weldon, who tried to go to the girl. But another cop shoved him on before he could reach her.

Just the facts, ma'am?

Okay, the facts are these. At about twenty past eight on the night of Saturday 19 October 1996, a few thousand people were enjoying the closing hours of an outdoor rock concert and market festival organised by Brisbane radio station 4ZZZ. By eight thirty on the same night Queensland police, assisted by the Australian military, had launched an attack which cleared the park and filled scores of paddy wagons with injured, frightened people. The chaos was made worse by a huge thunderstorm which erupted over Brisbane at that time. Police claimed that they initially responded to a brawl which broke out in the bar area. They say this got out of hand and they increased their presence to deal with the ensuing riot.

The police are lying.

Market Day, like Triple Zed, is an old and slightly notorious Brisbane institution. Long a rallying point for those northerners who refuse to line up with the System, the station has always been a target for the pimps and mercenaries who live off and defend that system. Triple Zed takes no advertising, relying on subscriptions and fundraisers like Market Day, a major leg of the station's funding strategy. Take it away and watch the whole thing come crashing down.

Market Day has grown bigger and gaudier and even a tad mediaeval in its gathering-of-the-tribes air. But the organisational machinery which makes it happen is as slick and professional as anything fielded by Big Day Out or the Livid Festival. Up to fifteen people run the organising machine, a crew which spins up to about 150 staff and volunteers on the actual day. Liaison meetings with the police, the council, ambulance and so on start months beforehand. October '96 was no different. Peter Rohweder, station treasurer and a Market Day coordinator, helped set up one such meeting at West End police station, the lockup nearest Musgrave Park, the site of Market Day. The meeting worked through the date, starting time, finishing time, the location of the stages, number of bands and stalls, and arrangements for selling alcohol and controlling underage drinking. Terry O'Connor, Zed's long-haired, cadaverous security guy, asked the police not to clear the park until the official closing time. 'Last time they began clearing an hour before the bands had finished,' said O'Connor.

West End understood and agreed. They also told Zed that the Public Safety Response Team would not enter the park 'unless there was a major incident'. The PSRT are the hard riders of the force in Queensland. They cruise the city in packs, stomping down on any sign of trouble without hesitation or pity. They are known for their aggression, their ruthlessness and the rakish blue baseball caps they sport—a little like the street gangs they are tasked with suppressing.

Rohweder copied full details of the final arrangements to West End two weeks before Market Day. There were no problems or late changes. The police presence was supposed to be minimal. On Saturday afternoon, however, at about a quarter past four, O'Connor was introduced to another sergeant from West End, a stranger, and told he was now the officer in charge. 'It was a bit of a problem,' he said ruefully. 'He hadn't been at the meetings and didn't know what the arrangements were.' Mark Simpson, the constable Triple Zed had been liaising with, was now out of the loop.

On the Monday after the riot, when a shaken Police Minister Cooper called Zed in for a meeting with his commanders, they claimed it had never been the case that

Simpson would be in charge. The sergeant was always meant to take over. A Superintendent had a thick wad of paper which he kept waving and pointing to, claiming that thirty police, not half a dozen, had been planned to prevent trouble, that this had been arranged weeks before-hand and updated on a weekly basis.

'At no point were we informed of any of this,' said O'Connor.

Police command did not cover themselves in glory during the meeting with Cooper. Expecting their conservative National Party boss would back them up, they were probably horrified to discover he might just leave them with their dicks in the breeze. Cooper was in no mood to eat the big dead cat on a stick his officers handed him. He pressed home the point that he wanted to see Market Day happen again. As he would a few weeks later, when police arrested dozens of mourners after the funeral of an Aboriginal elder, Russell Cooper refused to blindly support his troops. He seemed to have learned a lesson lost on previous National Party ministers: sometimes they just weren't worth it.

Michelle Vlatkovic arrived at Musgrave Park with a friend just after lunch. They had volunteered to tie arm bands for an hour or so, after which they qualified for a couple of cheap beers. They got their tickets, sat on the grass outside the doof tent, kicked back in the sun, listened to the music and relaxed. 'There were dreaded folk there, Mohicans, punk rockers, goths, all these different strands of the music scene,' she said. Young surfies mingled with indie kids, skaters, old hippies and ravers. There were plenty of families, kids in strollers and toddlers hanging out down at the bouncy castle and on the swings near the entrance to the park. Murries, who got in free, it being their land and all, grooved on to the bands and grazed amongst the food stalls with some ancient pensioners and trad punks. There were sixty or seventy stalls dotted around the grounds: a lot of food stalls run by local cafes and the city's ethnic communities; stalls pumping out the word for groups like Greenpeace and Amnesty; and commercial stalls selling jewellery and clothes and dumb stuff like face painting and vegan cookbooks.

'It's not the chambray shirt Country Road crowd,' said Michelle. 'But every kind of subculture turns up. Every shade of hair and skin, every style of clothes. They all come and get on and there's no slagging somebody off because they look different.'

For some that changed a bit come nightfall. The storm came as Michelle was speaking to a friend. 'I was holding an umbrella and getting completely drenched,' she said. 'It was ridiculous. I said, "Let's piss off." It must have been three minutes before the cops came.' She didn't know anything had gone wrong until the next morning. 'I turned on the radio and they were asking people to call the station if they'd been assaulted by police. I thought, "What the fuck?" I got on the phone and asked a friend what had happened. She said they just came in and beat the shit out of everyone.'

The cloudburst seems to have been the catalyst for the police coming in en masse, but there'd been a lot of action during the day. By nightfall a lot of people had been taken out for a variety of offences, many of them for pissing up against the trees rather than using the portaloos. But one incident behind the bar tent in the waning of the afternoon set the tone for the later troubles.

Linda Molony, a Newtown girl, found herself in Brisbane in October '96. She walked through the front gate at Musgrave at 3 p.m. A familiar story: she met some pals at the doof tent. Spent most of her day there, just sat and listened to the DJs. 'The bands weren't very good,' she laughs. 'The first time I noticed the police presence I was coming back from the bar. There were a few people looking at some kind of argument between this girl and two guys. Then suddenly, out of nowhere, about six or seven police turned up, the guys with the baseball caps.'

She was stunned by what happened next. 'It seemed like the police really made it worse. They immediately put this guy on the ground when he'd done nothing. His girlfriend was getting hysterical. A huge crowd was gathering. The police came out of nowhere and whipped up a frenzy. Shoved the guy to the ground, really violently. Put the cuffs on him. I went back to my friends and said, "There's a really strong police presence here that I don't think anyone is aware of."'

Molony blew off the next couple of hours in the doof tent, having a drink and a dance and talking to friends, but she had a feeling after that earlier incident that something might happen. The atmosphere, for her at least, seemed a little charged.

'When the storm came,' she said, 'it was like they were

waiting to pounce. But there wasn't anything going on. The crowd was going wild, getting into it, thunder and lightning. People were dancing in the rain.'

Police numbers had built up during the afternoon. PSRT had been lurking for a couple of hours before the sun went down, materialising suddenly every now and then, like they'd beamed down from the Enterprise to smack someone around. The deal with them staying clear unless there was a major incident, if it ever had been a deal, was dead. A witness at a nearby autoshop saw 'the guys in baseball caps' unloading their big kit bags in the middle of the afternoon. Hours before any trouble they were already tooling up for the night's festivities, unloading shields, batons and helmets. While patrolling the park supervising the bouncers, Terry O'Connor also kept an eye on the police. He spoke to Mark Simpson around five thirty when the police presence was beginning to escalate dramatically, not just in number but in the different types of units: PSRT, CIB and undercover. 'He had an air of defeat,' said O'Connor. 'Everything had been taken out of his hands. He had no role or authority in the situation.'

Others began to notice. Rohweder thought there were a lot more patrol cars and wagons parked up near the rear gate behind the main stage from about two o'clock. 'By seven there were a lot more PSRT,' said Rohweder. 'A lot of police in the streets around the park and walking through . . . I was alarmed, wondering why they were there in those numbers. I couldn't see a reason for it.'

As police numbers grew the crowd shrank, but not necessarily because of the increase. At day's end a wall of evil, thick green storm clouds began piling up over the city. You live in Brisbane long enough, you know what that means. Go home, bring the washing in and put the kettle on. Maybe fire up a joint and get ready to watch the light show from your verandah. When a strong wind suddenly swept over the park there were maybe two or three thousand stayers left watching the bands, chilling down at the doof tent, hoping for the best. But with a flash of white light and an explosive crash of thunder the best of the day was behind them. It wasn't all over though. Oh no. Not by a fucking long shot.

'Jeez,' thought Simon Bedak. 'Look at that.'

He was in the doof tent, shaking his big hairy booty all round when he saw a cop on a horse go charging by, swinging a baton like a polo mallet. A little odd, he thought.

As the storm began 'Brian', a stall worker (name changed), had looked at the skies, figured 'no way' and finished up. He walked down to the main gate, past the bar tent, the doof tent and the area in front of the stages where a few thousand people were still gathered. He didn't see any trouble until he reached the gate, where cops were running in. Patrol cars were screaming through the streets in a mad rush.

Over in the beer tent Tony Kneipp, an old Triple Zed hand and a newsroom staffer, had noticed that police were starting to pick people off around the edges of the crowd. 'When it started raining, most people left,' he said. 'A number started skylarking around in the rain. They were mud wrestling and kicking water at each other. I think that was the "unruly behaviour" the police took as being some sort of brawl.' Kneipp was standing close to the epicentre of the 'bar brawl' which the police claimed sparked the trouble. He didn't see it. All of the action he saw was outside, in the rain. Peggy Newman, another bar worker, didn't much fancy the atmosphere inside as the heavens opened up. She was pregnant and sensitive to the vibe.

'The weather was bad. People crushed in. A lot of them were drunk,' she said. 'I was a bit wary that someone was going to push one of the tables over and I was going to get hurt. I stopped serving and stood back.' She noticed other staffers had done the same. Somebody said they should just serve out the tickets already sold then wrap up. Newman walked away to get something to eat. 'I'm pregnant. I don't like drunks and I don't like people's attitudes when they get drunk. I was just . . . wary I guess . . . grossed out.' Gross they may have been, but brawling they were not. She noticed the large numbers of police too. 'A fair bit of the crowd was lit up. I saw police on horseback charging around and I thought, that's a bit silly. I just stood and watched. My friend Brendan appeared with a scanner and said he was on the police frequency. He said they had riot gear and were just about to come through. I thought, that's ridiculous! But I heard this drumming noise. They were beating on their shields with batons to frighten the crowd.'

As the storm clouds had built up Marissa O'Keefe, who had been on the front gate most of the day, hurried back to the bar tent, which also served as the HQ for the volunteers. Like Peggy Newman she was hungry, but there wasn't much food left, so she fixed herself a pickle and chilli chip sandwich. 'I was happily munching along when it started raining,' she said. 'It was so quick. It was just instantly pouring. I was thinking how lucky I was to be under the tent where I could be dry, munching my sandwich. The crowd outside were just going off. They were so happy, roaring with joy at the rain.' Another staffer raced into the tent and screamed that the police were charging their horses into the revellers. 'I remember thinking, what the fuck's going on?'

Someone in a headset was trying to put out a PA call telling the crowd to leave. But with the power off, the headsets weren't working. People were panicking, shouting at him, asking what was wrong, what was going on. He'd tried to tell the police that if they could get the PA turned on they could clear the park in five minutes. But a cop hit him and he fell under a horse. O'Keefe gaped out through the front of the tent. A huge, closely packed crush of people were still gathered out there. Then something hit them. 'The impression I had was like a giant hand. That something huger than the world had come in with a baseball bat and hit the crowd. It was like this amazing force hit the crowd and these thousands of people were all pushed in one direction. I ran to see what was happening.'

PSRT had formed a riot line with plain clothes and uniform police and marched into the crowd hammering their shields, shouting 'Move move move', clubbing and bashing anyone who came within range. Others were being threatened by a police dog, straining to get at them from the end of a taut leash. Even then some people hadn't clued in. O'Keefe was amazed to see dozens of party boys hanging around the front of the beer tent waiting to trade their tickets for beers. 'They hadn't caught on,' she said. 'We were like, "Can you see what the police are doing? Get the hell out of here!"'

Zed was slowly reacting, however. Brendan Greenhill from the newsroom was charging around with a micro-recorder, getting the screams and the chaos down on tape. Others were mobilising, calling lawyers and media. 'Some people were amazing,' said O'Keefe. 'They were already doing what had to be done.' She shook her head. 'There were people like that and there others like me who just crumbled and fell to pieces.'

Greenhill had seen the whole thing start in vista-vision, watching from raised ground outside the park. Spooked by the spiralling numbers of cops, he had lit out earlier in the night, scurried off home to pick up his police scanner. Taking shelter from the lashing rain on his return leg, he tuned in to hear the call for general assistance. 'As I was walking past the park I could see them all coming in and hear police asking for directions, where the band tent was and where to assemble on the oval.' Through the static and chatter he listened to the cops talking about closing the bar, a sure sign that communication between Zed and the police had broken down. The bar had been closed earlier, when the rain started. Pushing past hundreds of people who were already leaving, Greenhill could hear the sirens and see the weird blue strobe of police lights flashing. A lot of punters saw the lights but didn't recognise their meaning. Some in the doof tent mistook them for a laser show. As Greenhill made it to the bar, forty or fifty cops had formed up for the first riot line. They stepped off as he rushed in, trying to alert his fellow staffers.

'When the first line pushed through about one to two thousand people were moved,' he said. 'They swept through and shovelled the crowd in front of them. They returned and formed up again. I saw two police horses charge into the crowd. About forty people hurled their beer cans straight at them, all at once. The riot line moved again. I could see people being clubbed with batons. I saw the whole line wheel across the front of our beer tent and down towards the doof tent. There were all these hippies trying to chill down there, suddenly confronted with this riot line.'

Staffers asked a sergeant if they could try to clear the tent. One volunteer actually got in and managed to lift a side of the tarp, through which a lot of people escaped. But he was eventually clubbed away too. The police chant started up again.

'Move move move move . . .'

Linda Molony, still in the doof tent, had never seen so many police in her life. Everybody was scared, looking at each other, waiting for someone to explain. 'Girls were crying, it was really intense. There were so many police. They came out of nowhere. Everyone had this look of total shock, they couldn't believe it.' Somebody pushed her in the back, a hard painful shove. She spun around, confronted a baseball cap. 'I said, "Hey, do you mind!" I asked him what his name was but he wouldn't give it to me. So I chased after him, stupidly, like—I want your name. Then

I saw this Army guy. He was trying to provoke this much smaller man. He was sooo angry. Going "come on come on", asking for a fight! I said, "Hey leave him alone." But you know how it is when someone is so angry they can't even see you.'

Brendan Greenhill saw the MP at the same time as Molony. He took in the Army camouflage but had a little trouble processing the fact. 'I had another look and I realised he was a military police officer. His beret was stuffed into his pocket and he had a mate with him. I saw one of the civilian police gesture to them, an overhand movement, like "Come on, get in here."'

There was a lot of confusion about the MPs. At first the Army said they just happened to be there, but they didn't touch anyone. Police media claimed that some of the MPs were attached to local civilian units because of a military exercise in the region. Others were just cruising the streets, heard the call for assistance over the radio and took it upon themselves to respond as 'concerned citizens'. A fortnight later, when the Army had sniffed the breeze, they cut their men loose. Army spokesman Lieutenant Colonel John Weiland confirmed that his men should not have been there, had no power at all to intervene and were operating in direct contravention of Army rules and procedure. It opens up the possibility of some heavy lawsuits against the Defence Force should anyone assaulted by them care to sue. Greenhill witnessed one such assault outside the main gate.

'The police had forced their way down to the entrance,' he recalled. 'As they hit the street a number of civilian police were wrestling with some guy and the MP was trying to grab him in a head lock. He had about three or four attempts because this guy was putting up quite a struggle, getting thumped and kicked, getting his arms wrenched up behind his back. The MP got in front of him as the guy lost his footing and went down. The whole scrum collapsed, everyone on top of this guy. A pair of cuffs were produced and because the MP was the man in the best position he applied the handcuffs, left hand first, then right.'

David Weldon, who had seen the teenaged girl get wiped out, was lucky not to end up in cuffs himself. Standing at the gate with a big crowd waiting to squeeze out, he was clubbed on the back of the head by a cop in riot gear. He turned to protest that he was leaving as fast as possible but the officer flipped his baton round to use it as a jabbing weapon and drove it into Weldon's chest with enough force to break a rib and tear away some ligaments. Another cop held him back before he could finish the job and Weldon very wisely chose not to hit back.

'I know there's no point fighting with the police,' he said. 'You're only gonna come out a loser.'

It was a riot, said the cops. And they were right. But it was their riot. We were attacked, said the cops. And that was true as well. Some guys threw some beer cans at them. Even yelled out some things. Probably pretty hurtful stuff too. At least one lady cop got popped on the nose. Bled quite badly. That would have hurt. But no cops were attacked in coordinated assaults by squads of trained goons. No cops were baton whipped, or smashed with plexi shields, or speared into the mud by flying wedges of half a dozen burly men. No cops had attack dogs sooled onto them. No cops were trampled underfoot by horses. No cops were choked or strangled or clubbed to the ground.

'I would suggest that no further events such as these be allowed,' said Gary Wilkinson, the Police Union President. Wilkinson said his officers were fed up with Market Day. 'Every one of those things has been a disaster.' It was, he reckoned, a combination of alcohol, drugs and the type of music that caused the trouble. Wilkinson dipped into a grab bag of fantastic allegations following the rampage. He said that rioters had stabbed a police horse in the chest with a broken bottle and tried to kick its legs out. They had chanted 'kill the pigs, kill the pigs'. They had pelted police with beer cans full of urine, stolen watches from officers' wrists and tried to steal their guns.

At the meeting in Minister Cooper's office the brass came up with some good stuff of their own: a dubious cache of the 'weapons' confiscated from rioters during the disturbance. Terry O'Connor wryly recounts the story of the Superintendent producing a bag containing a couple of confiscated knives, a plastic pole with 'Woolworths' written on it, a Brisbane City Council manhole lifter and a sharps bin in a plastic bag which he somewhat perversely described as a can of capsicum spray.

Well, you don't get a lot of rocket scientists signing on with the Queensland police. One stall holder reported seeing a young man handcuffed to the metal fence near the police staging area at the height of the electrical storm. It's pretty obvious that the debacle of Market Day was largely a result of systemic failure in police command. Contrary to what Gary Wilkinson says, not every Market Day has been a disaster. Zed has been running them for twenty years without trouble of this magnitude. Partly that's because of the good working relationship built up between the station and the local police, because of the communication and liaison channels which have been refined over the years; channels which the police hierarchy chose to ignore on October 19. That answers pretty simply how these events came to pass. But why is another question and I don't think I can tell you that.

THE MOULDY SANDWICH
INCIDENT

I'm walking down to the beach with my babe. Guy at the end of my street is going to stop me and ask for money. I know he's going to. I can just tell. He has that look. That half-crafty, I can see you and you can see me and I can see you seeing me but let's all pretend otherwise look. For some reason it sets my teeth on edge and I deploy my own look. This gaunt, forbidding, slightly deranged expression I developed over the six years I lived around Kings Cross. Very much your angry loner, gun nut survivalist look. A great look for getting seats to yourself on the bus, fitting in at Pauline Hanson rallies and warding off the advances of hookers, spruikers, dope dealers, Christians and beggars.

I hadn't used it in a year. Maybe I was rusty. It had no impact on this guy at all.

We draw closer and he starts bouncing around on the footpath. Really. Like *boing-boing-boing*. He is the healthy leper from *Life of Brian*. He bounces up. Thrusts this thing under my nose. A packet of mouldy, two-week-old sandwiches he's fished out of a bin somewhere. He's dressed oddly, like a beach gypsy. And he says, 'I am going to give you the opportunity to save me from eating these sandwiches.'

Because he was, you know, so poor and hungry.

I stop and stare and he doesn't look like no poor, hungry street person to me. He's clean, for a start. And fit and healthy and his hair is washed and combed and Sunsilk fresh. He must have a lot of energy too, what with all this bouncing around. So I scoff, I shake my head, and I follow my babe, who has wisely elected to walk on by. It's strange. A sad reflection on my generation and our lowered expectations. We don't tell beggars to get a haircut and a job driving trucks for their country. We just mumble stuff like, 'Why can't you go get the dole like everyone else?'

I'm thinking, 'I seem to be asking this a lot recently, what with all these characters getting around town.' But don't get me wrong. I'm as big a fan of Dickensian street life as anyone. Bearded, red-haired guys with walking sticks and plastic orchard necklaces who'll massage your aura or just stare murderously at you for a dollar? They're really cool. And that old girl in the tunnel at Central Station in Sydney? Flapping her arms and singing her songs? You know her. Tuneless yowling, sounds like a cartoon cat being forced through a cheese grater? She's cool too. Always got a dollar for her. Because you can take it or leave it. Her act, that is. It's not like she jumps on your back, starts wailing and won't let go until you hand over your wallet.

Not like the mouldy sandwich guy. He just kept on at

me, skipping along beside me, threatening to eat this sandwich. The thing is, if he'd just asked for a buck I may have given it to him, or even bought him a new sandwich. But he caught me in a bad mood and we took a little trip to Testosterone Hell. I'm like, 'I don't give a toss if you eat it, I'm not giving you any money.'

I'd had a bad day. That's all. And he looked like he'd been surfing. I just wanted a walk on the beach and this doofus pops up like an evil clown, starts waving his pack of mouldy Gladwrapped horrors at me. Finally, I snap. I turn on him and shout, 'Go ahead, eat the fucking sandwich! See if I care. It's just a dumb trick.'

Well, he takes real offence at that, me calling his bluff. Because I guess he had plans for those sandwiches. Figured he could raise fifty bucks with them before dinner time.

'A trick?' he goes. 'A trick! You think this is a trick?'

I say, 'yeah' and he says 'right' and he takes a huge bite, like a mad dog, right through the Gladwrap, and he spits this wet, black lump at me. Oh boy. Now I'm psychotic with rage. He's carrying some sort of stick, for show, like 'I'm a free spirit walking the earth and this is my stick and these are my sandwiches.' But I'm like, just raise the fucking stick sandwich boy, just try, because . . .

Thankfully, my babe drags me away. A lucky thing because I know for a fact we would have beaten each other to a pulp over those mouldy sandwiches if she hadn't. Next time, maybe I'll just give him a dollar.

Two-fisted whiskey 'A

PSYCHOPATH KILLED HIS MOTHER.

HE WAS A DRUNK. HE WAS MAD FOR

A LONG TIME AND HE WILL DO

ANYTHING FOR PUBLICITY.'

PIMP DADDY'S LOCAL
MEMBER

I was a big fan of the Samios scallop. Ten cents they cost, these huge, round cakes of potato, grease and golden batter. There was a time a young bloke could eat his fill of them and still have enough change from a dollar for an icy cold Coke. Still, we thought they were an odd bunch, that Samios mob. Wogs for a start, in a town full of old Australians and ten pound poms. Along with a semi-mythical Chinese character called Jimmy Wah, the Samios clan were one of the pillars of cosmopolitan Ipswich. And Jimmy, being Asian, was considered even stranger than old Samios, of course. An inscrutable guy, his cheap Chinese takeaway was well-known, according to schoolboy lore, for thinning out the local cat population.

Messrs Samios and Wah suffered long and hard from this sort of egregious bullshit when I was growing up in Ipswich. Word on the playground was that they were always being caught peeling spuds on the dunny, frying goldfish in bread crumbs and grinding up dead dogs for their hamburgers. I never made it to Jimmy's place, which was over the river in the badlands. But I was into Samios' for a big feed of potato scallops every Friday afternoon. He never seemed short of custom so I guess all those deeply defamatory rumours about his poor spud peeling technique didn't count for much in the end. Ipswich knew what Ipswich liked and Ipswich loved a ten cent scallop.

I had time to dwell on these legends of my youth as I mooched around another home town landmark, Gillece's fish and chip shop, waiting for the red-headed harridan who has brought shame on humble fishmongers and Ipswich old boys everywhere. The Samios clan, I'd discovered, were no longer in business; not the greasy food business anyway. Their hot, dark chippy had gone the way of Cribb and Foote's department store, the Bakehouse Steakhouse and Tristram's soft drink factory. All such significant way points on the bright, crayon mental map of Ipswich I carried with me from childhood. All gone now.

Mr Wah had kept on keeping on, as best I could tell. I drove past his shop with Grant, an old school friend, late one night after a feed at the Cecil, which used to be one of the toughest pubs in a very tough town. It looks surreal now, a white, mission style building picked out of the darkness by powerful blue feature lights. The publican spent up big renovating the place when there was talk of a university being built on the old railway workshops across the way. The campus didn't eventuate, however—they decided to site it at the town's insane asylum instead—and I guess the poor bastard must have done his dough cold. At least Jimmy Wah hadn't blown his mad money on any ill-advised touch-ups. According to Grant, whose sister once lived upstairs from the takeaway, the place hadn't changed in twenty years.

I was grateful to Jimmy for that, tipping an appreciative nod of the beanie to his steadfast refusal to budge from the days of primitive pinball machines into the age of 'Mortal Kombat IV'. So much else had changed. The railway workshops, as I might have mentioned, were gone. Three thousand men pared back to less than one thousand and transferred up the line to Redbank, to something called a Centre of Excellence. The woollen mills, by contrast, had simply disappeared. And the miners, who contended for so long with the railway men to define the culture of the town, well, there were a few hundred of them hanging on . . . but I doubt you could back them at any money in a race to extinction with those poor, doomed dugongs which have given Keith Williams so much grief. The old, industrial heart of Ipswich was beating lower and slower, a thin, attenuated rhythm which struggled to pump life through the streets of my town.

Reading the dispatches you could be forgiven for thinking that sex crimes and Nazism were all that had replaced the town's hard-knuckled working men. The week I was home the local paper's front page was monopolised by the case of a man on trial for prostituting and raping his fifteen-year-old step-daughter. He had proffered the *Lolita* defence, that she had repeatedly made sexual advances towards him, happily performing on him Bill Clinton's favourite sort of sex act at least three times in the comfort of the family home. The defendant didn't think there was anything wrong or 'odd' about this. He had already fessed up to 'participating in the provision of a child for prostitution,' allegedly trousering the lion's share of the $120 to $200 she charged for a session. As I was hanging with a couple of staffers from the local paper, waiting to crash the One Nation press call in Gillece's fish and chip shop, the girl at the centre of the case stalked past with a small, fast-walking clutch of supporters. The paper's photographer—the same woman who had been spectacularly evicted from a Hanson press conference a few weeks earlier—scrambled to snap the back of their heads as they flew by.

They were an unremarkable group. Bad haircuts and cheap clothes, seething resentment and the underwhelming air of a bunch of bitter, shit-eating rubes who know they've been badly ripped off by someone, somewhere—or perhaps by everyone, everywhere—but they're just not sure of how, or why, or whether they'll ever get their money back. In other words, a picture-perfect snapshot of Hanson's favoured demographic, and a close approximation of the 'elite' view of Ipswich following the town's seemingly wholehearted embrace of Hanson in the election of March '96. I wondered, waiting for her to appear, what she would make of them and they of her. They would probably be starstruck, like the young family from Wollongong who nervously fronted her after her press conference to ask for an autograph. I imagined she would regard them with that powerful mix of distaste and withering contempt the lumpenbourgeoisie reserve just for their social inferiors, although nowadays I doubt she would be stupid enough to let this show; she needs their votes.

Sadly the gods were not in the mood to arrange a meeting of the two camps for my benefit and edification, Hanson and her minders emerging from the same quiet street as pimp daddy's little girl and her friends a few minutes too late to make their acquaintance. The effect on the media mini-circus gathered outside Gillece's was electric. Camera guys and soundos immediately hefted their kit, reporters flourished notebooks and searched frantically for pens and tape recorders as Hanson strode across the busy one-way road which ran outside the takeaway. Peter James, her diminutive, bearded state director, was with her, along with some no-name apparatchiks and a plain clothes cop. But Hanson was definitely the star. She had it. That same presence, that intensity of being-in-the-world which I'd seen in the air around some rock stars when working for *Rolling Stone*.

She was larger than you'd think from her television appearances, tall and quite raw-boned, not at all the shrinking figure of vulnerability which some learned commentators have tagged as appealing to the deeper protective instincts in her male fans. She was tricked out in a long cream dress, with an eye-boggling set of chunky golden earrings and a thick gold chain, from which hung a golden frog, perched to make the leap to safety from between her breasts. Up close, about two feet away as I was, her hair seemed unnaturally wiry and wrong. Her pug nose was even more pronounced than usual and her eyes were alive with both fear and loathing of the press, which closed in on her like a pack of wild dogs on a slightly rotten carcass. She was there to launch a farrago of lies and contradictions which passed for a small business policy, but that was the week *Four Corners* had aired its One Nation special, the program in which David Oldfield sort of called himself a National Socialist and a lot of former members publicly questioned the influence of extreme right-wing racists over their extremely right-wing and racist party. When she finished a nervy, warbling reading of her small business policy, the journalists exploded, bombarding her with questions about the large number of fascist nutjobs who seemed to find a warm welcome in One Nation. I yelled from my vantage point, some two feet away from her right ear, 'How many Nazis have you expelled from the party so far, Pauline?'

She turned only part of the way towards me, like a blind person, searching for a voice in a crowd, and said something like, 'I'm not here to answer those sorts of questions today!' It raised the prospect that maybe she'd answer them at some stage in the future but we weren't to find out as the press pack then veered off on another tangent, a standard query about the costings of her policy. The disorganised frenzy of the questioning, which only strengthens the suspicions of her supporters about the media's bias against their heroine, was also her greatest asset in this minor skirmish. There was no chance of pinning her within the confines of a single line of interrogation. Whenever one journalist seemed to be manoeuvring her into an untenable position, she simply switched her attention to someone else in the baying crowd. After five or ten minutes of this, Peter James decided it was time to give the networks their background vision and his charge was evacuated from the free fire zone of the actual conference into the safety of the day's photo-op; Pauline standing, grinning, over a fat fryer with a wire basket full of chips and scallops.

Oh Mr Samios, where are you now?

The day after the conference I sat in the bar of the Ulster Hotel with my dad, knocking back pots of Fourex and shots of straight whiskey with a half dozen or more of the regulars. The Ulster is an old style pub at the top of the one-way road out of town, no pokies, no Sky Channel, no piped music, no nothing but the earnest, unflinching consumption of cold grog and quiet conversation. My dad takes a drink there most nights and whenever I'm in town I'm usually of a mind to join him. My mother, to the best of my knowledge, has never set foot in the place. I used to play cricket with the publican's son, and some of the regulars, God bless them, have both paid for and read my books. It's not my place to tell you their stories though, which is a pity, because these are the people who supposedly visited the Hanson plague upon us and they have been misunderstood. They have no time for her at all.

Shortly after Hanson had been elected John Howard said he wouldn't necessarily infer from the result that there was a racist streak in Ipswich. He said the right thing for the wrong reasons. There is a racist streak in Ipswich, or rather there are clustered cells of racism in the town, as there are in the hearts of almost all people. I believe that Howard, who ran a campaign of cleverly insinuated racism, was looking both to polish his own alibi and to amplify the role of Paul Keating in his own destruction. Three hundred Ipswich people rallied against their new local member a few days after her election, as many thousands more townsfolk have rallied against her since, giving lie to the idea of Ipswich as a sink of ignorance and political brutalism. Indeed, some of the fiercest opposition to her has come from within her own heartland, and Hanson's elevation to the national stage was much more the result of a strange confluence of local forces than a racist, proletarian putsch against the ruling elites.

Before One Nation, before Oldfield and Pasquarelli, Hanson was just one of dozens of marginal seat candidates for the Liberal Party who were never expected to win. She had actually snuck onto the Ipswich City Council on the coat-tails of a former Labor mayor who ran as an independent after being crunched out in a factional brawl. She made almost no discernible impact before losing her council seat, and was chosen to run as a Liberal candidate in the federal campaign in part because she could fund her own campaign. The ALP's sitting member was a deeply unimpressive machine man whose hold on the seat was so insubstantial he would have been run out of town even in a Labor landslide. When the Libs disendorsed Hanson, it was too late to replace her on the ticket so she picked up the natural Liberal vote, the national swing against Keating and a personal swing against this clown courtesy of thousands of Labor voters who suddenly felt free to back her. She later described herself as a job seeker who landed a position she really wasn't expecting and admitted she was very scared by the prospect of moving to Canberra.

The deteriorating relationship between Hanson and the black and Asian community resembled a barroom brawl which starts with a few ill-considered words, degenerates into a bit of push and shove and quickly ignites into a wild free-for-all. Her original sin was to claim the Aborigines received too much help from the government—or 'gummint' as it is usually known in this line of argument—compared with poor white trash. In an election where Howard was desperate to hose down any smouldering doubts about his own form on the race issue, it was enough to see her purged. It was an ignorant comment, mildly offensive, and widely supported both in Ipswich and outside. It was the sort of bitter, unthinking statement you could hear a hundred times a day sitting in taxis or barbers' chairs listening to talk-back radio, and my guess is that its historical roots can be traced right back to the convicts of the First Fleet who both looked down on the natives of Port Jackson and yet envied them their freedom. The awful unspoken truth of Hanson's rise, only recently becoming obvious, is that millions of 'mainstream Australians' agree with her. Not to the extent of marching in lock step with the neo-Nazis of National Action, but enough to nod quietly when she attacks what she and the Prime Minister like to call the 'Aboriginal industry'. For many people, like Hanson and Howard, are not active racists. They do not have dark hearts. But they are uncomfortable with differ-ence. Diversity and change unsettles them. They honestly feel uncomfortable in the presence of strange foreign cultures and they fear displacement and even dispersal, although they will never make the imaginative leap of empathy from this to understanding the plight of the Aborigines.

Thus Hanson's first few months in 'power' were marked, as you would expect, by the cringe-worthy mistakes of an untutored provincial visitor to the centre of political culture. She said what she and many others thought and seemed surprised, and then outraged, when this drew increasingly hostile fire from the people she was attacking. And lurking, smirking at the edge of it was John Howard, happy to give the impression that he was enjoying the show—the lifting of a pall of censorship as he called it. Or at least he *was* smirking, until the brawlers in the bar suddenly turned around and beat six kinds of hell out of his coalition colleagues in the Queensland election. Up to that point the rapport between Howard and Hanson had been, as one wag put it, the love which dare not speak its name. Browsing through the clipping file in the *Queensland Times* I was struck by the rampant metooism of Hanson's reactions to the new Government's policy prescriptions. Howard cuts hundreds of millions of dollars from ATSIC's budget? Hanson says good start but there's plenty left to cut. Howard slashes away at the migration intake? Hanson applauds, but urges him to cut deeper and harder.

At the launch of Reconciliation Week Howard hopped into the assembled delegates, to effectively champion the white race's civilising mission. Hanson dismissed reconciliation as a 'failed concept [which] should be abandoned', and later said that she was 'sick of people bowing and scraping to the Aboriginal people. We have done nothing wrong. I consider this as much my land as theirs.'

As long as she confined herself to racial matters she was

no threat to Howard because, in the early days at least, they were of one mind. Hanson's rhetoric simply was not constrained by Howard's need to carry a 'broad church' with him. It was only when she engaged in a wider political discourse, firstly about gun laws and then, much more powerfully, about economic rationalism and globalisation, that her national appeal spread significantly beyond a hard core of actual, dark-hearted racists.

And here we return to the public bar of the Ulster Hotel. There was a man in there, a quiet, decent sort of fellow with whom I shared a few beers. I don't feel able to say too much about him, personally, for I was not interviewing him while we spoke. I think I can say, however, that he has four children, all grown to adulthood, none of whom has ever worked, through no failing of his. Had they been born into a luckier generation they would have found work in their home town in the railways, mines or factories. But these are gone now, or downsized, and the reasonably paid but low-skilled work they provided for thousands of Ipswich school leavers has gone with them and is never coming back. I doubt anyone has told them. Not in those terms anyway. I doubt anyone has looked them in the eye and said, 'I'm sorry, but you didn't work hard enough in school, you're unskilled, uneducated and untrainable. This country has nothing to offer you.' On the other hand I imagine that many, many political aspirants have patted them on the head and cooed sweet nothings into their ear about what a shitty deal they've had and how much better things would be if only they'd just vote the right way.

In the end, that's all Pauline Hanson is doing, except she has added the force multiplier of blame. Not just blame of the Government or Opposition, who are mostly remote media figures, electrons and sound bites, but blame of tangible, immediately accessible human beings. That Vietnamese baker. Those threatening black teenagers. That rich Chinese businessman in the silver Mercedes. She hasn't attacked the Jews, the gypsies or the cripples but no doubt they are tempting targets for some in her party. These sort of people have always been around, safely corralled into groups such as National Action and the Australian Nationalist Movement where they could do little harm because everyone recognised them for what they are. They ran a Senate candidate in the 1984 Federal election, for instance, fully expecting to pick up at least 50 000 votes. What they got was one tenth of one per cent of fuck all. Little wonder they are now signing up as One Nation members and candidates.

It's like Yeats said, the centre cannot hold. The best lack all conviction while the worst are full of passionate intensity. But it does not have to be that way. My last day in Ipswich I took a drive out to the insane asylum with a worker from the town's Art Gallery. The old small town Gallery is being remodelled into a fine regional facility, capable of exhibiting international shows. Along with the university campus and the City Council's active promotion of digital infrastructure it represents a different sort of change for Ipswich. The town is not a dead husk, as I fully expected. It is more of a chrysalis, changing from within. From a place with very few university graduates living amongst its population—save for the medical practitioners staffing its extensive hospital complex and many private practices—Ipswich will soon become a college town, with students and staff outnumbering the railway men at the height of their reign. The centre of town, now a confused strip where $2 bargain bin stores compete with $5 all you can eat greasy spoons, is slowly being transformed into a cultural precinct centred on the new gallery. The giant RAAF air base just outside town is being refitted as regional research and production centre for the Boeing corporation. It will be a ten to fifteen-year process but the new, knowledge-based industries which are rising from the town's rusted industrial carcass will bring with them thousands of highly skilled workers, attracted, in part, by the town's enormous stock of cheap, quality housing. It is possible to buy two or three renovated Queenslanders in Ipswich for the price of a one-bedroom apartment in Sydney's eastern suburbs.

The asylum which will house the new University of Queensland Campus sits on a commanding hill, surrounded by a golf course and, once upon a time, legend has it, a moat. We drove up there, not knowing it still housed the insane. Nobody stopped us as we drove in, parked and wandered around before coming to a halt perched over a fairway in the dying moments of late afternoon. The town was spread out in a sylvan scene below us and we talked as dusk fell. The gallery staffer, a white man, was married to a black woman and confessed himself shocked at the depth and virulence of the racism they had encountered since moving to Ipswich. He wanted to know whether I, as a local boy, thought the place had a dark heart. We kicked the issue back and forth as the insane and abandoned shuffled through the twilight around us. Eventually I said that I thought Ipswich probably had a hard heart, not a dark one, and that it was the work of his children to soften it some.

JAMES ELLROY: DEMON DOG

Here comes the Demon Dog. Foot tapping, finger snapping and kicking out the jams. He doesn't just sell you this song. He comes around to your house and installs it. An LA song. An evil, obscene, hilarious paean to the City of Quartz. He performs it with a jazz band in the States all the time. But he won't let you reprint the lyrics because he ripped the music off somebody else and doesn't feel like being sued.

That's cool. Even kinda funny and endearing, because it's still early. The day has not exploded in your face yet. It's ticking though. You can hear it when the crew from *A Current Affair* arrive. Those fucking bozos. I hate those guys.

James Ellroy the crime writer, the Demon Dog, is working out the kinks in a session with the Jackson Code. He asked the drummer if he'd like to be introduced to the audience as the man with the world's biggest penis. Sunday morning. Some skanky warehouse space in Glebe. Sprawling and claustrophobic at the same time. A recording studio with an old, *Flintstones* era video game, an old couch and a trophy wall of CDs by the entrance. The CDs fall down when the music gets too loud next door. The Demon Dog was late. Delayed by a mountain of pancakes and hash browns smothered in maple syrup and ketchup. He needs the fuel to keep up with the machine.

We are the machine. A pitiless, transglobal publicity turbine. Given half a chance we will run him into the ground and chew his carcass to bloody rags before we take our pictures. Because he is the Demon Dog of American Crime Fiction. A psychopath killed his mother. He was a drunk. He was mad for a long time and he will do anything for publicity. So say our editors. The trannies on William Street, they told us. Get some photos of the Demon Dog with the trannies on William Street. Doesn't matter which side of the street. Transvestite. Transexual. Doesn't matter. Just get some good-looking ones and make sure they sign the release forms. And some cops too. Walk him around the Cross with some cops. Get some shots of him near famous crime scenes. And some sex clubs too. Some really bad ones.

'We should take him to that motel,' I said. 'The one where they killed Nielson. Cut her throat in the laundry. It's got Atmosphere with a whole bunch of 'A's. And if the sex clubs won't let us take our happy snaps we might need that.'

'We should make a list,' said Lorrie.

So we had our list and their list.

Ours: Cops, crims, trannies, hookers, devo's, fags, hustlers, bikies.

Theirs: Recording studio. Book Awards. Dinner with the Premier, Mr Carr, and his wife. At home. The Premier is a big fan. The metro dailies will take photos before the first course.

It turned bad at the studio. First thing in the morning. I hate those fucking *ACA* guys. The soundo bumps me on the way through the studio. Words are muttered. But nothing comes of it. Not then, or a few minutes later when it happens again.

The session goes on.

The Demon Dog's minders advise that the trannies are not going to happen. Mr Ellroy is not like that anymore. He has a wife and a dog in Kansas City. They wouldn't understand.

Meanwhile, the Demon Dog is retailing some high octane gossip about the marriage of Mr and Mrs Nicole Kidman. And the predilection of a high profile English stage actress for frequent sexual congress with a canine.

And, say the minders, if the trannies are off, the sex clubs are off. Doesn't matter, I shrug. They told us to get fucked anyway.

This all took two, maybe three hours.

Then to the Book Awards.

The *ACA* guys were there. Everybody was there. Maybe 200 lit-critters crammed into the top floor of an Oxford Street bookshop. Bad wine and body heat and something close to idolatry.

The Demon Dog leaps to the stand and calls them all pantie-sniffers, peepers, prowlers, pimps and pederasts. He is a big man. Physically imposing. He stands with his feet maybe a whole metre apart. He calls everyone kangaroo fuckers.

The *ACA* guys will edit that out. The metro dailies might make veiled reference to it. In the crush around Ellroy as he signs books, the *ACA* sound guy elbows me in the ribs.

'See that soundo,' I muttered to Lorrie. 'Later on I'm going to trip him and stand on his fucking fingers when he tries to get up.'

I drank some cheap wine.

Lorrie didn't.

We locked the keys in the car outside the Premier's house. I waited for the NRMA. Luckily Lorrie had her stuff. She went in with the other press. I read *American Tabloid* out in the street.

Mr Frank Moorhouse, a writer, arrives for dinner just as I regain the car keys. I sneak in behind him.

The Premier's house is very nice. But there are no soft surfaces anywhere. Even the couch looks hard. The water view is nice though.

Mr Moorhouse sat with Mr Pounder, a bookseller, and Mr Coupe, a vaguely credentialled publisher of crime fanzines and a shotgun rider for the Demon Dog's visit. The other minder, an Alan Someone, was not there at that time.

The Demon Dog kidded the Premier by pretending to bribe him while Lorrie took a photo. The Premier explained that sort of thing didn't happen anymore. He had what Americans call a shit-eating grin. As Mr Ellroy pretended to 'shakedown' Mr Carr, the Premier rubbed his hands, laughed weakly and tried to explain his steadfast commitment to the process of criminal justice reform.

The Premier's wife, a successful businesswoman, rattled around in the kitchen while the menfolk did their thing.

Mr Moorhouse invited us to stay but we demurred.

The Premier was overexcited.

He forgot to introduce his wife as she served the meal and we understand that the Demon Dog took her for a house maid. Fortunately he kept his lip buttoned.

We bought takeaway, drank some wine and watched the *Ray Martin Election Special*. We were not in a good mood as we drove back to the Cross.

We met them at the Piccolo Bar. Got some snaps.

We walked up to the Police Station. I spoke with the Demon Dog. He said he was very tired. It was late. But business was business.

I had spent most of Friday getting authorisation from Police Media for the walk around photo op. They had faxed the authority to Kings Cross. But as we gathered under harsh lights in the station foyer it became obvious something was wrong. They knew of no photo op. They had no authorisation.

There were harsh words and some grinding of teeth. The Demon Dog was jetlagged and, uhm, dog tired. He hadn't slept for a few days. He swayed on his feet and stared resolutely into the vending machine. He shook his head. A lunatic wandered in and joined our discussion with the Patrol Commander's representative. A female parolee was unable to secure the attention of any officers. She became agitated.

Some things happened then.

Lorrie suggested I sort out this mess while she got some shots of Mr Ellroy with some bikies. Alan Someone, who had reappeared, nodded rapidly and ran away to ask their permission.

'What about me!' exclaimed Mr Ellroy.

He was told to stay here. But he too became agitated and wanted to know about these bikies.

They're just some guys, we said.

And the Demon Dog snapped. He began to scream.

'Well I ain't gonna do it. I ain't gonna get photographed with no fucking bikies, or junkies, or goddamn freaks or perverts, or hookers, or fags, or criminals or any of that crap. It's got nothing to do with me or my goddamn books!'

Lorrie stared at him.

'Okay,' she said.

They went to a pool hall instead. Was it jetlag, burnout, or just old-fashioned payback that made him send the cueball flying at Lorrie?

I stayed to argue with the police. They told me some journalists did have an authorisation for a walk-about photo-op, but they already been through with Mr Ellroy.

Last night.

They were from *A Current Affair*.

I hate those fucking guys.

SONS OF BEACHES

Flying into Coffs Harbour, you come down right over the beach. In bad weather it can appear quickly, just under your window, beach and breakers and a strip of swampy-looking, pissed-out bushland south of the town. It looks stone cold and primal through the rain, like you could plant someone in there and they'd disappear for thirty years or more . . . till maybe the brown water got drained off and the land dug out for a Taco Den or a K-Mart or something. You turn on a wing over the harbour itself, a postcard scene which has been used to sell retirement savings plans on TV. A thick finger of land—not seen on TV—shields part of the harbour. It has been half gouged out to provide rock for the breakwater. One tiny shack with a Land Rights flag on the roof sits in a clearing of raw scrub on the foreshore, isolated but giving offence to the scene just over the water. As you're sucked down towards the tarmac the flag slips behind and you fly over a sewage works. Something is happening down there.

The brown pools are threshing and foaming up a storm.

It's strange to be flying into the town. You've passed through before, many times in fact. Coffs—a caffeine break on the East Coast road trip, a point on a line going somewhere else. Caravan parks, motels, a Big Mac and a coke. Stop revive survive. But this time you stay.

You walk through light drizzle into the Coffs Harbour Museum, a cinder block bunker on one of the main drags back to the motel strip. The exhibits lean heavily towards pioneer rust but some space is given over to the area's original tribes. The photographs are interesting, their subjects a long way removed from the image of their great-great-grandchildren. They were tough-looking hunter killer types then, all strong arms, spears and attitude. You see their descendants walking the streets during the day and you might cross over the road. But the threat from their sullen, watery eyes says more that they've been robbed, not that you're about to be.

Some live in the house you flew over coming in. It was an old Public Works shack. Generations have lived there since the Second World War. It feels the strain. The roof lets through the rain, which corrodes the wiring and rots the floor. Fishing gear stands off to the side of the garden. Harry, their shrewd potbellied old patriarch, hopes that something might be done soon. He can't see much point in hanging around since his wife died and he is thinking of cutting out for Queensland.

In 1984 Laurie Brereton said they would never be moved off their land, but successive governments have not been so openhanded and after eight years Harry's people are still being bounced around. They are an obstacle to the exploitation of the area. You stand on Harry's shaky front porch and watch the fishing boats beating out to sea. You just know that the landpimps are wetting themselves to get in here and you smile, thinking that it would strike a disturbing, sub-aural note in the town if the locals bothered to listen and understand their own history. They are getting some of Harry's medicine now, a little taste of what it's like to get fucked around by fat greedheads with all of the guns and no respect.

The smarter ones, those with perspective and emotional distance, can see the change, a long subterranean shift in perceptions and allegiances. They tell you it broke surface during the last Council elections. Yahoos and vandals in shiny suits and white shoes spent a hundred thousand dollars running for unpaid office. They won handsomely and one of the new Mayor's first announcements was that a sewage outfall would be built just outside town at Look At Me Now Headland.

You walk out there the second day in town. On the previous evening some friendly natives have caused you to smoke a weed grown in these parts and your body, now packed in steel wool and grated glass, does not thank you for the fresh air and exercise. The headland sticks out into the ocean like a giant thumb. It is a fine, bracing scene. For the most part it is bare of tree and bush, being covered by grass and some rare form of lichen which you probably trample to death as you stagger about. Climbing up the thumb, to the trig point at the tip, you are forced to the edge by a bog which has settled around a long ditch scoured out by the dozers during the Battle of Look At Me Now.

Your guide is Williams, an American, an outsider and an unbeliever. He is large and bald. A bad leg gives him trouble. His breath comes hard, giving his words a harsh, exasperated texture. But he can make real an awareness which comes out of the mouths of others in halting half-formed thoughts, gestures of frustration and a fear that they are being pushed into the margins on their home turf. A growing concern, as a schoolteacher put it, that the town is becoming the sort of place where you don't count unless you've got money. And if you do have money then rules don't count.

At the high point on the farthest reach of land, most of what lies before your view is the Solitary Marine Reserve. Williams says there's good fishing down there, and great diving. Behind you and off to the south towards town, a long white beach fronts undisturbed bushland. To the north is the small settlement of Emerald Beach, setting for ICAC inquiries and surf competitions and, if you are not mistaken, inspiration for the town of Porpoise Spit in *Muriel's Wedding*. Beneath your muddy boots is the proposed site of the outfall. They weren't going to bother piping it out to sea. The pipe head would jut precisely one metre out from a cliff, about one hundred feet over the crashing surf. The shiny suits said some kind of 'fan system' would disperse the clumps of human grease and 'solid matter'. But standing over the spot, buffetted by a strong sou'wester and watching some board riders catch a long booming swell into the beach, you knew that shit wasn't going anywhere but right back in their faces.

'Corruption is innate in small towns,' says Williams. 'You need something done? Friday you get on the piss with your man in the Council. Monday, things have usually worked themselves out.'

These informal structures were okay in a small fishing village of a few thousand people. But fifty thousand live here now, half a million will according to the Mayor, and the place is falling apart. The shiny suits on Council want an International Airport but they've cut the library budget to shreds. Letters in the papers complain there are no parks for the kids to play in. Suburbs are going without kerbing and guttering for twenty years. Big resort development is fast-tracked, however.

'The business barons are looked after,' says Williams. 'But the basic people structures are ignored.'

You drive down the coast to two big resorts, Pacific Bay and Opal Cove. Once these places were known as Charlsworth Bay and Hills Beach. But that wasn't sophisticated enough, so the names were changed. One day things known for generations just didn't exist anymore. Unthought at the stroke of a pen on a cheque. Then the land itself was changed. Hills, bluffs, dunes and picnic grounds all disappeared, the landscape bludgeoned into submission.

There must be something in the air, or maybe in the proximity to the frontier with Queensland, close enough for some kind of mutagen to be carried out of that heart of darkness to nourish a clutch of little Kurtzs. This place is becoming littered with them. Doing as they please, acting out their own form of brute creation in the forests as they subdivide, slash, burn and concrete the whole fucking thing over for condos, golf clubs and full-bore 3D Irwin Allen-inspired disasters like the Big Banana.

The Banana was one of the first Big Things now littering the tourist routes. It was a working banana farm where families on driving holidays could break the east coast trip and it featured on 60 per cent of the postcards sent from Coffs Harbour. People would stop in for an hour or so, have a cup of tea and a banana sandwich, learn interesting facts about bananas and have their photo taken in front of a largish fibreglass banana before leaving. The syndicate which bought out this worthy enterprise planned a thirty million dollar Banana Disneyland. A monorail would run all over the valley, out to Pacific Bay and Opal Cove, before looping back to a shopping mall around the side of the Banana mountain. For ten bucks you could catch a ride and see the million dollar mechanised bunyip, the mountain top space station ('Bananas in the 21st Century!'), and the withered grey fruit trees which had been sought out from afar and left to die on the side of the mountain.

The Banana was a lemon. Doomed from the start. The receivers moved in. They are hoping to get two or three million dollars back. Scores of local contractors will not be paid, a nasty shock to a small town economy.

The new manager of the Banana walks you around the place and tells you that the idea was fucked in its conception. There was never a market for an international theme park in this part of the world. He has gone back to basics, to the family market. Half-way up the mountain he points to the coast, to the multistorey Pacific Bay resort. Finished nearly two years ago, it has never opened its doors. It cannot hope to sustain the occupancy rate it needs to pay for its overheads. Nearby, Opal Cove is not deserted. It just seems that way. The condos built in the middle of a fairway for those golf crazy Japanese are empty. Who wants to live in the flight path of a thousand little white missiles? Some species of killer ant has taken over the greens. Driving through, you mistake their anthills for thousands of little doggy turds.

An inauspicious debut for big dollar international tourism. But other developments are racing ahead with that special full throttle high octane feel you remember from the days when guys like Skasey and Bondy were lauded as heroes for bankrupting the country. One of these, the Big Golf Course, was the work of one of the geniuses behind the Big Banana. He left town in a hurry claiming the Yakuza had taken over the project. The new backers say he took two million bucks of their money then had to leg it out of Dodge City pursued by his creditors. The new backers make the national media when they are allegedly caught flogging a prospectus around Tokyo touting developments for which they have no planning approval.

The push for an international airport does not strike you as weird. There are people here who would eat their own young if they could get a fast return on the deal. With hundreds of millions of dollars tied up in dead assets, they are going to scream like strung-out junkies unless some high volume fat margin tourists come online, and that means plugging into the Japanese.

Item. Coffs Harbour Council File No 191890. Development Applications. A report of the City Planner on the Indian Pacific Resort says that the State Pollution Control Commission supports a reticulated sewage system for the resort, but advises that the town will need to increase its licensed sewage dumping levels and that approval for this is 'unlikely until an alternative disposal system is found'. An outfall.

Normally your Emerald Beaches are conservative places. The police concern themselves with lost dogs, garden gnome vandalism, traffic infringements and, on 23 May 1992, the disappearance of a Buttercup bread truck, last seen exiting the Sawtell Reserve Caravan Park through a new hole in the fence. The citizens of such places do not front as anarchists and Luddites. They are drawn from the professions. Lawyers, architects, GPs and accountants. They pay taxes and vote in elections, conservatively. They would not normally find themselves arrested in job lots, as they would not normally set themsleves against Law and Order. They would not normally deface their houses and clutter the streets with crude, handpainted signs declaiming their government and councillors as progenitors of a proto-fascist state.

Item. Statement of Albert D, 60, arrested during protest at Emerald Beach outfall site.

I'd injured my leg and had sat down to rest when a constable told me to move on. I explained I had hurt my leg and he assisted me to my feet. While he helped me across the track Sergeant Macdonald came along and said arrest that man. I was taken into Coffs Harbour after about an hour's wait in the paddy wagon. We were in the cells for four hours then. There were twelve of us there when eight police came in and told us to line up against the wall. We were picked out one at a time to go to a single cell. Two young people were told to strip in the cell yard. I was told by a constable to empty my pockets. I emptied them and he told me to strip. I refused. He went through the contents of my pockets. He told me to remove my tee shirt, which I did, then to remove my jeans, which I refused. He said we have ways of making you do this. I pointed out that I was old enough to be his father. He said take off your boots, which I did. I was upset. I was humiliated. I am a grandfather of 60 with seven children and five grand-children. I am retired on a pension.

Item. Statement of Michael W, arrested during protest at Emerald Beach outfall site.

I was up on an excavator when they grabbed me, asked if I was coming down. I said no, so they threw me down, grabbed me and walked me back to the wagon calling me scumbag, fuckwit and maggot. Two had hold of me, twisting my arms painfully. When they got me to the wagon they opened the door with the spare tyre on it straight into my ribs with force. Mark Ingelby witnessed that. I was charged with three offences, two resisting arrest and one watch and beset.

On October 12 the Mayor had announced that the sewage outfall would be built at Emerald Beach, just outside town and in the middle of the Solitary Marine Reserve. The first protest meeting was held on Bluff road, near the site, two days later. The unions declared a picket the following day. On October 16 the first big crowds of residents appeared, drawn by local TV coverage.

They lined up on the banks of the dune system at the base of the headland. This sort of thing felt new and awkward. A police sergeant, MacDonald, told them they were causing an obstruction. They would be charged with a breach of the peace unless they moved. There were 26 arrests that day. Those women present with children were threatened with neglect charges and told the children would be taken by Family and Community Services.

Note. Statement by Micheal N, 14, arrested during protest at Emerald Beach outfall site.

I was up a tripod when one cop grabbed my toe, another got my foot, and five or six came for me. I went down, then they were kicking, grabbing and punching, twisting my wrist and arm off. My mum was there as they dragged me to the wagon. They threw me against the wheel nut and cut my back. My mum was allowed to take me to the station. They gave me six charges, told mum she was an irresponsible parent. I told them to fuck off and they charged me with offensive language.

These were the early days of skirmishing and organisation. Outsiders began to arrive from other protests:

Chaelundi, the South East Forests, Aidex—this last name puts a shiver on the back of your neck. A military trade fair in Canberra, a byword for state sponsored brutality. A thousand peaceniks in mediaeval caravans camped outside the National Exhibition Centre. Squads of cops in overalls with riot batons. None shall pass. For three days you sleep in a ditch by the side of the road. You see the price paid for 'nonviolence' as time and again the protesters' lines are thrown back with maximum prejudice. You see madness. Eyes rolled back to yellow. Lips drawn up over long fangs. Batons whipping through the air in a blur. Bones cracked. Heads run into the road. Trucks and wagons ploughing through the centre regardless. Tripods, like the martians of HG Wells, built from stripped pine trees, twenty metres high, appearing without warning to block the access road. Protestors scrambling up to sit in the crow's-nests formed at the juncture of the poles. The cops bringing up their star forwards, TRG, 'hut hut hut hut hut', thick necks, strong arms and stone faces. Their violence more controlled than the desk riders with night sticks. Focussed, a single spear hand strike to the kidneys clearing a hole where three cops going crazy with batons had no effect.

Those tripods drove the cops insane. After a few days they began to appear at Emerald Beach. As the tents were rigged up in the dunes and the first tripods climbed towards the sky, the town folk weren't sure they wanted the outsiders' support. They called them feral. They were dirty. They lived in the forests and had become wild. They seemed the embodiment of savagery. Already fighting for their homes against the shiny suits, these wild people threatened to hijack what litle margin for action the locals had left.

But as the numbers of arrested increased and as the ferals stood by them day after day, on the barricades and in the cellblocks, as they took their beatings and kept coming back, they earned their place on the beach. At dawn and dusk families from the middle class villas overlooking the ocean would struggle down through the beach grass and sand with loaves of bread and big steaming pots of soup for them. In return the ferals would dive under the blades of the dozers, tie themselves to excavators and bury their bodies in the path of trucks. On the 21st of October the locals threw back the machines, bounced them right off the headland and back to square one.

While the cinematic action played itself out down at the beach, another fight took place in the courts and on the floor of Council. Injunction, appeals, bus trips to Parliament five hundred miles away, all provided a lull until 5 a.m. on October 28.

Residents monitoring a police scanner picked up a message to the media that the big expected raid was on. An elaborate phone tree lit up within minutes and the streets overlooking the headland filled with alarms, cars, parents and children in pj's rubbing their eyes. They ran to the dunes where the first defences were already down. Some who had been onsite ran to the newcomers, mixing up their words, whipping their heads to and fro searching for any more nasty surprises. They described scores of men in balaclavas and jungle cams taking to the tripods with machetes. Residents ran past to take up positions, chained themselves to trees and machines, climbed tripods, lay in the path of police vans and workers. All hesitation was gone now, the fundamentals established a long time ago. Three wagons' full were taken off.

They were no longer shocked to see an uncle or sister frogmarched away. They were not surprised to see Aaron James pulled from an excavator arm to fall onto the shovel. They understood when Mark Whittleton said a policeman tried to gouge out the eyes of a protester who was sitting on the ground with arms locked around his friends. They did not consider it unusual that Susie Hope got a fisting for asking an arresting constable his badge number. They understood the way of things now.

But there was a strange, otherwordly feeling of suspended animation when the mayor made an appearance at 7 a.m. to address the crowd.

'Just let me say,' he told them, 'I am a Christian.'

They fought up and down that headland for weeks, and even though they won in the courts and on the ground, with the cops and the machines having to pull out in the end, nothing was really resolved except the Council's intention to prevail at all costs. They have now hired a PR firm to sell the outfall to the same people they were beating on so recently. The static and bullshit has got so thick you need your decoders going full-time just to get through the day. People who have lived in the town for generations are moving on.

The gut truth of the thing can be found in silence. In the empty corridors of Pacific Bay. The rooms ticking away in their stillness waiting for the tourists from El Dorado. No locals will stay in those rooms, or swim on the beach or picnic in the forest. They are not wanted. They are irrelevant. They do not factor into the balance sheets. They have become like Harry's people down on the foreshore, sold out and moved on, packed off into the margins.

THE CITY

William 'Joey' Hollebone was a man with a thirst for cheap wine. In an era when men drank beer by the schooner or took a broken glass in the face for their presumed homosexuality, Hollebone presented as a heavy-set, Brylcream thug with cold axe-blade eyes and a taste for flagons of sickly sweet claret. He once glassed his wife after a day-long vino binge, walking away from her as she screamed and pawed at the raw flapping wound on her face, a forty-stitch job. He was a standover specialist, but not a blusterer or a man with any need to self-promote. His friend, Chow Hayes the gunman, recalled him as a good listener and emotionally self-contained. The explosions, when they came, were more often a matter of cold fusion than a hot temper. When he was nineteen years old he drew a ten-year stretch for kicking a fruit seller to death.

While he was inside on a charge, older but no wiser, a small timer named Alfie Dawes broke into his home, stole Hollebone's clothes and backhanded his wife, Hazel.

Hollebone's old lady was not the stoic sort and ran straight to jail with her story. Joey quietly insisted she tell nobody. When he was released he made for Dawes' home in Waterloo which was, in those days, a sort of hellish edge of darkness shanty settlement, the type of raw urban wound peopled by the worst inhabitants of Jim Thompson's vicious disconnected noir novels. Hundred-year-old sewage boiled up from the poisoned soil. Toxic industrial waste contaminated the air, the ground, the water, and such houses as existed were often little more than crude humpies constructed of stolen construction material, packing crates, rusted iron. Waterloo was not a place where the odd bit of gunplay caused much comment.

On 29 August 1946, Hollebone changed that. He drove out to the Dawes' family residence, a 'squalid wooden shack' according to the tabloids of the day, walked in carrying a large calibre pistol and unloaded it on the occupants. He capped six people, killing three, including Alfie Dawes, shot through the right eyeball. Joey's trigger finger was on song that night. The other lethal shots nailed Marjorie Nurse dead in the centre of her face and Douglas Graves in the side of his head. Hollebone also shot Alfie's girlfriend in the shoulder, perhaps a sharp-shooting act of mercy, as she was breastfeeding their three-week-old baby at the time. Probably not though.

Hollebone was acquitted of all charges.

If you peer through the rush of static pouring out of the city's legions of boosters, the civic spin doctors and commercial hucksters, you'll see these sorts of stories begin to resolve themselves more clearly and more frequently. The tourist illusion leveraged into global brand—a clean hot sun glinting off a harbour of Perrier water and friendly visiting Disney whales, the eternal arc of the Bridge, those frozen sails of the Opera House, jolly old convict memories of cheery pickpockets and put-upon Irish rebels, Skippy, Fox Studios, laughter and forgetting. The illusion, pursued fiercely enough, can even become material. But it still conceals deeper levels of meaning.

Sydney, the southern PacRim corner of an LA–Tokyo global trade triangle, the entrepot for billions of dollars worth of hot, liquid capital sluicing into and out of Australia is also the Sydney of unbelievably grim slums stretching over miles and miles of hot baked arid plains on the city's western and southwestern fringe; slums where hopeless poverty is passed down through families like a hereditary virus, damning generations unborn. Sydney the painfully beautiful city of water and bushland, blessed with dozens of beaches, uncountable secret coves, hundreds of parks and gardens and examples of virtually every architectural style known to the world is also the Sydney of rapacious development of neo-brutalist, antihuman concrete slab monuments to stupid, unthinking greed and arrogance. It is the city which ate itself in an orgy of ruin, burped for a moment in the time of the Green Bans, and continued on its baneful course. It is also the city which gave the world the term 'green' movement, Germany's Petra Kelly being so taken with those bans that she and her allies freely borrowed the idea of organising resistance to the blitzkrieg strategies of modern development from the building workers and heritage protesters of Sydney. Sydney the migrant creation, along with America the last great hope of the wretched and dispossessed, is also Sydney the home of a micro movement of Australian neo-Nazis, and the natural breeding ground of a lumpen underclass drawn increasingly to the racist insanities of One Nation and their lesser imitators.

Sydney is a wide open territory, where any can try their hand, amass a fortune, snatch a measure of gold and glory from that vast, ripping torrent of global capital rushing through her streets. She is also inherently corrupt, fucked in the core and at conception, where the spoils, the power, and power's righteous splendour goes only to the strongest, the most cunning and the creatively evil; the sort of place a good looking, sharply dressed guy like Joey Hollebone can lay waste to a room full of nobodies and come out smiling on the other side. The city's story is, when viewed from this vantage point, a corridor of mirrors receding into darkness and the inscrutable void. A natural haunt of the morally ambiguous, with a soundtrack by Portishead and screenplay by David Lynch.

It is possible, from outside the city gates, to misunderstand. It is common for tourists on package deals to spend three or four days rolling from one photo-op to the next, from Manly to Bondi via the Quayside souvenir shops. After a few days of relentlessly skimming across the bright plastic surface they slump and tire and a weary disappointment comes over them. Tour guides complain that buses full of Japanese office ladies and retired insurance brokers from the American Midwest will all eventually whisper an awful secret. That this place has no soul. They are wrong, but not for the reasons you might think.

Travellers commonly mistake the incorporeal spirit of a place for a bunch of old stuff lying around. The Colosseum, the House of Lords, the Bastille. Manifest expressions of bloody contention, of repression, revolt, endurance, transcendence, of the best and worst of humankind. The folds of the harbour, as delightful as they are, seem to offer no frozen moment of indirect contact with the base matter of human savagery. This grossly misreads the city's narrative.

It is not really possible to compare Sydney with Rome, Athens, Cairo or even London, her mother city. They are all centres of the old world. In the case of Athens, the very crucible of western civilisation. And in Cairo the foundations of civilisation itself. The ghosts of cities swallowed by the sand stalked Cairo's bazaars thousands of years before the Romans scratched out the rough, muddy tracks of Londinium. Sydney by contrast is only three human lifetimes old. It winked into existence during the afternoon of 26 January 1788 on the edge of a continent presumed to be empty. That meant that, unlike London, there was no established and ossified power structure to distribute the wealth of the new land. In England a land-based class system, slowly evolving into a mercantile and industrial elite, had maintained a stranglehold on the keys to the kingdom for over a thousand years. The same standover racket was not possible in Sydney.

To survive, the colony had to exploit the talents of every single human being who made the trip to the dark side of the globe. The whole continent lay open to plunder and a hundred-year labour shortage in the underpopulated settlement rendered obsolete the old, imbalanced power relationships of the mother country. Be they pickpocket, murderer or merely broken-down drunk, the new city offered salvation to all who arrived. It would take whatever they had to offer. The city remains generous in that two-faced, self-serving way. There is no old money oligarchy here. If the city thinks she can make a dollar off you, she will come and put her hot mouth all over you, to misquote Michael Herr.

She is not a museum piece of crumbling empire artifacts. She is an engine of pure capitalism, she is greed metastasised. You look at the metro-centres of the old world and can see in the fabric of their buildings and streets the whole cloth of dead history, patches of time in which church, state, various commercial interests, the universities, the landed gentry and the emergent middle classes all contended for dominance. In the cities of the new world these moments are not frozen. The clash of the big battalions, the cities' power blocs and axes of influence spark and hum beneath the surface of everyday life, distorting shape and structure, raising some on high, casting others down utterly.

Sydney stands, as she has from the first day of her white history, at a confluence of fantastic energies, with tidal flows of money and people warping and contorting the structure of space within her boundaries. In fact so great is the pressure of riches flooding in through the gates that wealth effects spin off in swirls and eddies, inflating the price of property, cappuccinos and cocaine in rival and satellite cities along the entire eastern seaboard of the continent. Within the city nucleus, inside the highest towers, her new elites create raw, formidable wealth and power by manipulating symbolic artifacts on flat plasma screens. Millions of lives are daily channelled in new directions for good or ill by the decisions of fund managers, forex traders, merchant bankers, media tyrants, development moguls and even, occasionally, the city's old political commissariat in Macquarie Street, Trades Hall and the private gentleman's clubs. A metropolis lacking an inborn hierarchy, she has become a Hobbesian experiment in the protean nature of power, a digital urban domain where private muscle is beholden only to itself, where fierce, uncertain currents of creation and destruction rage against each other.

To understand these forces is to see the modern city anew, to penetrate to its otherwise intangible soul with a sort of x-ray vision, which reveals the underlying structure not to be concrete and steel, but rather lust, greed, hubris and a ceaselessly shifting but morally inert and insatiable will to power. Is there any chance of some rube from Arkansas busily working his Nikon at Taronga Park Zoo actually zooming in on this stark vision? Doubt it. Because to peer deeply into this ghost city, the one lying beneath the surface of things, requires some concentration. You have to squint to see past the dazzling light and understand that Sydney does have a soul and that it is a very dark place indeed.

And yet . . . you know, the light is just so dazzling.

There are harbours, like Rio, just as magnificent. There are Manhattanised skylines more imposing and hinterlands, such as Seattle's, which are infinitely more striking. There are even cities within Australia whose internal life is more finely honed. Melbourne, basically, with its bookshops, libraries, nightclubs, bars, cafes and restaurants, all five years ahead of the curve in Sydney. But within the magic circle of the harbour city, wherever salt water might be easily reached, there life can be lived as well as at any place on the globe. And it can be lived for the most part freely, with no fear of casual tyranny or state-sponsored terror. It is a striking paradox, perhaps the city's pivotal enigma, that a place born of insensate cruelty can have become a home so kind to its chosen, so beloved by newest arrival and oldest native alike.

Imagine riding the first ray of dawn as it spilled over the edge of the Pacific and streamed in towards the broken, biscuit-coloured cliffs of the city's eastern extremity. Atop miles of those cliffs, virgin bushland, sanctuary for some of the oldest, oddest forms of life on the planet. Where the bluffs drop down to receive the ocean's kiss, long stretches of nearly empty beach, spotted here and there by joggers, walkers, the occasional unauthorised kelpie or labrador. The long curling waves harnessed by surfers. The massive bay at Bondi trawled by a handful of swimmers, some of them performing a personal ritual begun six decades earlier. On the harbour the ferries trailing long white wakes as they deliver the keenest workers to their toil. At a thousand cafes the smell of muffins baking and coffee brewing, the sizzle of bacon and eggs. A hundred thousand newspapers being wrestled into some sort of order on the first commuter trains. The sports pages read first and then the comics. Trawlers at the fish markets delivering the morning catch. Coppers in paddy wagons outside the Magistrate's Court doing much the same. On Oxford Street a gaggle of queens spilling from the Taxi Club, bleary-eyed and totter-heeled. At Kings Cross a drunk asleep in the little garden outside the Goldfish Bowl. In Lane Cove five hundred Pajeros supplying one thousand private school students to a dozen bastions of exclusive privilege. At Cabramatta offerings to Buddha carefully placed at shopfront shrines. In Bankstown a centuries-old family recipe for Vietnamese rice noodle soup brewed up for the customers of Hiep Chi Phan's Pho restaurant. Rowers on the Woronora. Bushwalkers in the Royal National Park.

All human life is contained within the sandstone bowl of the Sydney basin and as such cruelty lies next to sympathy, stupidity with wisdom, rapacious greed with great generosity. The city which annihilated its original tribes with smallpox and musket fire is the same city which sheltered escapees from the Nazi Holocaust and marched in its hundreds of thousands to call for reconciliation with the survivors of its own indigenous holocaust. The contradictions are a source of tension but need not destroy each other. If the modern city declares for anything it is the triumph of complexity. With every major and most minor languages of the earth spoken on her streets, with her slave state past and uncertain, conflicted future, with her wealth and power, Sydney will always confound, infuriate, engage and seduce. She is provider/destroyer, madonna/whore and prophet of the main chance. She is hated, feted, loved and envied. She cares not. Self-obsessed and cosmopolitan, tacky, shallow and deeply serious, she knows her own worth and vainly overstates it at every turn—as when one speaker at the last Premier's litfest dinner favourably compared the old tart with the Florence of Michelangelo. The gasps at the dinner tables were probably in surprise that anyone could think to bracket Sydney with such a provincial backwater.

In the end though she is, if nothing else, a place of redemption. For thousands of the lowest, most wretched lumpenproles exiled from their mother city. For millions more refugees and escapees, the desperate and dispossessed of two awful centuries. Even now she draws the poorest souls into her arms. Modern day slaves and indentured serfs.

I spoke to two of them while researching *Leviathan*, an Indian and a Chinese man, a cook and carpenter respectively. They had both travelled to Sydney from their home countries at the invitation of powerful business figures. They had both been imprisoned on their arrival and forced to work for free, threatened, abused and treated as the nearly worthless property of their masters. Both eventually escaped with help of workers who discovered them in their extremity. Both then lived in fear of the swift and terrible vengeance which had been promised should they ever attempt such a thing.

But both live free now. The city, which has at times been so cruel or at least indifferent to the plight of other fallen travellers, took them within her protection. Police officers swept in to guarantee physical safety. Lawyers took up their cases before the courts and in Canberra. Journalists and other troublemakers campaigned on their behalf. And they were liberated to take their place as free men of the harbour city.

THE JOY OF SCRUFF

Mason's cafe, which opened in 1910, described itself as the original and the best. A generation of indigent rock journalists can testify to the truth of that. Located just around the corner from the former offices of *Rolling Stone* near Central Station in Sydney, it had a tattoo parlour and a hostel for substance abusers as neighbours. For nigh on ninety years it also had the best chips in Sydney. Fried three or four times in beef tallow and piled up next to T-bones as thick as tectonic plates. All washed down with real, honest-to-God milkshakes in battered metal beakers jewelled with condensation.

It had once been home to another generation of dubious Sydney identities, gunmen such as Chow Hayes and Joey Hollebone, who ate there during the Depression. You could get a three course meal for six pence then, but the cutlery was chained to the tables. A waitress with a damp cloth would wipe the knife and fork after you were finished and there were no condiments. The proprietor

Harry Lawrence wore a suit vest with salt and pepper in the pockets and if you wanted either, Harry would dole out a pinch between his fingers.

Mason's is gone now. The whole block on which it sat is to be redeveloped. The once scabrous neighbourhood is now home to increasing numbers of design warehouses and loft conversions, and anyone looking for a frightening steak experience has to head uptown, where the local outlet of the Chicago chain Morton's will ping you eighty bucks for a feed. It's doubtful whether Mason's entire menu would have added up to half that. Prices seemed not to have changed since Gough Whitlam drew his first pay cheque as PM.

Of course Morton's eighty dollar steak is the future. And it would be churlish to diss the joint just because a lunch there will unburden your wallet of roughly the same weight in bank notes as you'll eat during the main course. But to restrict yourself to the silver circle means missing out on the low rent pleasures of places like Mason's, or the infinitely classier but still quite naff Leo's in St Kilda, or suburban surprises like The Bodega in fabulous Ipswich, spiritual home of the prawn cocktail and steak diane. When you pull into the car park of the Spanish ranch style Bodega, the man-sized champagne bottle spewing imitation bubbly into a giant champagne glass is a lay-down guarantee that something special is afoot. No million dollar fit-outs here. No painfully abstract Italian seating or polished concrete floors or unisex toilets. But the permanent attraction of this suburban bistro and of places like Leo's and Mason's speaks of a widespread desire to fall behind the cutting edge and collapse into the safety of the beanbag, the Chiko roll and the uggy.

There is a reason the trash mags devote 15 per cent of their available pages in any given year to grainy, out of focus photo spreads of the world's most fabulous celebrities struggling with outbreaks of zits, cellulose, and—if we're really, really lucky—the odd case of flesh-eating bacteria. It's proof positive that these paragons of glamour can get down with the worst of us. Most of us simple village folk know our lives will never remotely approximate the aesthetic totalitarianism being pimped by the likes of *Wallpaper** or even, God help us, *Domain*. Thus it's comforting to think that when they imagine that the last of the paparazzi and spin doctors have packed up and crawled back under their rocks for the day, even the most polished celebrity will slip into a rancid pair of Dunlop Volleys, slump down in front of the box and start pushing Chicken McNuggets into their face like some stinky, slumpy McNugget-eating slug. Just as the Nobel Prize-winning poet occasionally needs to take a break from the rigours of painfully impenetrable free verse by furtively dipping into a Matt Reilly hyper-thriller, so too must the most constipated style Nazi eventually cave and opt for the sticky beanbag over the Alastair Keating Design Ward Seven Series wheeled seating cube. (Inspired by the clinical aesthetic of the medical profession, its seemingly pure functionality holds a scalpel to the throat of form!)

It is not always the polished, slimline Starke or Alessi which takes our fancy. It is difficult to love one of those War of the Worlds invading Martian orange juicers, for instance. Or a $62 magic bunny toothpick holder. But the battered enamel mug, the faded and chipped Peter Rabbit breakfast bowl, or the ancient imitation crocodile skin stubbie holder: these can be held as dear as the most long-lived childhood teddy bear. Their very tattiness speaks to some unkempt corner of the human heart.

We're not talking Rachel Ashwell's Shabby Chic here, a design ethic that seems to consist of compressing enormous tonnages of painfully twee knick-knacks and garnish down to neutron star density in already over-crowded rooms. If you're looking to purchase your indy scruff, you'd come a little closer to the mark with some-thing like Melbourne's Wunderkammer, in Elgin Street, Carlton. If you have some space that needs cluttering up with the skanky refuse of a bygone era, they can supply you with a certified strand of woolly mammoth hair, an artifi-cial leg, or a William Burroughs-approved hypodermic syringe set from the 1920s. It's the same dorm room sen-sibility employed by generations of medical students who draped their articulated skeletons in jaunty football scarves. And Wunderkammer is less frequently haunted by angry loners and disenfranchised Goths than you'd imagine. Rather, its mummified cats and confronting anal probes draw in a steady stream of Melbourne's urgently hip, all looking to unburden themselves of a small wedge of the folding stuff in return for the sort of street cred only something like a half-dissected human head can give a two million dollar converted warehouse apartment.

This urge to purchase the raffishly decayed has some deep root within our response to the demands of universal entropy. If the whole cosmos is indeed winding down towards an infinite long weekend, why bother keeping up appearances? Why wear the unwearable Gaultier when K-Mart and Target are so damned comfy and cheap? Why pay elephant bucks for that genuine Meiji futon base when a dozen or so stolen milk crates can do the same job—or can, in fact, do a better job doubling as filing cabinet, laundry basket and/or modular couch? During my own stint at batching it I managed to construct nearly an entire apartment out of those handy little buggers. I can guarantee you they'll stack together more easily than any piece of Ikea, and their ubiquitous nature meant that moving house was no longer a matter of booking a couple of hefty men and a delivery van. It simply meant denuding my new suburb of eighty or ninety poorly guarded plastic cubes. It's not really stealing because you never permanently deprive the world of their use. You simply push them back onto the footpath when you're done, where they'll soon be scarfed up by the next interior decorator with an eye for a bargain. This endless cycle is even more efficient than mother nature's circle of life. It operates on a larger scale whenever your local council schedules a pick-up day for major items of rubbish. For sure, tons of broken-backed brown couches and non-functional microwaves are discarded onto suburban streets. But only a fraction ever make it to the landfill site. The major part of those mounds of garbage simply migrate a few doors up or down the street, where they take up residence for another five or six years, until being recycled again.

Perhaps this is partly a reaction against the sort of painfully puckered aesthetic fascism which led one ultrahip

New York boutique hotel to line its bookshelves with hundreds of identical but empty volumes. The covers were all blank and red, presenting a machine-stamped uniformity to the world, all being exactly the same size and shade. This ploy solved a problem which has been keeping constipated art directors named Sven awake at night for years; how to impose a pleasing conformity on the inherently unruly domain of a bookshelf. The hotel's solution was elegant, in a way, but also profoundly anti-human.

At Australia's best second-hand bookstore cum coffee shop, Bondi's Gertrude and Alice, the staff quickly discovered that the punters would come over all distressed and persnickety at any attempt to impose order on the shop's groaning, chaotic shelves. To straighten up a section when nobody was looking invited retail retribution as sales from the newly tidy area would plummet until a bit of confusion and jumble was reintroduced. It was almost as though the idea of having to prospect through a random pile of tattered old books was more attractive to the hordes who have made G&A their second home. With scratched tables, a magnificently tatty brown couch and cane baskets full of books which are sometimes emptied to double as impromptu baby capsules, G&A has the feel of an eccentric's private library. It is the ambience that huge megabarn booksellers like the American Borders chain are shooting for when they drop a coffee shop into the middle of one of their operations. But you can happily finger a sticky piece of baklava while fondling G&A's merchandise. That sort of thing will bring the Tidy Cops running at Borders.

Perhaps it is something to do with the beach. As a nation clinging to the shores of the continent maybe we've been worn down by the eternal process of erosion which is so pronounced at the intersection of land and water. Everything rusts at the beach. Sand gets in everywhere. The winds come blasting off the ocean, abrading exposed surfaces, dulling clean windows with salt spray, ripping branches from trees and occasionally tiles or chimneys from the roof. At the beach you're always on holidays. That crumpled newspaper can be picked up tomorrow. Those pizza boxes don't need to go out till Tuesday. Does it really matter if you wear the tracky-daks just one more time without a wash? We are all heading towards decay and dissolution, and on the beach that doesn't seem like such a bad deal.

THE ROUGH BEAST

Violence is out of style. Not everywhere, of course. Not in Hollywood or Chechnya. But in the middle class world it has been deleted from the hot list, and even Hollywood occasionally feels compelled to mouth excuses for the endless reels of splatter porn spooled out every year. Witness Schwarzenegger's and Stallone's claims to 'strong anti-violence messages' in *Last Action Hero* and *Rambo III*.

It wasn't always so, of course. It has only recently become *déclassé* for chaps to settle their differences by pounding each other into a bloody pulp. Author and biographer Peter Corris believes it was the noble and manly thing to do well into this century, disappearing from polite society only after the Second World War.

When, at a Hollywood cocktail party during that war, Errol Flynn said something wretched about a very close lady friend of John Huston's, an infuriated Huston called him a lying sonofabitch. Flynn, drunk or mean or possibly both, asked Huston whether he'd like to make anything out of it.

'And I decided that I would,' said Huston.

He recounts the contest which followed in *Ringside*, an entertaining if somewhat unfashionable anthology which Corris has edited with Barry Parish. Huston writes that the two made their way to the bottom of David O. Selznick's garden, removed their jackets and sailed into each other. Straight away Flynn, a fine athlete and a good boxer by Huston's own testimony, knocked the director to the gravel where he landed painfully, injuring himself so badly that for years afterwards small slivers of bone continued to emerge from his right elbow. Huston, his blood up and a few drinks into the bag, ignored the pain and leapt back into the fray. The thumping and grunting continued for an hour, with both getting bloodied and badly messed up, but fighting the whole time according to Queensberry's rules.

As the party ended and departing guests discovered the punch-up, they came running to separate the two. Flynn, whom Selznick suspected of starting the brawl—such was his reputation—was bundled off to a hospital. Huston stayed over with the Selznick family, checking into a different hospital the following day.

He writes that the next morning Flynn called him, '. . . wanting to know how I was. He told me that he had two broken ribs and I said that I had thoroughly enjoyed the fight and hoped that we would do it again sometime.'

In contrast, modern manners generally require an exchange of solicitors' contact details rather than blows. Huston would no doubt be disappointed, feeling something worthwhile had gone from the world. For while fighting has an overtly effective character—i.e. it changes the world in some way, such as rearranging the ill-mannered Mr Flynn's ribs—fighting also has an affective quality. It alters the nature of those involved. It is assumed to brutalise them, of course, but there is more to it.

Corris boxed as a youngster. 'That's forty plus years ago now,' he says. 'I had about four bouts and in the last I was struck on the nose and wept. That was the end of my boxing career.' Decades later he fondly remembers the thrill of lacing the gloves. He remembers the fear, too, and the pride of getting through something required of him as a man. Another writer, Norman Mailer, was himself a keen boxer until his knees gave out. Writing in *Esquire* magazine, he admitted to never feeling as virtuous after giving it up. Something vital to his manhood remained inside the ring when he left it for the last time.

Mailer's *Ringside* piece, an extract from his book *The Fight*, is one of a whole section dealing with the Ali phenomenon. It is not the standout piece, however. Surprisingly Jose Torres, himself a world title holder, has it all over Mailer on the page, just as he did in the gym where they often trained together. *Ringside* is fat with great writing, which may confound those who think of boxing as a witless pursuit, surpassed only by the killing of ducks with shotguns. It has always drawn great writers, many of whom, like Mailer and Hemingway (who also boxed, of course), are represented in this volume—although there are some notable omissions, Pete Hamill and Hunter S. Thompson foremost amongst them.

A few women such as Mae West appear, testifying to the

sexual magnetism of savage, near naked men. Bev Wills, who attended Melbourne's Festival Hall in 1969 on 'the first night ladies were admitted free to the fights in the company of a man', writes: 'I was surprised to find myself stirred at the sight of their rippling muscles, beautifully formed legs and handsome heads . . . a boxer's body is perhaps one of the best from an aesthetic point of view, and much to a lady's taste.'

In his *Esquire* article Mailer also wrote that to be born into the middle class is to be brought up not to strike others, which is perhaps why Mailer found something in boxing missing from other sports. He wrote that fighting aroused two of the deepest anxieties men contain: 'There is not only the fear of getting hurt, which is profound in more men than will admit to it, but there is the opposite panic equally unadmitted, of hurting others.' He and the other amateur pugs who laboured away at the Gramercy gym in New York could rarely, if ever, resolve the conflict. When he did, one day against the actor Ryan O'Neal, who had just humiliated one of Mailer's gym buddies, the angels sang for him. He ripped into O'Neal like an avenger, smashing and pounding his valuable face with lusty abandon and boxing better on that day than at any other time in his life.

'You punch sharper than anyone here,' muttered a ragged and impressed O'Neal during a clinch.

'Go fuck yourself,' replied Mailer.

Appalling behaviour, but enormous fun, as I must confess. It's been nearly eight years since I hit anyone, but sweet mother of God, I enjoyed it. Really gave this obnoxious Young National something to go on with. I biffed him during a frenzied demonstration cum riot in Brisbane and amidst all the shoving and violent anarchy it felt like my life had come, very briefly and powerfully, into alignment.

'I was the little warm centre that the life of the world crowded around,' writes *Fight Club* author Chuck Palahniuk, who seems to understand these things. Things like the mythology of regeneration through violence:

> You aren't alive anywhere like you're alive at fight club when it's you and one other guy under that one light in the middle of all those watching. Fight club isn't about winning or losing fights. Fight club isn't about words. You see a guy come to fight club for the first time, and his ass is a loaf of white bread. You see this same guy here six months later, and he looks carved out of wood. This guy trusts himself to handle anything. There's grunting and noise at fight club like at the gym, but fight club isn't about looking good. There's hysterical shouting in tongues like in church, and when you wake up Sunday afternoon you feel saved.

Fight club is fifty guys in a basement, beating nine kinds of hell out of each other and loving it. Sort of an encounter group for a generation of men who were raised by women, as first time author Chuck Palahniuk's nameless narrator puts it.

This guy likes to hang with support groups for people coping with terminal diseases. No one is ever suffering from, or dying of, these diseases nowadays. They're coping with them or living with them, as though AIDS, for instance, is an uninvited house guest who might be persuaded to leave any day now. *Fight Club*'s hero took up his habit because like every rootless 30-year-old Gen X wannabe his life is like, you know, meaningless. So he crashes these groups as a vicarious therapeutic pick-me-up because he leaves them feeling more alive than he's ever been before.

It's vaguely reminiscent of the character who puts herself through an AIDS test every few days in the movie *Reality Bites*, another Gen X icon. In fact Douglas Coupland's *Generation X* seems to alternately haunt and inspire Palahniuk's story. He makes such frequent reference to the same existential talismans. To list but a few: McJobs, self-mutilation, Swedish furniture, liposuctioned yuppie fat and odd, slanting references to skin cancer in the antipodes. However, putting him down as a mere imitator would do *Fight Club*'s author a grave injustice. It hits hard for a first novel, frequently stunning the reader with short rhetorical jabs, like his narrator's reaction to the avid sexual advances of a woman dying from brain parasites: 'Normal times, I'd be sporting an erection. Our Chloe, however, was a skeleton dipped in yellow wax.'

In contrast to Coupland's legion of mimics Palahniuk mines a much deeper, richer vein than twenty-something anomie. At the dark, mordant heart of his story sits a question as old as America itself. Can violence ever work as a transcendent device or is the very idea inherently corrosive, doomed to failure?

Simone de Beauvoir did not think so. In *The Second Sex* she argued that violence can be the legitimate recourse of a free man and despaired for women who were, by their nature, deprived of its hard lessons. Woman 'may feel herself alone in the midst of the world,' she wrote, 'but she never stands up before it, unique and sovereign. Everything influences her to let herself be hemmed in, dominated by existences foreign to her own . . .' A boy, she said, learns early to take care of himself, contending with his fists, emerging beyond what is given and asserting himself above others. While de Beauvoir conceded that brute force was largely inappropriate in the adult world, she knew that brutality still haunted it. She wrote that much of men's behaviour springs from a root of possible violence: 'On every street corner squabbles threaten; usually they flicker out; but for a man to feel in his fists his will to self affirmation is enough to reassure him of his sovereignty. Against any insult, any attempt to reduce him to the status of object, the male has recourse to his fists, to exposure of himself to blows . . . Violence is the authentic proof of each one's loyalty to himself, to his passions, to his own will.' Her bug-eyed boyfriend, Sartre, went even further, stating that 'irrepressible violence is man recreating himself' and that only through mad fury could the wretched of the earth become men.

It was all too much for Hannah Arendt, repelled by what she called grandiose rhetorical excesses. In *On Violence*, a small book published in 1969 examining the violent upheavals of that period, she sneers at Sartre's belief that violence, like Achilles' lance, can heal the wounds it has inflicted. She was aghast that anyone could justify violence on the grounds of creativity, which seemed to be the existentialist's position. 'The practice of violence like all action, changes the world but the most probable change is to a more violent world,' wrote Arendt.

If *Fight Club* has a point, this may be it.

Palahniuk's narrator, in the tradition of a long line of vaguely tormented, dissolute protagonists, from Coupland's Andy back to Salinger's Caulfield, is heavily put upon by an uncaring world. In truth, however, he is something of a co-conspirator. A product recall campaign coordinator, he decides whether the cost of recalling a faulty car or electrical appliance is greater than the cost of probable lawsuits on behalf of those injured and killed by the exploding, disintegrating or malfunctioning product. He feels his life drowning until he meets Tyler Durden and asks his mysterious new friend to save him.

Tyler agrees to let him move into his filthy, run-down house on the edge of an industrial estate but he asks one favour: 'I want you to hit me as hard as you can.'

They fall into a brawl in the car park of a bar, watched by a circle of drunks and other existentially cramped, put upon guys. These are the first members of fight club, because this fighting thing takes off, a bit like boxercise and snooker and racquet ball. Except it isn't just for yuppies. It's for men. Every weekend these guys get together and beat the crap out of each other. And within weeks they're turning guys away, having to open new secret fight clubs all over the country. It touches something raw in the male psyche.

Who guys are in fight club is not who they are in the real world. Who I am in fight club is not someone my boss knows. After a night in fight club everything in the real world gets the volume turned down. Nothing can piss you off, your word is law, and if other people break that law or question you even that doesn't piss you off.

Nothing was changed when a fight was over, but nothing mattered anymore, which is the rub. Violence doesn't only erase your problems. It is instrumental, something we turn on the world, but it is also an entity in its own right; a rough beast always straining to break free of any restraints we might impose. Given a chance it will erase everything.

Thus *Fight Club*'s story opens as it ends, with our narrator and Tyler Durden locked in a mortal embrace on top of the world's tallest building. Tyler has a gun jammed down his friend's throat. A few floors below them, other members of fight club are throwing desks and filing cabinets and chairs out of the windows, raining them down on the crowds below. Explosives strapped to the pillars in the basement of the building are a few seconds from exploding. The violated dream of violence, as Arendt called it, has led not to some higher plane of knowledge but to madness, desolation and despair.

Even Arendt, however, accepted that violence had a legitimate role in the personal sphere. Occasionally, she acknowledged, 'acting without argument or speech and without counting the consequences—is the only way to set the scales of justice right again . . . In this sense, rage and the violence that sometimes—not always—goes with it belong among the natural human emotions, and to cure

man of them would mean nothing less than to dehuman-
ise or emasculate him.'

It is the restless energy of the rough beast, its constant
straining at the leash, which renders vexed the question
of whether it can ever be more than a destructive force.
The liberal mind, so uncomfortable with absolutes, seems
unable to quarantine it, instinctively drawing a connection
between the smaller acts of personal aggression and a
wider, general contagion. Who is to say, in this schema, if
or when a violent act is justified?

In fact it is not that difficult. There are no fast answers,
no formula for working out degrees of justification. But as
justice can only exist in a moral universe we do have
recourse to another, much neglected, faculty; our con-
sciences. A reasonable man who raises his fist will know
within himself whether it was justified or shameful. If he
can satisfy this inner voice he may rest easy. Thus the
declining incidence of personal violence in public life, of
an avenging Huston willing to thrash a cad like Flynn, may
be related to the triumph of moral relativism. In a society
where nobody is guilty anymore, where no one is really
responsible for their actions, the ground slips away beneath
the man who wants to stand and fight for any principle he
holds inviolate.

The dirty little secret of violence is not that it is ugly
and unjust. It is that it promises so much but delivers so
little. This promise, that by a strong arm and valiant heart
a man may bend the world to his will, is a recurring
dream. Who doubts, asked Arendt, that the poor dream of
the possessions of the rich and the oppressed of setting

themselves up in the oppressor's place? Dreams which almost never come true.

Professional boxing is littered with broken men who were sold the oldest dream of all, that they could contain the world within their fists. *Ringside*, a much more conventional foray into masculine ferocity than *Fight Club*, is nonetheless peopled with the heroes and victims of this mythology and their stories are haunted by the same contradictions which drive Palahniuk's narrative.

Saddest of all, sadder even than the trembling shell of Muhammad Ali, was Joe Louis, champion of the world, one of the first black men to deal with the white power structure of America on his own terms. He ended his days crippled by strokes, a sorry, shattered wreck in a wheelchair, pushed into the foyer of a Vegas casino to sit in front of a giant statue of himself and greet conventioneers, lodge men and low rollers as they streamed through to hit the Mob's fifty cent slot machines.

Ah, but when he was the Champion of the World . . .

The Reverend Martin Luther King told a story, recounted in *Ringside*, of a young black man, the first to be executed by gassing in a southern state of America. The microphone placed in the chamber recorded his last, terrified words on Earth.

'Save me Joe Louis, save me Joe Louis, save me Joe Louis . . .'

MR BRILLO HEAD GOES
TO JAIL

I sat within two feet of Keith Wright through both of his sex crime trials. I had to be up real close where I could keep an eye out for surreptitious erections. He was that sort of dude. Politics and religion shaped his public life for 25 years, underlain by a third unseen dynamic, an intense, aberrant sexuality which finally betrayed him. He was another control freak, a man driven by a fierce Will to Power, who would do anything to make the world conform to his own projected impulses. Ugliness was so fundamental to his character that it became externalised. Deep lines scourged his face, which turned the mottled, livid colour of bad blood and meat sickness towards the end of the trial. The skin was tight around the eyes but loose and fleshy at the lips. His fingers were old and dry, incredibly wrinkled, and the skin between them was occasionally raw and chafed. His hair was a flat, thick mass of wiry curls, cut like Elvis on a really bad day. The other journalists were looking to hang tags on him like disgraced

MP and former morals campaigner. But for me that haircut meant he would always be Mr Brillo Head, a child molester in a clown suit with a shit-eating grin.

Wright's mother had died when he was young, leaving his father, a grocer, to raise five kids alone. They grew up poor, in sight of the mansions built by Queensland sugar barons, cultivating a deep sense of an unjust world. The desire to impose meaning on this world and to change it lay strongly within Wright. In 1959 at the age of 17, the same urge drew him to a Billy Graham crusade at the Exhibition Ground in Brisbane. There, amongst the sawdust and cow pats, caught up in the fevered gameshow pitch of the American evangelist, young Keith realised he was a 'vanquished' person. With a great swelling in his chest and rubbing the tears from his eyes, he came forward and was born again.

The other calling of his life, politics, manifested itself in 1966 when he joined the ALP. Wright quickly gained pre-selection and entered State Parliament with a huge and unexpected swing. The 1970s and early 1980s were Labor's bleakest years in Queensland. Individually, Wright prospered in public, starring in Parliament and establishing a very successful publishing company. His private life maintained thematic consistency, though. It was an unrelenting downer.

His first wife was plagued by kidney problems. She underwent surgery more than twenty times and was told she would not walk or talk or live through the week on many occasions. Her condition depressed Wright. Returning from hospital one night, he stopped at traffic lights and heard hymns blasting out of a Baptist church. The powerful, stirring chorus drew him into the church and eventually led him to the United States in 1979 and 1981 as a lay preacher. Wright claimed the sabbatical cured him of serious illness. So impressed were the Americans with him that they invited him to study for a doctorate in theology and to lead his own fully tooled up evangelical SWAT team.

This religious background, regarded as weird by some in the party, was an advantage in the Deep North. Wright denied he was morally conservative. Like Pierre Trudeau of Canada, he believed 'that governments should stay out of the bedrooms of the nation'. He quickly added 'the nation's adults', because, he insisted gravely, he was a passionate protector of children. In November 1982 he was elected to the leadership of the ALP in Queensland.

The last Saturday in March of '83 was a good day for Keith Wright. The conservatives were crashing and burning all over the country. He'd watched Malcolm Fraser chased from office like a blubbering girl a few weeks before. Even the Bjelke-Petersen regime looked just about ready to turn up its toes, poisoned by hatred and unable to cope with the new Opposition leader; a baby-kissing born-again son of Our Lord.

Wright was a radical break from the beery, dull-witted monsters who'd run the ALP like their own Jurassic Park for as long as anyone cared to remember. Apart from an occasional glass of white wine, he did not drink. He did not smoke or play cards or take the Lord's name in vain.

He believed swearing showed a lack of self-discipline. He understood the media and always presented himself like a frontman for the Reserve Bank in dark, well-cut suits and sober ties. He stood ramrod straight, spoke with a deep, well-trained voice and illustrated his points with fine manicured hands.

Even opponents noted and praised the change in style. The Liberal's boss Llew Edwards described Wright as perceptive, fair, and able to deal with issues that were beyond his colleagues. His leadership had re-energised the ALP, which had spent nearly twenty years turned in on itself, in bitter internecine warfare. The bookies had him streets in front of the field.

So that weekend, as Keith Wright drove to a campaign launch in Ipswich, just outside Brisbane, he had good reason to feel pleased with himself, to sit a little higher and smile a little wider. He had come a long way from poverty row in the canefields of North Queensland. That very morning the *Australian* newspaper had run a long glowing profile on him, placing him amongst the new generation of Labor leaders sweeping to power all over the country. Under Wright, it said, the party had its best chance of taking government in 26 years. The Nationals had trouble demonising him because of his strong Christian beliefs. But that did not stop them trying. Wright had been forced to defuse rumours about his marriage by admitting his private life was 'no bed of roses'. His enemies looked pretty bad for kicking a Christian family when they were down. Keith threw it back in their faces, saying, 'The paragons of virtue in the government and the Ministry will be the ones that are hurt—and at their own hands their families will suffer the most.'

Motoring up to Ipswich, however, he could put that shit on the back shelf. The Believers who greeted him at the campaign function weren't buying any of Bjelke-Petersen's poisonous swill. Keith was their leader. He was the Man. And he was going to deliver them from the wilderness. His political crusade had become infused with this sort of personal evangelical fervour. As he passed through, their bright faces beamed a heated focus at him. You could almost feel the wave carrying them to government.

He had a lot of these functions to attend, of course. So nobody thought less of his leaving before the night was over. No doubt he had a speech to work on for the big Palm Sunday peace rally the next day. But Keith did not go home to brush up on his speech. An hour or so after he left them with his best wishes and a renewed faith in their prospects he was lying on a couch with a thirteen-year-old schoolgirl.

The affair between this high-stepping, passionate child protector and a vulnerable schoolgirl would eventually expose Wright as a fraud and a user. As she grew up, he deployed a cunning array of emotional weapons to maintain the relationship in the face of her increasing revulsion and reluctance. When she finally drew the line and said no more, he raped her.

Wright once took the girl, whom we will call Lisa, on a date to Parliament House. He showed her around and arranged for her to watch a sitting. Later, in his rooms, they sat on the side of the bed while he embraced her. He stroked her body and placed his hands inside her pants, but she said, 'No, I don't want this to go on anymore.' Wright got up from beside her, walked around the bed and lay down next to her. Lisa explained that she had been molested before. He patted her arm reassuringly and said, 'I know.'

Wright's control of the affair, the hold of an older sophisticated man over a child, was demonstrated when Lisa turned sixteen. She went to his office to pick out a birthday present and they discussed where to go and have sex. She said, 'I don't know, you're the adult.' Wright shot back, 'We're both in this together, we're both to blame, we're both equals in this situation.' She accepted that. She was sixteen, after all. But she said, 'I was quite miserable about it. It was quite terrible, a terrible split. I was living two separate lives at the same time.' She reluctantly accepted her role in the relationship and they had sex on his desk.

Some time later, as he drove her to school, she again said she wanted to end the whole thing. Wright pulled the car over and seemed to agree. He said okay, but shortly afterwards he found his way into her home. He was giving off a dark, ugly vibe and she said, 'No, go away.' Wright said nothing. He pushed her down and raped her. She fought but could not dislodge his body weight. When he was finished he got up and walked out without saying a word.

'I cried and cried for hours and hours,' she later testified. 'The sort of crying that is howling without making any sound at all . . . and I took the nightie off, I wiped myself, wiped all of the semen off me. It was a nightie that my grandmother had made me, I remember it really clearly, and I threw it into a cane basket and I couldn't even look at it for weeks. I just left it there. I never wore it again.'

When Lisa finally gathered the courage to expose him she said he rang her to threaten blackmail, inventing a story about her sleeping with a schoolteacher. When she told him he was lying she said he burst into tears and sobbed, 'I'm sorry, I've got to go,' and hung up.

In 1984, a year after he had first molested Lisa, Wright unsettled his colleagues by giving a strange interview to a religious magazine called *On Being*. 'Once you enter the political arena there is no protection other than the ongoing promise Christ has given us that his angels shall surround us,' he said. 'I take tremendous strength from the promise that we can stand on the rock with the enemy encircling us, and yet we shall not have harm come to us.'

He talked about the strains on his first marriage, which was a sham by that stage. He still dragged his cheated, chronically ill wife along to selected public appearances. But he was abusing Lisa and carrying on another affair, the latter one with a more conventionally aged partner. Asked how he dealt with the rough treatment of his 'family life' he replied that, instead of being constantly bitter, he had learned to pray.

'When a guy does me over in Parliament I quietly pray, Lord change that guy,' he said. 'And it's happened. A Minister did me over recently and I prayed about it— and he came up and apologised. That's the work of the Holy Spirit.'

Sadly, the Spirit was lacking when it came to going the fiddle with little girls. A move from state to federal politics at the end of 1984 changed nothing. It meant only that he was out of the spotlight. Wright was unheard of in Canberra, except for one attack on foreign investment and a proposal to tax imported antiques. It wasn't until August of 1992 that he popped up on the screens again, in an increasingly bizarre series of appearances after Lisa had gathered the courage to report him to the police.

The grim details were still a mystery but as stories began to circulate that he would resign from Parliament, Wright went on TV to say he just had some health problems including headaches and memory loss. He baffled reporters by telling them he did not have to have a shunt to remedy 'ventricles' leading to his brain, he just had a heavy cold. After declaring himself 'off limits' for one week, he re-emerged for a press conference, saying he would answer questions about neurology but not about personal matters. An ABC reporter asked him about rumoured sex charges and was abruptly cut off.

By early September '92 all 24 federal reps from Queensland were bitching that they were the subject of speculation about sex charges. They wanted him named. They got their wish when he appeared in the Magistrate's Court on charges of having molested a number of girls. The press lovingly detailed the allegations, Wright supposedly having told one girl, 'I have been carrying around a condom for months in the hope of making love to you,' and that she 'needed an older man like him.' The ALP dropped him like a white-hot turd.

Things took a turn for the weird after that. Keith announced he was launching a new career as a songwriter and novelist. He said he had already penned 138 country and western hymns of love, hope and optimism. He had a murder mystery ready to go, along with a joke book and a guide to superannuation. God had steered him to write because, he confessed, 'I want people to know Keith Wright—the human side.' His human side was further exposed on Christmas Eve '92 when news of a planned 'study trip' to Belgium, Britain, the US, Spain and Greece was revealed. The Foreign Affairs Department was puzzled. They said the holiday season in those countries would limit the availability of officials for talks with the roving Australian. The Government cancelled his taxpayer-funded tour. Perhaps they recalled the minor diplomatic incident arising from an earlier junket to Eastern Europe when the Poles complained that Mr Wright could not keep his hands off the lady comrades.

Wright's last act as a politician was to cast a vote for himself in the '93 federal election at Rockhampton's Berserker Street School. He stood as an independent and got 6.5 per cent of the vote, which is kind of worrying when you think about it. He took public solace in the Bible after bowing out, talking at length to his home town paper about a passage from Isaiah which recommended forgetting the past and starting anew. 'It just leapt out at me . . . it was quite prophetic,' he said. As part of the 'healing process' he had written many letters, including one to Sir Joh, who wrote a 'very nice letter' back.

Wright approached his first trial, the one that fell in a heap, with a disconnected, other-worldly air. He refused Judge Tony Skoien's invitation to sit at the bar table while defending himself. He refused to argue about evidence or even to speak unless directed to. He intoned deeply, 'I am prepared to sit back . . . even though it might mean that I go to prison for something I didn't do, I intend to remain silent.' He was shooting for a dignity defence; a good man somehow cast into a Kafkaesque nightmare of unfair trial and humiliation. He would not be cross-examining the girl, he would not be calling witnesses, he would not be doing anything. When asked how he pleaded he replied, 'I shall remain silent, sir.'

The dignity thing lasted until lunch on the first day, about as long as it took to get Lisa up to testify. After that Wright realised he was down the shit chute and dignity would have to go by the wayside. He jumped to his feet after lunch and asked could he make a statement to the jury about the girl's evidence. Unfortunately the only way he could say anything to the jury was through the witness box, which he eventually but reluctantly entered.

His evidence came out in frustrated bursts, alternately vicious or vague, and frequently cut off by the Judge for being radically out of order. Mostly, it was an eruption of word salad that slewed chaotically between conspiracy theory, self-justification and leering innuendo. 'Now Lisa is a beautiful person,' he said. 'I care for her very much. I can only say to you that she was very well rehearsed. She is a drama teacher by profession.'

Just before three o'clock that afternoon he admitted he

had molested the girl. Just after three o'clock he uttered, 'I don't recall,' for the first time. He looked like a second-rate actor doing a greasy, lust-crazed preacher in an off-rating sitcom—clasping his hands, shaking his head and rolling his eyes to heaven. The whole performance had the hammy feel of a poorly rehearsed soliloquy delivered at a drunken football club talent night. 'I have brought shame to my God and to the name of Jesus Christ,' he said, trying to squeeze out some tears.

The trial aborted the next day when Wright leapt to his feet first thing in the morning. He had new information and witnesses, come to light that very day. They would prove he was innocent. Judge Skoien took off his glasses, rubbed his eyes like he had this killer migraine coming on, and explained to Wright that he just wasn't allowed to ambush the Crown's witnesses like that. But Wright was busy flapping his papers around, babbling about having been on trips to Rockhampton, to the hospital, to the dark side of the Moon when he was supposed to have fucked with the girl. He was cranking the Judge up, hopping from foot to foot and burbling interjections like, 'Justice, sir! Justice is what I want!'

The Judge was trapped. He couldn't allow Wright to throw a bomb into the trial, but the transcript was full of him saying that he would be denied justice if Skoien refused the requests. Skoien aborted the proceedings. He promised to come back and hear the next trial personally.

Thoughts on meat sickness . . . Keith pulled an eight-year jail sentence when the lawyers wrapped up his case a few weeks later. It was one of those hot, bad weeks in

Brisbane, when things seem out of place and slightly off balance. Arriving there was like pressing through a membrane into some vital but corrupted aesthetic; Northern Gothic, postmodern period. Contaminated flesh was on everyone's minds. A shipment of beef had gone to market dripping with DDT or Agent Orange or something and folks just burned up talkback radio worrying about it. They were concerned the poison could build up in your system and come back to get you years in the future. It was sound thinking which Keith Wright would have done well to heed.

At one stage in his second trial Channel 9 got a letter to him in the prisoner's dock, a long one, asking for an interview. He read it through, and it was testimony to his complete disconnection that he didn't just tear it up and throw it away. He didn't understand that nobody cared about him anymore. We were there to eat him alive but he was still playing the game.

There was a time he drew energy from the stares and interest of others. The attention was a metabolic necessity for him. Now people stared, but with undisguised animosity. He was an outsider, marked as of the Beast. He kept a straight back and never cast his eyes down during the trial. If he had media trainers they had done their job well over the years. More likely, though, he was just a natural. Genetics had thrown him up, a predator, the same way it can deliver a two-headed dog or a chicken with a hole where its heart should be.

It would be wrong to think he was special though. He

was a freak, one of nature's failed experiments. There was nothing special about that or about the way he crashed and burned. His type always do. It's an object lesson. Beware of men who wrap themselves in the shroud of the Lord and start telling the rest of us how we should live. It's just not normal and nine times out of ten neither are they.

TRUE CRIME

The first instalment of 'Chopper' Read's criminal memoirs opens with a strangely cheery Chopper digging his own grave. Nabbed by an anonymous would-be hitman whilst returning from a trip to the corner store, Chopper is cold cocked, bundled into a car and driven into the bush, where he comes to with a gun at his head. Given a shovel and told to hop to it, Read seems only too happy to help out. Merrily digging away, chatting and laughing like a madman, he breaks the earth in which he is soon to sleep and powers into his task with so much energy his bemused assassin may have thought he was hoping to escape by digging to China. Dropping his guard in the face of Chopper's relentlessly sunny disposition, the man—whom you may have surmised is no longer with us—strays too close to the pit's edge. Read scoops out one last heap of soil and swings the heavy blade of his shovel into the gunman's knee with all the force and élan of a champion Tasmanian tree-feller. Economic rationalists might nod here with the grim satisfaction common to their ilk. Raw competition triumphs and Mark Brandon 'Chopper' Read—killer, extortionist and successful author—was free to go about his business, which used to involve filling mortuaries but is now largely restricted to filling bookshelves.

So popular have the chronicles of Chopper been with the reading public that his memoirs have extended to four volumes and he has penned another two works of fiction. His *How to Shoot Friends and Influence People* jostles for shelf space in Dymocks and A&R Bookworld with the likes of Neddy Smith's *Catch and Kill Your Own*, seeming to indicate a fondness amongst underworld authors for criminographic exactitude in their book titles. Not for Australians the American squeamishness over criminals profiting from their villainy via book and movie deals. Whilst legislatures in the US have enacted laws to keep killers from their royalties, our rambunctious publishers hover over their chequebooks anxiously awaiting the first member of Cabramatta's 5T Viet youth gang smart enough to eschew pushing smack for pounding a keyboard.

Ostensibly marketed as nonfiction, all of these worthy attempts at reskilling by our celebrity crooks undoubtedly nudge into Demidenko territory on the issue of candour. Sitting in that grey area between truth and concoction so familiar to frequent occupants of police interview rooms, they are also an engaging manifestation of what Stephen Knight has called a characteristically Australian sub-genre of crime writing: the criminal saga. Whilst criminal heroes are occasionally celebrated in American and French culture (simultaneously in the case of Tarantino's *Pulp Fiction* at

Cannes), only Australian literature has observed a long, unbroken fascination for the prosaic, workaday concerns of the ne'er-do-well. Less dashing, less attractive and generally just much less inspiring than his foreign compadres, the criminal anti-hero of Australian literature has nonetheless proved more resilient. Knight describes him as a lowlife plodder who is understood and sympathised with, but not for romantic reasons: 'Without glamour, usually rather unimpressive in personal terms, the criminal seems to see a life of law breaking as the only path open to him, is not particularly thrilled by it, yet has a reasonable range of anti-social skills and illegal procedures that are carefully and approvingly revealed by the story.' Two hundred years of affection for this dodgy Everyman speak to Knight of 'a deeply held and almost routinised sense that any move against conventional authority is to be admired.'

Knight's history of Australian crime fiction, *Continent of Mystery*, delves deeply into the yellowed, flaking leaves of two hundred years' worth of writing to tease out a number of such themes, drawing them together strand by strand to effectively demonstrate the role of crime writing in the creation of our national myths, and the role of such myths in shaping the genre. The two-century survey reveals how the shamelessly populist enterprise has also charted and mirrored the development of our values. For instance, in the earliest days of the colony and the genre, very few stories revolved around a murdered or missing (usually murdered) person. Crimes against property were more commonly written of than now. Individuality seemed to lie more in material possessions, and even the immaterial concept of a man's honour, than in the corporeal body.

Just as isolation and a unique environment bred up species seen nowhere else in the world, Australia's unusual white history has given rise to a rich tradition of crime writing which has mutated and grown in ways quite different to its cousins overseas. A sympathetic fascination with the criminal as hero is but one example, and perhaps not that startling in a country with our convict origins. A culture which celebrates and values the individual over the state will tend to celebrate fictional characters who rebel against oppression and 'the system'. But as Knight points out, there is something decidedly unusual 'about the readiness with which the Australian crime novel accepts the viewpoint of the criminal and outlines with sympathy the wrongs committed against him.' Almost as though his crime were a legitimate response to an unfair world. Robert G. Barrett's monster-selling Les Norton stories and Gary Disher's beautifully realised Wyatt novels bracket the modern school. Respectively concerned with the comic adventures of a beer-loving, hard-punching underworld ingenue, and the grimly Darwinian existence of a Melbourne-based armed robber, they both represent a 'less idealistic' version of the outlaw tradition, best embodied in Robin Hood, where lawbreakers define true justice through their otherwise illicit exploits.

The logical by-product of the criminal as hero is the detective as villain and Knight does find a healthy local taste for the idea of corrupted authority. He makes a telling quip about local fears and prejudices when examining a book set in Melbourne by a touring English writer. Which Australian author, he asks, could write, as she did, of 'two powerfully built detectives' without some sense of irony or anxiety? The detective, of course, is a powerful icon in crime fiction: explorer, confessor, destroyer, avenger. That power is often inverted in the antipodes. In *The Forger's Wife*, published in 1855, we meet the first recognisable Sydney detective and can only wonder at his contemporary feel. Modelled on a real life detective called Israel Chapman, the fictional George Flower was a hard, sharp-witted thief taker not far removed from those he hunted. Retained by a client whose writing desk has been stolen, Flower simply 'knows' whodunit. He seeks out a fence named Nelson, beats him up, knocks him down and places a boot on his throat, snarling, 'Gurgle up the receiver, or I'll squeeze out your poisonous existence.' Spiritual godfather to generations of real life Sydney plainclothesmen, Flower gets the name he needs, recovers the desk and trousers a stray £50 for himself. Students of the Wood or Fitzgerald Commissions will bathe in a warm glow of familiarity at this point. Others with a more immediate interest have even tried raising the defence of 'it was ever thus' before those very inquisitors; one poor, benighted rozzer excusing himself in the dock before Justice James Woods by simply shrugging and laying blame for hundreds of years of muscular corruption at the feet of the Rum Corps.

Even more interesting, however, is the tendency uncovered by Knight for local authors to remove the police, or in fact any sort of investigators altogether, from their narratives. Comparing British, American and Australian crime fiction, he discovers a not unexpected preference for private eyes in the US and gifted amateurs in the UK. In Australia, however, the largest category of stories belongs to a tradition Knight labels zero policing. There simply is no investigator. Events themselves lead to resolution, and vengeance, if and when it is exacted, is often through the inanimate agency of the land itself. Until quite recently Australian villains were always falling off cliffs or into rivers, being bitten by snakes and toasted by bushfires.

Strange then that Knight should find the concept of 'place' reducing to a vanishing point almost as quickly as the role of the police. Although place plays such an important role overseas—Chandler's LA can be considered a character in its own right, for instance—the reverse has been true in Australia. Before Peter Corris' Cliff Hardy started driving around Sydney less than twenty years ago, local crime fiction often had no sense of place at all. The laconic, if not iconic, character of Hardy changed that and may even have had a hand in the recent resurgence of female crime writers. Marele Day, one of the new pioneers, had not read any crime fiction, let alone 'feminist' crime fiction, before she wrote *The Life and Crimes of Harry Lavender*. She says she simply wanted to write about the city and thought of the crime genre as an excellent lens through which to examine her subject. 'The private eye has both social and geographic mobility,' she says. 'They move across the city and up and down its social ladders, gaining entry where others cannot.' Interestingly Day, whom Knight describes as having a clear though not over-pompous commitment to feminism, says having a female investigator was more of an afterthought than a consciously feminist project: 'I'd just hope people see her as a woman of the nineties. After I decided to use a female character I wanted her to be able to look after herself.' In such ways are paradigms subverted without really trying.

Both Hardy and Day's Claudia Valentine cast a 'witty evaluative eye' over their city, and have an 'intimate privacy' with it; a clear break with the tradition of previous decades when you could read dozens of crime novels without receiving a single clue as to their setting. This seems to be unique to our country, a situation Knight describes as being 'simply blank, not so much a space on the map as a failure or refusal to map at all.' It was partly a result of English publishing preferences but also, he seems to feel, partly a result of threat of the locale. As if the land which so often consumed hero and villain alike was simply whited out of the story by an unspoken agreement between authors and readers dangerously isolated on an empty continent on the dark side of the globe.

Knight's weakest argument grows out of this; a thesis that Australian crime writing and the abovementioned themes he lays open so well can best be analysed in terms of post-colonial criticism. Rejecting standard explanations of Australian distinctiveness such as distance, terrain and climate, Knight turns to a conceptual framework which seems more relevant to the study of West Indian and subcontinental writing. Post-colonial criticism, as might be surmised, attends to the relationship between the coloniser and the colonised, which in this context generally means between the British empire and the native peoples of those lands it subjugated in the eighteenth and nineteenth centuries. The economic, social and racial conflict between the British and those indigenes, and the effects this had on the cultural development of colonised societies, is the grist of post-colonial theory's mill.

Transplanted to Australia, the friction is not a simple matter of the white invaders oppressing black natives. For here, unlike in India for example, the natives were dispersed and played a very minor role in the economic exploitation of the country. The conflict, between coloniser and colonised, the sine qua non of post-colonial theory, is now located entirely within the white community, between the 'land-taking squatters and those who filled the role of a mass labouring class.' Between the bunyip aristocracy and the workers who built up their estates. Or, as Knight puts it in the argot of the period, between 'sterling' and 'currency'.

He claims the most powerful and successful texts were those 'hybrids' which drew together the concerns of both groups, thereby creating the basis for a national mythology. To get to this point, however, involves doing violence to the historical record which would make Chopper Read blush. Aligning himself with Robert Hughes, who described the convict system as an eighteenth century sketch for our own era's terrible fresco of repression, the Gulag, Knight sees an underclass of serfs and slaves in the transported prisoners and the poor immigrants who followed them. They were treated as a colonised group, he writes, and fulfilled much the same role in our culture as the oppressed indigenes elsewhere in the Empire. Stretching the analogy to breaking point, he asserts, 'there was even an element of race in the strong Celtic component' of the labouring class.

The trouble with these intellectual gymnastics is that while they themselves seem to sit quite snugly within the folds of national mythology—the idea of starving farmers and hapless Irishmen down on their luck and forced to steal to feed their sooty-faced urchins, thereby sentenced to the brutalities of transportation—the reality is not such a comfortable fit. Conditions were undeniably harsh and occasionally horrific for the convicts and later immigrants. Yet by the late 1840s Australia was seen by the English poor as their last best hope. A chronic labour shortage—a whole continent lay ready to be taken, remember—meant that workers in Australia could earn much higher wages and live in much better conditions than their peers in the UK. The discovery of gold encouraged witnesses appearing before British Parliamentary committees on crime and punishment in the 1850s to predict that some would be tempted into lawbreaking by the prospect of a free trip to El Dorado. Even children were pressed into service, making money unheard of 'at home'. In *Our Antipodes* GC Mundy, who bemoaned the stories he found in Australia of criminals made good, wrote of a twelve-year-old waiting on tables in a hotel, a four-year-old carpenter's apprentice, and Joshua Holt, making a king's ransom—£60 a year—as an overseer of a gang of twenty convicts. In the 1870s when a mass movement against the immigration of Chinese labourers laid the basis for the White Australia Policy, working men's associations led the battle, aware that they enjoyed one of the highest standards of living in the world and unwilling to see it eroded by the importation of cheap coolie labour; i.e. the same 'colonised' masses Knight hopes to equate with the white, antipodean working class.

In spite of all this, however, *Continent* still stands as a great work of academic detection. Knight's revelations about the unique characteristics of Australian crime writing are groundbreaking and much to be admired. In the last pages of the book he recognises that many readers will not hold with his over-arching post-colonial analysis, but generously allows that its purpose is not to set an ironclad framework in critical concrete, merely to encourage discussion, comment and engagement with the field.

S 1 1

His lips were, dare I say it, unAustralian. They were lavishly, almost lasciviously, pink and seemed unnaturally full, as though injected with collagen in the minutes before going to air. His hair was blonde, and maybe thinning a little, but not ruinously so. Just enough, perhaps, to lend a little gravitas to an otherwise childish face. His eyes shone, but with a synthetic flicker. They were like lovingly polished marbles which threw off the blaze of the studio's high-powered lighting. He seemed to pause before speaking, just long enough for a smirk—I was sure it was a smirk—to form on those curiously feminised lips.

'So much for nonviolence,' he read.

I actually gasped. I had been prepared for something special, this being Packer's network after all. But the arrogance, the contempt and the reflexive, unthinking stupidity compressed into that fleshy pink smirk and those four brief words were still literally breathtaking. The news reader was two or three pars into his lead story, the first morning of the S11 protest in Melbourne, before I recovered sufficiently to follow what he was saying.

Violence had flared, angry scenes had broken out, clashes had erupted between demonstrators and police. A sixteen-year-old code cutter could have hacked up a simple piece of software to generate the story from a database of network approved phraseology. It might have been a little more challenging to load the computer-generated script with the appropriate subtext, a narrative of brave, beleaguered officers standing fast against a violent threat to civilised society. But it wasn't that subtle a subtext, so I'm guessing it could be done. And the news reader, with his eyes of glass and the heart of a tape recorder? Could he also be replaced by a CGI construct? A third or fourth generation Max Headroom to give protohuman expression to his ultimate owner's will to power? It would certainly be more efficient, more economically rational, and less harmful to the immortal souls of those currently forced by their lucrative contracts to utter such malicious bullshit as, 'So much for nonviolence.'

I doubt these thoughts bothered my pink-lipped friend though. He sailed on with a sort of spiteful cheeriness, throwing to vision of a flying wedge of police officers ploughing into a seething, screaming mass of protesters. The cops were attempting a rescue of WA Premier Richard Court, who had unwisely decided to emulate Bob Askin by 'driving over the bastards'. Unfortunately the bastards had surrounded his vehicle, cutting it off and subjecting the occupants to a sustained barrage of abuse and anti-mandatory sentencing graffiti. One Aboriginal activist mounted the bonnet and danced a jig while informing Court he was under citizen's arrest for state crimes against indigenous people. The Premier, he announced, now knew how the country's first inhabitants felt, being held to ransom for two hundred years.

It was a wild scene, as baton charges always are, but it was unrepresentative. Most of the first day actually passed off without significant conflict, as the police struggled to counteract the fluid tactics of the blockaders. Mobile phones and message runners gathered reinforcements to any point where it seemed the blockade might fail. Horses were ineffectually deployed against picket lines, which had been trained to close up against them, leaving no gaps for the mounted police to break through. No central authority existed to organise the dozens of disparate groups which composed S11 and that lack of a command structure seemed to unhinge the police response. A number of megaphone-wielding enthusiasts from the International Socialists, the Democratic Socialist Party and its youth wing Resistance did try with varying success to marshal numbers into a couple of flash points, but many of the anarchically-inclined protesters reacted as badly to their demands as they did to the cops.

Despite the emphasis on conflict which dominated the mainstream news coverage, the reports of hundreds of eye-witnesses which quickly flooded onto the internet spoke of hours of inactivity, punctuated by shorts bursts of intense turbulence at isolated locations where Forum delegates attempted to run the barrier. These moments provided the sound and fury on which television reporters insist if they are to have a story worthy of air time. They constituted only a fraction of the day's content, however, with thousands of people protesting peacefully while trying to stay dry in the morning's downpour. Streakers against globalisation jogged past a swami-for-justice sitting on a bed of nails. Christians prayed, and true believers from One Nation railed against worldwide conspiracy as dreadlocked forest dwellers broke out the drums, rolled some joints and got jiggy with it.

The baton charge to rescue Court, in which one man lost seven teeth, provided much of the broadcast media action. The balance was down to one freelance guardian of the Forum delegates' right to assembly—who sailed into a knot of picketers, windmilling his fists until taken to the ground with a bloody nose—and a group of three men tagged as neo-Nazis by some witnesses and Casino security by others. They attacked a thin line of protesters after a brief conversation with nearby police. One was alleged to have used a set of keys held inside his fist as a weapon.

The media, which had been indecently tumescent at the prospect of a week of Seattle-style street warfare just before the Olympics in Sydney, seemed unable to deconstruct their own imagery. Having composed a narrative in which foreign activists joined forces with domestic nutters to sabotage Australia's fifteen minutes of fame, many journalists and almost all commentators were incapable of understanding a simple premise. The vast majority of protesters were, in fact, nonviolent. Many had been trained in nonviolent dissent. Just as many had extensive experience of nonviolent protest. For all of their fearsome imagery, for all of the savage, howling mayhem of protest, the violence, when it came, was initiated by the agents of authority, not by the dissenting citizenry. Citizens do not launch baton charges or mounted attacks. They are the targets of baton charges and mounted attacks.

Allegations of protester villainy did surface, with the *Age* retailing instances of 'fish hooks being dangled from bridges to try to disable police; nuts and bolts being thrown at police; and ball bearings being thrown under police horses' hooves.' The Nine network also carried a story of unidentified anarchists invading an ambulance and assaulting the crew. At no time, however, were any of these allegations proved. Indeed, no evidence in support of them was even advanced. No urine-soaked police uniforms were produced. No assaulted ambulance drivers were interviewed. No dangling fish hooks were ever photographed despite the presence of hundreds of still and video cameras. A horse which was supposed to have been stabbed turned out to have a grazed nose, according to police media (most likely sustained in the charge against a picket line full of vegetarian animal rights activists).

This crucial disconnect between the world of real things and the world of fantastic narrative was to prove disastrous as the week progressed. With somewhere between one and two thirds of conference delegates barred from the Casino on the opening day, the rhetoric of press and electronic coverage shifted from a sort of preemptive Schadenfreude to spluttering, belligerent outrage. Tabloid attack dogs and Victorian Premier Bracks alike called on the police to bring down the hammer. The protesters were 'unAustralian' (even 'unVictorian') and therefore seemingly unentitled to the due regard of those authorised to use deadly force on behalf of the society they had so publicly betrayed and embarrassed. Bracks was reported to have said that the protesters deserved everything they got. Although he did not elaborate on whether these deserving victims of muscular law enforcement also included those hundreds of school students, previously characterised as innocent victims of a Resistance recruiting campaign, who were also in attendance. Apparently, in crossing over the Rubicon of civil disobedience, they too became unAustralians and thus unworthy of any previous concern for their wellbeing.

I suppose I should guard against a hint of outrage entering my tone. Weary resignation would be more appropriate. For what happened at S11 is an old, old story and I have both heard and written it many times before; in Queensland through the 1980s, at Aidex in Canberra at the turn of the decade, at any number of places in the last ten years, Coffs Harbour, Sydney, Parliament House, the waterfront. I have seen enough political violence to know that far from being unAustralian, it is in fact completely banal. And that rather than being the result of wild, antisocial renegades, it is almost inevitably an outcome of tactical decisions taken by the police commander on the scene, occasionally at the behest of political interests further up the food chain. I also know, down in my meat, that when the beast is unleashed the most dangerous place to be is not on a police line, but in front of one.

My first encounter with a police riot took place in 1989, at the University of Queensland. I was covering a series of demonstrations on that campus for *Rolling Stone* magazine and was lucky enough to be present when about thirty or forty cops stormed a sit-in. The students knew the raid was coming and had voted to carry on the occupation, but only with volunteers. Most wisely abandoned the building. About a dozen remained. Following the advice of the late Tasmanian war correspondent Neil Davis—that it is always safer to go in with the first wave—I charged in with the cops rather than waiting with the occupiers for them to arrive. I wasn't all that surprised at the chaos within. The vicious fights between weedy, underfed college students and Bjelke-Petersen's praetorian guard were predictably one-sided. But I was totally blown out by the sight of one young, probationary constable who was so far gone in the moment that when he could find nobody to punch, he launched himself at a wall-mounted telephone and ripped it right off its moorings before throwing it to the ground. Perhaps it was an unAustralian telephone.

After that I made the study of police officers during violent demonstrations something of an avocation. I travelled to the National Exhibition Centre in Canberra for the infamous Aidex Arms Fair riots, which I still regard as the most frightening police rampage I have ever personally witnessed. For three days I slept under a bush in a ditch by the side of the road while a mediaeval caravan of greenies, ferals, vegans and communists fed themselves into a threshing machine. I saw one cop shoot his entire wad, his eyes rolled back to whites, thin lips drawn back from his teeth in a canine grimace as he flayed into a knot of hippies with a PR-24 riot baton. The nightstick was a blur, like a particularly impressive special effect, which conjured up flying clumps of scalp and gouts of blood wherever he cared to lay it. I saw another cop smashing the head of a female reporter from a community radio station into the side of a police wagon as yet another diverted metres out of his way to crack the kneecap of a woman who had broken through the line and was threatening to carry the demonstration a couple of metres closer to the arms manufacturers ensconced within the Exhibition Centre.

This too was another nonviolent demonstration. Like S11, Aidex was a largely uncoordinated effort by dozens of different groups, most of them green rather than red. Decisions were mediated through a sort of mass fishbowling conference held at the start of each day, with the angry left of the ISO and DSP—or the Socialist Workers Party as I think they still were then—unable to swing the numbers behind a more confrontational approach. Nonviolence was a sort of mantra the majority of protesters invoked to protect themselves from some imagined karmic backlash. Its efficacy against a real world backlash was questionable at best. One of the saddest things I ever saw was a couple of hundred of these poor dumb bastards joining hands and dancing onto the road in front of the Centre, like children playing ring-a-ring-a-rosie. A baton charge broke them up in less than ten seconds, hundreds of blows falling on the exposed forearms of the enchanted circle people while the hard-core Left, who had opted out of that particular doomed action, watched on with spastic rage.

I have never known the media, which is always prompt with reports of injury to individual police officers and fictional ambulance drivers, to fully detail the casualties on the receiving end of the baton attack. To wander through the camp outside Aidex each day was to bear witness to hundreds of broken ribs, fingers, wrists and jaws amongst an abundance of livid bruises, weeping wounds and black eyes. At S11, volunteer medical staff totted up a similar butcher's bill. One first aid coordinator posted to the indymedia website that on the first day at Crown they treated about one hundred and thirty protester injuries, sending eleven to hospital by ambulance. On the second day, they tallied another two hundred, with thirty-one hospitalised, before he stopped counting. Most required stitches to the scalp and face, many from baton strikes to the fingers, kidney, liver and breasts (in the case of women). After being interviewed by a Melbourne newspaper the aid worker was upset to find his figures rounded down to about 'twenty hurt' on both days.

Fortunately the atomisation of reportage by the internet has meant that we are no longer hostage to the likes of Kerry Packer's pink-lipped vassal for accounts of such civil atrocities. Cheap digital recording equipment transformed hundreds of witnesses at Crown into reporters. Even those without access to camcorders could and did post extended personal narratives which invariably contradicted the mainstream media's initial reporting. (After a number of journalists were assaulted by the Victorian police their enthusiasm for Steve Bracks' enforcers was noticeably diminished. By late in the week some had even shifted their rhetorical ground enough to openly speculate on topics such as 'police brutality'. It's amazing how much the change from observer to participant can alter one's perspective on these matters.)

Dozens of hotlinked websites now carry thousands of pages of first person narrative and video footage from S11. It would be a great pity if this archive were to be lost to future researchers as I believe it is an infinitely more accurate depiction of what happened there.

AC, writing on the Melbourne indymedia site, captured some of the frustrating but reasonably peaceful tactics of the police (the following extracts are reproduced verbatim):

> . . . the day quietens down, but there is a sense of danger that is more palpable than monday. a sound system is set up at king's way on the overpass, which is teeming with people. this afternoon at king's way, police engage in an exercise of pyschological warfare designed to confuse, and tire the remaining crowd. squads of police change formation, march from one entrance to another, put goggles on, remove goggles, display canisters of capsicum spray, put them away . . . the dog squad is brought out and lined up inside the compound. unfortunately for the cops one of the dogs bites his trainer. riot police march through a foot overpass back and forth from building to building. it works. the crowd expends its energy running from one entrance to another, is revved up by marshals, engages on one boring chant after the next—in other words reacts exactly as to be expected. it's easy to say this in hindsight, of course. at the time, how do you tell the

difference between a formation of riot police designed to psyche you out, and a formation of riot police about to charge?

A young woman named Maya, in an article entitled 'How I was clubbed like some baby seal (or, thank god for the black bloc)', described her panic and what she thought of as her own cowardice when she realised she was the weak link in a picket line which would soon be targeted. (The 'black bloc' refers to groups of masked anarchists):

. . . then people were hugging me and telling me i wasn't weak, i was strong and asking if i wanted to go further back or leave altogether. nothing could have made me leave after that, but a little while later they attacked us and i couldn't hold the line. the truth is, even though i'm not very strong, i wasn't really holding on that tightly. i think i was panicking already. i was panicking. i started panicking the second they moved the nimbin hippie bus.

. . . one of the cops hit me in the throat with his baton. i went straight down and thought i would be trampled by the police that were running past our former front line. the cop dragged me up by the neck (throat), which at least stopped me being trampled. i was screaming 'i can't breathe, i can't breathe, you're killing me, you're killing me.' of course i can't identify him. a lot of the riot cops' masks were completely fogged up from their breath.

after about 30 seconds or less, this cop picked me up

and threw me backwards. i don't remember all of this. i know i ended up on the ground with a group of other (mostly) women from the blockade, and a group of at least four or five just went for us. if you could manage to get away, they would drag you back in. during this, one of the uniformed cops bit me. i have tooth marks in my arm. i don't know if this happened to anyone else. the truth is, i'll never be able to get my head around any of this. at the time he was still yelling 'get back! get back!' while he was holding on to me to prevent me getting away.

after the cop bit me i was really, really panicking. either him or another cop picked me up and threw me at the police line. i wasn't really thinking straight at this point, but we could see that if you got too close to the line, they would just beat you and throw you back in. i was terrified of the cops, i was terrified of the horses, i felt like i was about to die. there was no way i could have gotten out of all that by myself.

someone grabbed me. i don't know who. i think, (i think) he was with the black bloc. i'm pretty sure i saw a mask or balaclava. maybe i just think that because i couldn't see his face very well.

but this black bloc guy grabbed me and dragged me through the line and no one touched us. i don't even remember how, but he got me out of the fighting. maybe he saved me from a broken limb. maybe he saved my life.

then he left me with someone else and went back into the fighting.

thankyou thankyou thankyou thankyou. i hope i'm

not over-doing it. i hope this is an appropriate forum to thank you a billion times and still feel it's not enough. i don't think anything is enough . . .

By the third day of the protest, some mainstream journalists, who realised they may have backed a loser on the opening day, began to log on to the independent sites to access this motherlode of alternative data. It is possible that the net's erosion of the old media cartel, organised around the twin poles of the Murdoch and Packer empires, influenced the eventual response of both the cartel and the State. Just as some of the media at last changed tack in the face of a terrible and sustained assault on a small group of dissenting citizens, so too was the political superstructure forced to adjust to a new reality. Steve Bracks began the week by claiming that the protesters deserved everything they got and finished it by inviting the heroes of the emergency services to a State-funded barbecue. But he was soon forced to withdraw the invitation after sections of his own party sided with the churches in condemning the actions of the police. Even the Forum delegates began to get the message. Those who managed to attend the first day's much-depleted sessions had to accept that theirs may not be the only story worth hearing.

It may be argued then that the violence at Crown had a positive, heuristic effect. Had the protests taken the form preferred by critics like Bracks, Court, and Bob Carr—that is, had they been nothing more than a meaningless piece of irrelevant street theatre which had no discernible effect on the lives of the conference goers—they would have been contemptuously ignored. That is the subtext whenever a politician supports the 'right to protest' as long as it doesn't interfere with the legitimate concerns of others—I think 'people going about their business' is the preferred phrase. To label anyone who demurs from that line as unAustralian is an attempt to define them out of civil society. In the past this proved easier because of a commonality of interest between the owners of the means of communication and the State which protected their interests. (And because those threatening that arrangement were often so easily demonised anyway.) It may prove less so in future with the web providing the demons with their own means of mass communication.

The use of the term 'unAustralian' seemed to cause nearly as much anger online as the tactics of the police. More than one internet correspondent drew out the hypocrisy of political leaders trying to shame the demonstrators for violence which was actually the chosen strategy of the State itself. Because of course political violence is inherently conventional and those describing it as unpatriotic or anathema to some presupposed national culture are either deceiving themselves or, more likely, trying to hoodwink a wider audience as their own interests come under attack. The Prime Minister, with whom I credit very little, at least understands this. His attack on black armband history is a calculated assault on an emerging narrative of Australia, a narrative more accurate and faithful to the sorrows of this land than the sanitised pantomime history he was taught in primary school.

Australian history is debauched with violence: the

institutionalised savagery of the convict era; the massacres of both black and white on the frontier in the nineteenth century; the slaughter at the Eureka Stockade; the anti-Chinese pogroms on the gold fields; the street wars of the Depression between fascist and communist private armies; the civil rights demonstrations in Queensland; the vicious attack by NSW police on Sydney's first gay Mardi Gras. These are all defining moments in Australian history, occasions when the nation's cultural narrative stopped and turned and lurched off in a new direction, driven by violent impetus towards light or dark, but always onwards, never back.

DIRE STRAIT

I grew up in Ipswich, a long way from the sea. The only body of water nearby was a river, but not many kids were attracted to it. You wouldn't want to sail a raft along its sludgy brown meanderings, or try to fish there when you knew what the local abattoir and factories pumped into it. In 1974, however, before I had turned ten, I spent two weeks sitting on the back verandah of a friend's house watching that forgotten river burst its banks and eat half the town alive. We lived on high ground, so I could watch with cruel enthusiasm as street after street disappeared beneath a growing inland sea. Toward the end of the big wet, my father drove me to a valley where a small weir crossed the normally dry river-bed. It was gone. The flood waters ran fast there, at least a kilometre and a half wide and very deep, tossing giant gum trees, dead cows and old car bodies along like leaves in a gutter.

The waters subsided eventually but they left their mark on more than the face of the town. The river got a lot more respect afterwards. People would keep an eye on it, show some deference before nature. I retained a fascination with such elemental forces and can still be reduced to gape-mouthed wonder by the smallest echo of their power. I find it difficult, for instance, to come in out of a bad-looking thunderstorm.

That is why I found myself braced atop the open bridge of HMAS *Warrnambool* as it picked its way through Sydney Harbour on a cold, quiet day last winter. Cunningham, the patrol boat's Commander, had agreed to let me hitch a ride to Bass Strait. It is a rough passage under normal conditions, but during winter the sea can turn malevolent and hungry on a whim. I once went out on the Navy's largest ship, a fleet tender vessel from which I watched a destroyer climbing giant green mountains of waves. The ship would reach the top and keep going, so that a third of its hull was exposed to the air, before tipping forwards and spearing down into the black trough on the other side. As she hit and went deeply under, the few men working on deck were over-whelmed by tonnes of exploding seawater. Despite the robust motion of our own ship I stood transfixed by the spectacle of it, ten years old again. This was the edge of a cliff I had to get a little bit closer to.

Warrnambool rode over a feeble swell through the heads, pulled around to the south and worked up speed. The storms which crept over and hit us later were actually one long storm system, connecting four major squalls. As it rose up, it affected a strange schizoid disturbance of the ocean around us. To port, stretching off to the clean horizon, the sea was blue and undisturbed. To starboard, between the *Warrnambool* and the coast, the water turned inky black, spoiled by roiling white streaks and gashes of foam. The dividing line between these two contrary seas was our green wake in which a couple of dolphins played as the warmth leaked out of the day.

Four strange inverted pyramids blocked our passage: clouds, grey giants. As we beat into the deepening swell, they turned and stretched and slowly grew into a wall of rain which hid the coast and reached around in front of us. Some way ahead, a tiny trawler tried to crawl away to shore, edging alongside the storm curtain like a timid thief. The curtain quickly wrapped itself around the tiny vessel. Two hundred metres in front of us, the sea began to break up. Then, all about, strange grey circles of violent mist began to swirl and dance like incantations. These demented visions whipped in on us and the storm slapped down.

The wind and lashing rain briefly flattened out the sea and bludgeoned down the waves and chop. But larger cycles prevailed and the sea grew ugly. Lurching white caps threw *Warrnambool* around like a child's toy in a washing machine. The boat's design was rugged and it seemed less complex than a racing yacht, even with all the guns, aerials, life rafts and so on. As she muscled into the cannonading waves, I was reminded of watching a boxer close up his guard and walk through a volley of really heavy hits. Technically simple, but hard. Great crashing walls of spray smashed into the windows of the wheelhouse as somebody—the fourth officer, I think—told me about a French scientific ship recently hit by two 18-metre waves, south of Tasmania. The first smashed the windows of the bridge and the second poured through after it.

Fifty metres off to port, I saw a deep, black canyon yawn open in the water, the sort of thing I had imagined the parting of the Red Sea to look like as a child. Between us and the canyon's lip, the water was relatively flat, but then it dropped away down a sheer black cliff, beyond which I could see the far wall of the other side, giving the thing the appearance of a great rift valley, except this one was alive and moving away from us. Able Seaman Kalick said he had seen birds sheltering inside those canyons.

This wretchedness lasted an hour and a half. As it started to abate, Cunningham received a report that the boat's radar had broken down. Then the radio warned that worse weather was to come as we entered Bass Strait, one of the most dangerous stretches of water around Australia.

The Bass Strait of geographers is a narrow corridor of water between Tasmania and southern Victoria. A submerged land bridge with an average depth of 65 metres, the passage is roughly 200 kilometres north to south and 550 kilometres east to west.

For a geologist, Bass Strait is the submerged bridge to a portion of land, Tasmania, which moved away as the super-continent Gondwanaland broke up. For a while, Tasmania was headed south fast. It just failed to plunge into the deep trench which opened up between Australia and Antarctica. Then, over millions of years, the Tasman Sea and southern oceans came spilling over the ridges guarding the edge of the elongated, taffy-like structure which attached the island to the mainland.

The ocean scientist's Bass Strait is a weird confluence of systems; wind, waves, tides and land forms. Winter in particular combines and warps these elements into chaotic synergy. It is winter which brings the monstrous, unseen, 320 kilometre-long underwater cascade off the eastern edge of the floor of the strait. The water in the strait is colder and thicker, and kind of 'stickier' than the deeper waters of the neighbouring Tasman Sea. When the icy current meets the warmer flow at the eastern edge of the strait, it dives beneath it, falling 600 metres from the lip of the submerged land bridge to the bottom of the ocean floor. The force generated is great enough to gouge a canyon in the continental shelf and affect sewage patterns off Sydney's Manly beach, 1600 kilometres away.

A mariner's Bass Strait is something more than all of these; a place defined by disappearance, swallowed fear and madness—primitive references but as accurate in their way as any science. Its discovery attended just such circumstances.

Sydney Cove, carrying 32 000 litres of rough Bengal rum, sailed from Calcutta into savage and relentless seas in 1796. By the time she rounded Tasmania, three men had died of exhaustion at the pumps, more than a metre of water lay in the hold and a sail had been drawn over the bow and around the bottom of the boat in a useless attempt to bandage the leaking timbers. Just before it could be dashed on the rocks, the ship grounded in a channel between Rum and Preservation islands off northeast Tasmania. A good deal of the cargo was salvaged and shelter built on Preservation. Eighteen men then set off for Sydney aboard a longboat. Within a fortnight, they were wrecked on the coast of Victoria and forced to walk the rest of the way. Only two survived to get word to Sydney.

After being sent to rescue the *Cove*, Matthew Flinders became convinced that a strait, rather than a large bay, lay between Van Diemens Land and the continent. Despite fearful weather, Flinders, naval surgeon George Bass and eight volunteers circumnavigated the island by sail and oars. Flinders recommended that the strait be named after Bass, his childhood friend. The opening of Bass Strait cut hundreds of kilometres off the trip to the new colony. It also added a new name to the list of the world's infamous sea passages. Within a few years of the *Cove's* foundering, more ships had followed it and the toll in lives began to mount.

In 1845, the *Cataraqui* came out of Liverpool for Melbourne carrying 369 marriageable women for lonely colonists, 73 children and a crew of 46. One day from Melbourne, the master, Captain Finlay, hove to as the ship battled high seas and heavy rain. The weather had been so foul that Finlay had been guessing their position for days. He expected to make land around Cape Otway, west of Melbourne, at 4 a.m. Instead, at 4.30 in a raging pitch-black night he struck rocks about 100 metres from the shore of King Island, closer to Tasmania than Victoria.

Dozens of women and children who made it to the decks were swept away as soon as they arrived. Many others drowned below when the pounding of the waves broke all the ladders. Finlay kept the sails on, hoping to drive over the rocks, but the *Cataraqui* was firmly wedged and canted over, tearing as she went. The rocks were close to razor sharp and many of the people thrown overboard were cut to pieces.

At dawn, 200 clung to the wreck, but they grew fewer with each wave. Half went to their deaths at four o'clock that afternoon when the *Cataraqui* parted amidships and many who had lashed themselves to the wreck were dragged down with it. She parted again an hour later. By the morning of August 5, only 30 people were alive, mainly strapped to the forecastle, which was beginning to disintegrate. They undid their lashings, hoping to float ashore. Nine made it. Of these, only one was a passenger— a man called Solomon Brown. (Three years later, he drowned in a creek near Melbourne in water half a metre deep.) Bodies, 414 of them, were strewn along the beach for kilometres. They were buried in four mass graves.

The loss of the *Cataraqui* remains our greatest maritime disaster outside of war, but smaller episodes could be just as revealing of the desperation of early life in the strait. Bass and Flinders were not alone in heading south after the wreck of the *Sydney Cove*. A Captain Bishop of the *Nautilus* went, too. While the first two men set about discovering the strait, Bishop and his crew were already exploiting it, clubbing and skinning thousands of the seals they found on Cape Barren Island. Seals and whales were to form the basis of the strait's first oil industry, a grim venture which often called forth the worst in men. Even Flinders, whose liberal and humanitarian qualities were then far in advance of most seafarers, described killing a few seals he found. 'The terrors of the young cubs, who had not yet dared to take to the water, afforded us a great deal of amusement,' he wrote. 'They huddled together among the rocks, putting up a dozen noses through the cavities and expressing their fears of their tormentors by piteous looks and moans.'

Such cruelty was not reserved solely for the animals. Amasa Delano, an American sealer, describes being tipped from a row-boat which was swamped in a rough passage of water in the strait. The five occupants, including his brother William, were tipped into the sea, where Amasa found a bundle of sticks to cling to. He had started paddling for land when he noticed one of his sailors, a Swede named John Forstram, making for him 'with all possible exertion'. Amasa, convinced the man would drag him down, kicked away from his struggling shipmate for all he was worth. Forstram chased him but eventually succumbed to the raging waters and drowned.

Delano later wrote that though, 'I never until then had experienced any satisfaction at seeing a man die . . . I remember but few incidents in the course of my life, that were more gratifying to me than that of Forstram's sinking; for I was not only relieved of the dread of his involving me in his own fate, but I likewise had the oar he relinquished within my reach, which I immediately seized, and headed again for land.'

As the last light guttered out of the day, the gathering gloom smudged the features of the men on the bridge of

HMAS *Warrnambool*. They became, briefly, silhouettes; the Commander leaning back in his chair, staring out over the dramatic rise and fall of his ship's bow; the fourth officer, a neat and compact figure bent over his charts and maps, bathed in a soft orange light; an old petty officer propped against a gyroscope in front of the commander, chin resting on his hardened hands, a baseball cap pulled low over his eyes; a young helmsman and a lookout in blue overalls, their rimmed and burning eyes grown painfully tired. They were all very quiet. Their thoughts had been submerged beneath the thrumming of the engines, the squawk and chatter of the radios, the rhythmic turning of the vessel's useless radar and the ceaseless motion of the sea.

It had been quiet below decks for a day and half. Anyone without a job had taken to his bunk to sleep through the weather. Staggering around the boat's deserted, narrow corridors at night, I was overtaken by a sense of incongruity at the violence of my tossing, pitching, slamming, painful progress down such quiet passageways. Such are the little things that rub and chafe a sailor's patience during a rough journey. He cannot smoke below decks. His coffee and tea slop everywhere. He gets seasick. He has to sit down for a piss, a grave affront to any man's dignity. The crazy, tilting decks make it difficult to move about, to wash or even to climb into his bed. (I was speared into my top bunk every time, my head jammed hard enough to one side to make the gristle crackle in my neck.)

The strait contains many oil well platforms and *Warrnambool* traversed the restricted zone around them for a day or so. The weather died back, although the boat still jumped around enough to make the short walk from my quarters to the mess a shuffling affair of carefully selected steps. The platforms lay all around us. Even in the grey distance, they were fantastic visions which contrived to make you feel oddly out of place. The physical battering of the last three days had strung everybody out. Even so, crossing the restricted zone felt like passing through another world—a water planet inhabited by strange, dark structures, each illuminated by a single giant tongue of flame.

In reality the platforms looming up to more than 100 metres above the water are akin to isolated worlds. They are phenomenally complex structures, exotic hyper-complicated labyrinths of machinery, pipes, struts, grills, valves and wheels, metal everywhere. When you get onto them, you discover they even have their own weird weather patterns. There are wind tunnels to be avoided, up-draughts strong enough to send salt water into your face, wells of warm, dry, stable air the older workers know about, exposed bridges where you keep three points of contact all the time or risk being whipped over the side by the gales. Each platform has a colony of seals, which shelter among the giant steel legs anchoring the structures to the sea bed, and go surfing. An unexpected side effect of the strait's second oil industry has been to benefit a species almost annihilated by the first.

The older men among *Warrnambool*'s crew could remember tying up to buoys in the restricted zone for weeks at a time. They were there to protect the platforms from ter-rorists who never came and poorly guided merchant ships which sometimes did. A shit job, as they recalled. Boring on the good days, hell on the bad. I got a glimpse of the bad days from watching the *Flinders*, a huge, red tender ship, wallowing beneath a platform in a chaotic four-metre swell. High above, a crane lowered a hook to the big metal containers crammed onto the ship's long traybed. When the waves were lulled for a moment, two men ran out, grabbed the hook and set to work on a container. But the sea boiled up and the stern disappeared, scooping up vast amounts of seawater. The men dived behind a couple of containers as a series of giant deck waves thundered down on them. When the water sloshed away, they tried again—three times before they got it right—and then they ran as fast they could while the crane winched away the load.

For the younger sailors, the platforms were a source of free-floating envy. They speculated that the pay would be enormous, the days off endless, the food lavish, and best of all the beds—in splendid air-conditioned privacy—would not betray their occupants in high seas.

The oldest member of the crew, The Buffer, could not allow that life aboard *Warrnambool* was hard. The old Navy, *that* was hard. (*When ships were made of wood and men were made of iron.*) But I thought their lives seemed hard in a way that goes beyond the physical conditions they endure. Hardest really in their lack of options. They once trained heavily at sea for two weeks, got back to port, had all leave cancelled, and put to sea again for seven weeks. I don't suppose they went happily or even willingly. I guess they went bitter and resentful, as any normal person would. But the thing is that they went, because there was no option. Options were not part of the deal they signed on for and never could be. Not when the bottom line was that you maybe had to die one day.

Braced in a corner of the wheelhouse, only an arm's length from them, I stood at an impossible remove. As we left the worst of the weather behind and the journey assumed the tired, aching dullness of the long haul's dying hours, I found myself intrigued by something less visible than giant waves and storms. I caught a flicker of it in the bloodshot eyes of a weary, seasick man as he climbed behind the wheel to start his watch. It was after midnight, halfway through the voyage when the turbulent seas were at their worst. I had spent most of the day in bed and, having no responsibilities, approached the prospect of a night in wheelhouse with good humour. I did not have to be there. I had options. But the helmsman did not. He had given them away when he had made a choice to go down to the sea, not knowing what lay waiting for him. In the end, that fascinated me more than anything I saw that trip—a tired man's ability to get out of bed and drag himself into the violent night.

With the big issues beyond control, small wonder that the men took pleasure in the little ones: the rare sight of a whale metres from their guardrails; a cup of hot, sweet tea brought to them on watch at night; a minute wrapped up in their warm dry beds; a Cherry Ripe consumed with added relish as *Warrnambool* anchored at last in Western-port, their journey's end.

THE BRAVE ONES

The Battalion's nickname was strictly and bitterly ironic. 'The Brave Ones'. A fighting unit with a proud history of child murder, rape, plunder and riot. You could tell when Battalion 745 had passed through because of their signature legacy of shallow graves, burnt buildings and drinking wells crammed with the mutilated remains of the dead peasants they were pledged to protect. In September 1999, they were quartered at the eastern end of Timor, at a barracks complex just north of Los Palos, a forlorn sort of place which had never really recovered from the fighting of 1975.

The town, a market centre, sat on a wide plain, a plateau really, the remnant of a huge primordial lagoon which had been pushed up out of the sea with the rest of the island millions of years ago. The ground rose slowly to hills in the south and lay within the confluence of two climatic systems, arid and baking to the north, wetter and somewhat milder to the south. Primal forest survived in these parts, around the base of the mountains where *Falintil*, the armed wing of resistance to Indonesian rule, had retreated before the advancing invaders in '76. Mostly, though, the land was given over to grazing and rice paddies, one of the few areas of Timor not dominated by the soaring, broken-backed cordillera running down its spine. Within Los Palos, low-rise, prefabricated steel buildings threw back the sun's glare as fiercely as the whitewashed limestone walls of the surviving Portuguese architecture, the best of which could be found in a Catholic college about five kilometres north of the town centre. Los Palos had been abandoned by its inhabitants during the invasion, most of them fleeing to the apparent safety of the nearby mountains, and the Indonesians, taking affront, had sacked the town.

Still, as one traveller wrote later, it wasn't so much that Los Palos had been savaged in the war. More that it had been depersonalised, like a settlement at the edge of a volcano's footprint, where the 'habit of living for the moment is engrained'. The people lived here, thought the writer Norman Lewis, not by choice but by an accident of fate, among temporary structures of corrugated iron, and they somehow kept going with a minimum of security and hope. The area had always been a centre of resistance to the invasion. A lot of young boys from Java, Madura and Bali had died around here, and the Indonesian armed forces had taken more than a generous measure of revenge on their behalf. When Lewis journeyed through the district shortly after the travel ban on East Timor was lifted, he found an empty land known locally as the 'dead earth', because those who had filled it were gone. Driving along the coast road, it was possible to see traces of disappeared villages, outlined by strange geometrical beds of wild flowers or phallus-shaped gourds which had grown up within the boundaries of their ruins. Human activity, wrote Lewis, had come to an end.

Battalion 745, the Brave Ones, were tasked by Jakarta with making sure things stayed quiet. They were a territorial outfit, a bunch of second-raters, with a good percentage of their numbers made up by local men. Their training, equipment and operational doctrine were all inferior to the main force units of *Kostrad*, the army's strategic reserve, and *Kopassus*, the fearsome and much-hated special forces. They were not quite as bad as the militia, the military equivalent of those scabrous, stringy-legged wild dogs that haunt the streets of so many towns throughout the archipelago. But 745 were not what you'd call a disciplined or even a remotely formidable military force. Unless you happened to be an unarmed Timorese *paean*. In that case, as Ambrosio Alves discovered on Thursday, September 9, an encounter with the Brave Ones could be just about the worst thing in the world.

The ninth was a busy day. Nearly a fortnight had passed since the referendum on East Timor's independence, and Jakarta's vengeance, the razing of the new nation, was well advanced. World attention, so distracted in 1975, had hardened against the Habibie government's mishandling of the ballot, but Jakarta seemed to be playing it out, buying as much time as the TNI (the Indonesian Armed Forces) and its militia surrogates needed to finish their work. On that particular day, Indonesian Foreign Minister Ali Alatas called for 'more time' to allow Indonesia to restore order. APEC foreign ministers meeting in Auckland had just demanded that Indonesia stop the killing, but Alatas and his ambassador in Canberra complained that a 48-hour deadline 'was unreasonable'. A fair-enough assessment, given that the 23 000 heavily armed troops and para-military police on duty in the province had so far proved themselves entirely incapable of stemming the violence.

On the same day, the Australian government, facing a karmic payback on two and a half decades of weasel words and collaboration, announced it was doubling the size of its contribution to any peacekeeping force. The Governor of the 27th Province, Abilio Soares, who had deployed all the resources of state at his command in the effort to secure a vote against independence, said that Indonesia might not ratify the result anyway. TNI chief, General Wiranto, insisted that East Timor had become calmer after martial law, a claim dismissed by the Secretary General of the United Nations and met with weary contempt by the rest of the world. The United Kingdom and New Zealand demonstrated their faith in the General's word by dispatching warships to the island; the United States Congress prepared a bill cutting off military aid as UNAMET's (United Nations Assistance Mission East Timor) compound in Dili came under heavy machine-gun fire. The few remaining staff were refusing to leave, saying they feared that one and a half thousand East Timorese who had taken shelter within their walls would be butchered as soon as they left. As New York delayed their departure, Jose Ramos-Horta said the United Nations would be leaving them to almost certain death.

The world's attention had pulled in tight on that compound. That was partly a practical matter. There was little else it could see. The UN's regional staff and the hundreds of monitors from human rights groups such as Amnesty and the Carter Centre were going or gone, many of them hustled out of the province at gunpoint by the military. The position of hundreds of journalists, both Indonesian and international, who had covered the ballot and its aftermath, was increasingly untenable as they became the target of vicious harassment.

Matt Frei, from the BBC, described running towards the UN compound as a Timorese man nearby was 'hunted down like an animal'. A colleague of Frei's filmed the attack while hiding in a shack opposite the compound gates. 'It took only 30 seconds to hack the man to pieces,' said Frei. 'The attack was so ferocious that bits of him were literally flying off. The sound reminded me of a butchers' shop—the thud of cleaved meat, I'll never forget it.'

Keith Richburg, from the *Washington Post*, was struck by the resemblance of the Indonesian-sponsored militia to those he had struck in Africa during the Rwandan genocide. He took the blunt edge of a machete in the back from a militiaman while covering an attack near the UN headquarters that reminded him of similar close encounters in Mogadishu. It would all come back to him, he wrote, 'in my room at Dili's seaside Turismo Hotel, barricading the door against intruders, pulling the mattress to the floor to avoid stray bullets, positioning a tree branch near the bed to use as a last defence in case they made it through my flimsy fortification'. He'd left his bullet-proof vest in Nairobi, never believing he'd need it again, 'at least not in Indonesia, not for what was supposed to be an assignment covering economically booming Southeast Asia, in the last year of the century'.

There was one crucial difference, however. The danger in Africa had been random and spasmodic, a wrong place and wrong time deal. But Richburg and the other members of the press corps felt themselves specifically targeted by the military in East Timor, 'to close off the world's eyes and ears, so they could do their dirty work unimpeded'. In Mogadishu, he said, the media could cut a deal with the devil, hiring the militia to protect them as they went about their work. But the same primitive shake-down racket did not seem to operate in Dili. After the machete attack, Richburg and a few colleagues did pay local police, the *Brimob*, to guard the Turismo Hotel where they had holed up. The journalists even ponied up for the cops' meals and drink tab, putting it all on their hotel bill in the hope it might buy a little protection should a posse of goons from the *Aitarak* (or 'Thorn') militia decide to come over the walls. 'But by the third day,' he said, 'one of our protectors confided a secret to *Washington Post* special correspondent Atika Shubert, who speaks Indonesian: If the militia came, he told her late one night, he wouldn't shoot them to save us. He agreed with them, he told her: "They are doing good things for the country."' Richburg decided it was time to leave Dili.

The fact was, a good number of *Aitarak* members were

really TNI territorials and *Kopassus*, moonlighting as half-crazed savages who'd run amok after the vote. Various observer groups compiled dozens of statements from East Timorese who recognised members of the Indonesian military in the natty black tee shirts of Eurico Guterres' nominally private army. The destruction of Dili was so thoroughly well organised and the intimidation and occasionally violent harassment of the observers so finely calibrated that the Indonesian government's obdurate, po-faced denials of state involvement were almost magnificent in their perversity.

By the ninth of September, however, they had achieved their aim. What the world knew of the crisis in East Timor was confined to a few hundred square metres of downtown Dili, comprising the UNAMET compound and the stories of those trapped inside. Conversely, of course, there was a blowback effect for the TNI. The shadowplay of the militia's vengeance, with the military as puppet master, had drawn the world's attention. Indonesia was getting its fifteen minutes of fame, but for all the wrong reasons. The tactics that had worked so well in earlier conflicts and covert operations, such as the original invasion of the Portuguese colony or the annexation of West Irian, proved less fruitful this time. In '75, Western governments connived at the ruse for geopolitical advantage. Non-aligned Indonesia was valued as an anti-communist foil and allowed or even encouraged in its misadventures. By 1999, a decade after the fall of the Berlin Wall and right after the implosion of the Asian economic miracle, the situation had changed.

On the ninth, all that mattered was the compound.

Throughout the night, the air above was constantly rent by automatic gunfire, with tracers zipping past into the hills behind, making escape impossible. Thousands of people sheltered in a school next door, all fearing an attack which came with militia charging the campus, while TNI troops and *Brimob* fired on the compound. The panic induced was so great that many parents simply threw their children onto and over the barbed wire which sat atop the wall guarding the UN buildings, hoping to get them away from the marauders. A 26-year-old woman described the assault for Amnesty International after she had been evacuated to Darwin:

> They came in with swords which they were swinging at people, but they did not hit anyone ... The people inside the compound were panicking and some were so scared that they jumped over the fence which had barbed wire on top. Some parents were so terrified for the safety of their children that they just hurled their babies and young children over the fence. Many of them were cut on the wire or hurt when they fell on the other side. I could see that the army were playing a very direct role in this attack. They were shooting in the air trying to frighten and panic the people and looting all our possessions.

Vision of the attack was beamed out on satellite links, a squalling, claustrophobic catherine-wheel of images. Screaming women and children, wild-eyed men, UN staff and even other journalists—yelling, gesturing wildly for blankets or cardboard or coats, for anything to lay over the wire, all of them flinching and ducking instinctively at the roar of automatic weaponry outside. Only rumours, terrible and perhaps archetypal, relayed any sense of what was happening beyond the immediate range of the cameras. The *Guardian*'s John Aglionby said he'd been told by villagers of men being marched to the waterfront then gunned down and bayoneted, an echo of atrocities from the invasion in '75. Others spoke of bodies, headless and limbless, stacked to the rafters of police stations. Perhaps it was true, but probably not.

The urgency of those horror stories, the way they sparked and jumped so easily from the lips of a terrified refugee and onto the front pages of metro dailies all over the globe, testified to the moral bankruptcy of the Indonesian regime. Their credit was gone, and it says a lot about the attachment psychosis of the New Order regime that it still couldn't help but play out the game. The essence of politics is conflict, but in stable societies this is ritualised and channelled into non-destructive forms. There are limits to action. The New Order, however, which came to power via the enormously bloodthirsty coup and counter coup of 1965–6, seems never to have internalised this lesson, that political development proceeds from anarchy to order—not just to organised terror. At the heart of its extreme reaction to any form of challenge there must have been a corrosive doubt in its own legitimacy. For a regime apparently so certain of its command prerogative, it invested hugely in repressing the merest hints of defiance throughout the archipelago. Freedom was evil, dissent was subversion and its own citizens could not be trusted. That deeply ingrained pattern of political psychosis was allowed a full flowering in East Timor—and so, while the siege of the UN compound in Dili served variously as metaphor and melodrama, and as a channel for the world's frustrated rage, in the dark beyond CNN's failing, constricted field of vision the blood-dimmed tide was loosed. The Catholic Church announced that six nuns in Baucau and a priest in Suai had been slain by militia. The first intimations of a genocidal evil began to seep out of West Timor. And Ambrosio Alves encountered the Brave Ones.

Little is known of Ambrosio's last hours. He was grabbed up in the village of Asalaino by soldiers from Battalion 745 and members of the Team Alpha militia. He was beaten to death and found two months later, in a shallow grave with another, unknown victim. The significance of his passing lies in the fact that he is the first known victim of 745's withdrawal from the province. We know a lot about the passage of the Brave Ones through East Timor because one of their last victims was Sander Thoenes, a Dutch journalist. He had the bad luck to strike a couple of battalion outriders, either territorial or Team Alpha, the same crew who bailed up British reporter John Swain on the second day of INTERFET's lodgement.

Swain had hired a taxi with an American photographer, Chip Hires, and was crawling through the hills outside Dili when 745's convoy enveloped them. Motorcycle riders began hammering at the vehicle, pulling on the handles. One of them turned his rifle on the driver Sanjo Ramos, smashing him in the head with such force that he lost an eye. Swain later said that as Battalion commander Major Yacob Sarosa pulled up, he yelled at the journalists. 'These people are East Timorese too. They are very angry, very angry with [the] UN and you Westerners. You must understand.' The Brave Ones then 'arrested' Swain's interpreter, Anacleto Bendito da Silva, forcing him into a truck at gunpoint. The westerners never saw him again, but a Battalion sergeant, Hermenegildo dos Santos, a *Falintil* informer who later returned to East Timor, revealed that he had been murdered during the battalion's stopover in Dili.

The Brave Ones were really taking care of business that night. An hour later they're thought to have ambushed Thoenes, the Jakarta correspondent for the *Financial Times*. A local motorcycle chauffeur testified that he gave the Dutchman a lift to the suburb of Becora, where three uniformed soldiers opened up on them with automatic weapons. A single round took Thoenes in the back, ripping through his heart and lungs, causing death within minutes. He was mutilated post-mortem. A nearby TNI post did not intervene in the shooting, or offer the journalist medical aid, nor bother to contact INTERFET.

Between the murders of Thoenes and Ambrosio Alves back in Los Palos, the Brave Ones racked up nearly two dozen civilian kills, some bodies left burning in ditches by the side of dirt roads, some dumped in rice paddies, others in shallow graves or simply in fields where they had been shot in the back while trying to flee. Quite a few were dropped down village wells—a disposal technique with a bonus pay-off, the poisoning of scarce water supplies during the island's severe dry season.

They made a mistake killing Thoenes, though. One of his freelance employers, the *Christian Science Monitor*, was so appalled that they dispatched another reporter, Cameron Barr, to chase down the story of Battalion 745, which seemed to have marked its route out of East Timor with a trail of corpses and ruin. As he traced their withdrawal, along the coast road and through the dead earth, Barr heard that the Brave Ones had wiped out six people as they swept through the town of Baucau. A young man in Fuiloro, near Los Palos, explained how 745 had snatched up and murdered his brother. Investigators confirmed they were sure the battalion was responsible for Thoenes' death. And in Los Palos he found Sergeant dos Santos, who gave Australian police officers detailed information about his former outfit's war crimes.

Barr's reconstruction of the Brave Ones' last days shot holes in the TNI cover story that the unholy disorganised bloodswarm which blew through the eastern half of the island was chaotic, objectless and unplanned. It was, as everyone could see—and as many had warned for months before the referendum—a state-sponsored program, part vengeance and deterrence, but also encompassing barbarism for its own sake. The only question was, which state? The formally recognised government of Indonesia, headed by President Habibie and represented abroad by Ali Alatas? Or another state? A ghost nation existing within the formal structures of the republic, a revenant of Suharto's New Order regime. For that vast, conflicted network of military and corporate combines, well-connected robber barons, state apparatchiks and First Family business concerns did not pass away with the untimely departure of their Emperor. As former Indonesian minister Lakesmana Sukardi put it, 'The pathologies of the previous regime remain in the system.'

It is inconceivable, given the magnitude and the logistic demands of the scorched earth operation in East Timor, that army chief General Wiranto was unaware of its existence. The broad outline of the strategy was exposed time and again by foreign journalists and aid workers with direct access to the territory in the months before the ballot.

Operation *Wiradharma*, as it was known to senior *Kopassus* officers, 'would have required at least his [Wiranto's] condonement', according to the United Nations' special investigator, former Australian diplomat James Dunn. Dunn's investigations found that the spasm of 'so-called militia violence' that culminated in massive deportations and destruction in September '99 was not a spontaneous outburst by those who favoured integration, but rather the outcome of a plan by TNI generals, executed for the most part by officers of elite *Kopassus* units. His report found that the Indonesian military sponsored the establishment of the militia, providing training, arms, money and even drugs on occasion.

While Dunn has often been maligned by Suharto apologists as a diehard member of Australia's East Timor lobby—a charge which did nothing to stop the UN appointing him to such a sensitive position—his report to the UN merely restated the conclusions of Indonesia's own National Human Rights Commission. The Commission reported in January 2000 that there were strong links between the TNI, various arms of the Indonesian police (POLRI and *Brimob*), the provincial government and the militias. The violence was 'the result of a systematic campaign' based on 'extensive planning'. The militias were 'under the direct co-ordination of the TNI', not just one or two rogue, lowly placed officers. Their mobilisation 'was in line with various policies of the military leadership' and 'was accomplished through political terror. Murder, kidnappings and forced displacement were committed by members of the TNI, POLRI, government bureaucracy and the militias':

> After the popular consultation, violence increased drastically throughout East Timor, including murders, kidnappings, rape, property destruction, theft of homes and property, the burning and destruction of military installations, offices and civilian residences, with the goal of forced deportation. Members of the TNI, POLRI and the militias were the key figures responsible for this campaign which involved the creation of conditions, choice of acts committed, scheduling and planning of the forced deportation. This campaign was initiated to convince the international community that the results of the popular consultation should be doubted and that the people of East Timor would rather choose to live safely in West Timor . . .

Of course, that was a choice denied the two dozen unlucky souls who chanced across Battalion 745 on their own journey to the west. The day after Ambrosio Alves fetched up in a hole, two brothers, Florentino and Florencio Branco, were strongarmed out of their village, Home Baru. Their bodies are believed to have been dropped into a well inside the Battalion compound to rest with a few of their neighbours. When Cameron Barr pulled through on the trail of his colleague's killers, he found the well surrounded by tall cornstalks and partially covered over with rusted corrugated iron. It was possible, with the sun in just the right position, to make out the tangle of rotting limbs and torsos at the bottom.

Three days later, another two members of the extended Branco clan joined Florentino and Florencio. On the night of the 12th, Martinho Branco had fled into the rice paddies with his family and their friends, the Belos. 745 tracked them down and fired over their heads, threatening to kill everyone if they made the troops wade through the paddy sludge to lay hands on them. Barr writes:

> The families reluctantly stood up and walked toward the waiting soldiers. Belo and Branco were immediately arrested. Without explanation the 745 soldiers also grabbed each man's eldest child, two teenage boys uninvolved in politics. Juliao de Assis Belo's wife, Filomena de Jesus Freitas, was devastated to see her son in the hands of the soldiers. 'If you want to kill someone, take me, not him,' she pleaded. They ignored her and marched the men and boys along a dirt road that divides two large rice fields. Ms. Freitas and Branco's wife, Maria do Ceu, watched their husbands and sons

walk out of sight. Gunshots were heard a few minutes later. The women prayed.

At mid-afternoon Freitas found the courage to go to the Battalion 745 compound to ask after the men and boys. She was told that they had not been arrested. The next day the people in the neighbourhood began to search. At dawn on Sept. 15, they found Belo, Branco, and Branco's son Marcelio in an area about five minutes' walk from where the families had hidden in the fields. The corpses were partially burned, but Freitas recognised her husband's face and trousers. Her son, Elder, was nearby, at the bottom of a well.

The Battalion was occupied for the next few days breaking down their HQ and transporting the bulk of their personnel to Lautem, a small beach settlement by the Wetar Strait, from where they would be shipped back to Java. Those troops remaining in Los Palos ransacked their barracks and burned about three-quarters of the town, including the UN buildings, the market, and the power, water and communications facilities. Their work done, they saddled up a convoy consisting of dozens of army trucks, some stolen civilian vehicles and a few dozen motorcycles—the latter driven by Team Alpha members. Sergeant dos Santos told Barr that the convoy was not filled with overwrought men bent on revenge. The soldiers were happy to leave and indeed seemed delighted with their orders to carry out a scorched earth retreat. As Battalion CO Major Yacob Sarosa stood by, a lieutenant told

dos Santos, 'If you find anything on the way, just shoot it.'
According to the NCO, Sarosa had previously warned his
men that if Jakarta's preferred option went down in the
ballot, 'they would have to destroy everything.'

The 21st was the Brave Ones' last full day in East Timor
and they held nothing back. It was also a day on which
they brushed up close against their own destruction and all
but touched off a war between Indonesia and Australia.
Their first victims were Abreu and Egas da Costa,
murdered just a few minutes after the convoy had left their
own barracks ablaze at Laga. Their deaths were witnessed
by Zelia Maria Barbosa Pinto, who hid in an irrigation
ditch as she heard the convoy approaching. The da Costa
brothers, doubling on a motorbike, weren't as lucky. Their
own engine noise masked the approach of the trucks until
it was too late and the battalion outriders were on top of
them. Somebody in the convoy yelled out that they were
terrorists, and as Abreu backed away from the motorcycle
and screamed at his brother, 'We're going to die,' the
soldiers opened up on them.

Someone shot Abreu's leg out from under him as he
ran. He fell, staggered up and made it a few more feet
before a round slapped into the back of his skull and
pitched him into the paddy water. His brother didn't get
that far; he was shot in the stomach before he could run
more than ten feet. Zelia Pinto watched a soldier walk over
and bayonet him.

The da Costas had been about a hundred yards from
the turn-off to their home in the village of Buruma. But it's
a moot point whether they'd have lived if they'd made their

run just a few minutes earlier. 745 moved inexorably through Buruma and the sister village of Caibada that morning. Lucinda Da Silva took a shotgun blast in the chest. Elisita da Silva was machine-gunned while cowering behind a bush with her baby daughter, Cesarina. The toddler's grandmother witnessed the shooting, which killed Elisita and shattered Cesarina's right thigh. A few miles down the road, a couple of soldiers straggling behind the convoy killed Victor Belo, who was returning to his home thinking the danger had passed. Carlos da Costa Ribeiro, a former teacher who had stayed hidden in his house, was hunted down and shot in the head.

Later in the day a couple of Timorese youths, who remain unidentified, were arrested, beaten and taken to Manatutu. They were never seen again. The village itself was annihilated, with 98 per cent of the buildings razed to the ground. When the UN came through a few days later, not a living soul could be found in Manatutu and the surrounding countryside appeared to have been emptied of life.

745 and Team Alpha drove through the old Portuguese quarter of Baucau, the second city of East Timor and a major staging point for TNI operations throughout the centre and eastern reaches of the island. From there they took the coast road west for Dili, where they bundled up the journalists Swain and Hires, before killing their colleague Sander Thoenes. As the convoy moved along the main Becora road, with gutted, burned-out houses slipping by on both sides, soldiers in the back of the trucks whooped it up, firing into the air. A local who was caught out in the open, Manuel Andreas, was shot in the back as

he tried to escape down a ruined side street. The convoy halted for a few hours at the TNI barracks in Dili, where they refuelled, ate dinner and murdered John Swain's interpreter. Before they drove out later that evening on the last leg of their retreat, a local military commander asked them to refrain from further bloodshed. Within half an hour they had driven into a potentially catastrophic showdown with the Second Cavalry Regiment of the Australian Army.

The Australian modified light armoured vehicle, the ASLAV to its friends, is really not that light. Or friendly. It weighs in at about thirteen tons, depending on its configuration. 2 Cav runs up to half a dozen variants based on three different hull types. The ASLAV 25, an eight-wheeled, three-man reconnaissance vehicle, carries an M242 25 mm Bushmaster cannon, a chain gun which can discretely place a single high-explosive incendiary cartridge into the heart of a problem, day or night, from up to 2000 metres away. Alternately, should you prove reluctant to come around to the Cav's way of thinking, the Bushmaster could hose you down at a rate of 200 rounds per minute. The ASLAV 25 can also mount two machineguns in its turret, which is fully stabilised and equipped with a thermal imaging day/night gun sight. Its sister vehicle, the ASLAV PC, which is designed to carry seven troops into harm's way, comes with a 12.7 mm machine-gun and a day/night gun sight at the Crew Commander's station. Standing next to an ASLAV, your average machete-wielding nogoodnik is immediately dwarfed by its blunt mass and, more subtly, by the promise of mayhem contained within its brutish frame. As the Australian Army's Third Brigade secretly worked up a concept of operations for lodgement in East Timor (a week before President Habibie invited them in), 2 Cav's heavy persuaders were among the first units chosen.

The ASLAV's offensive capabilities and the training and commitment of the men who drove them were the reasons why armed peacekeepers were never going to be welcome in East Timor in the pre-ballot period. General Cosgrove made it abundantly clear at the start of INTERFET's mission that trying to intimidate his soldiers would be a very different matter to lording it over unarmed civilians. With a neutral, heavily armed force in place, the TNI's scorched earth policy would have been prohibitively expensive, or even impossible to carry through in the face of opposition from the likes of the Second Cavalry Regiment. The antipathy and reserve of the Indonesian forces which prevailed in Dili when INTERFET arrived was partly an expression of that. The TNI had many more troops in place, but behind the comparatively small number of INTERFET personnel stood the threat of intervention by the armed forces of those states that had contributed them, including (though not limited to) Australia's traditional allies, the United States and Great Britain. The appearance of that foreign armour on Dili's ruined streets signalled to all sides in the East Timor conflict that things had changed; specifically, the immunity to armed sanction enjoyed by pro-Jakarta forces had ended. This transitional phase was the most dangerous moment of the crisis, the point at which miscalculation by

INTERFET or foolhardiness by militia or TNI units could easily flash into a wider, international conflict. Into this situation rode the Brave Ones.

On the night of 21 September, the second day of INTERFET's mission, half a dozen ASLAVs, disbursed in two groups, were squatting astride the main east-west road through Dili. While the TNI's senior officer in East Timor, Major General Kiki Syahnakri, had proved co-operative and had indeed rendered invaluable assistance to INTERFET during the taut period immediately before and after the arrival of Australian combat forces, Dili was still infested with hundreds of militia bandits and ill-disciplined Indonesian troops. At all hours of the day and night they tore through the devastated city in trucks and cars, screaming abuse and levelling their weapons at the Australians. Under the rules of engagement they could have been shot at any time for making such threatening gestures, but the Australian troops restrained themselves despite the heat and stress and physical demands of carrying full combat loads.

That stress should not be underestimated. Foot patrols ran all day and night. Sleep was snatched in short bursts among rubble and burning refuse. Bob Breene, in one of the first serious military accounts of the INTERFET mission, described the environment as an assault on the senses. 'Smoke, stench and dust filled nostrils and stung eyes. Buildings were on fire or smouldering black shells.' Rubbish, dead dogs and human filth lay everywhere, piled up into mounds wherever large numbers of East Timorese had sheltered in the last hours, such as down at the port.

Very few civilians remained in the town proper and nobody walked anywhere. Everyone ran. Night-time was even weirder. 'Bizarre and dangerous', according to Breene, a city of the dead under a smoky red glow, with long convoys of trucks crammed with soldiers and loot rolling through the streets while spasmodic gunfire and explosions could still be heard in the distance.

The first Australians ashore, an advance group of about 1500 paratroopers, special forces, assault pioneers, cavalry and airborne infantry, worked in a hyper-stressed, uncertain atmosphere. Indonesia still had tens of thousands of armed men on the ground, and despite Syahnakri's genuine desire to avoid any conflict, everyone was aware that these were the same troops General Wiranto had supposedly had so much trouble controlling over the past month. Ramping up the tension, the Australians, most of them very young men, were at last close enough to reach out and touch the material consequence of the TNI's failure. Bodies rotted in drinking wells, drainage ditches and ruined buildings. Some, writes Breene, had been burned to destroy evidence, leaving behind nothing more than ashes and bone.

Some bodies bore signs of torture and all had been mutilated. In some cases, hands and heads had been cut off in a crude and brutal attempt to hide the victim's identity. The body of a young woman, her hands bound and throat cut, abandoned in a toilet area awash with her blood, was a shocking discovery for the diggers who found her. For many young soldiers these were the first bodies they had seen. Soldiers who had to recover and place remains in body bags, or re-bury bodies for health reasons, recalled that they would never forget the smell and how it lingered on their clothing long after they had finished their gruesome duties.

In some buildings there were signs of multiple murders, the dark brown of dried blood accentuated by white tiled floors. At several sites floors were covered in blood and gore; bits and pieces of people. There were thick sprays of blood and brain tissue along walls at a height suggesting that victims had been forced to kneel before being shot through the head. Limbs, chunks of flesh and entrails were scattered about in other buildings amongst pools of blood suggesting frenzied attacks with knives and machetes. The diggers followed blood trails of victims who had been hacked, and then fled, bleeding profusely before succumbing to further blows; dying before their bodies were dragged away. There were machetes and clubs covered in gore, abandoned after being used to butcher victims. Bloody drag marks suggested that scores of bodies had been dragged away for disposal.

In contrast to the 23 000 TNI and *Brimob* troops, who had been strangely ineffective in the face of this slaughter, INTERFET's comparatively small number of personnel began locking down the city immediately. The ASLAV roadblock was part of a campaign to quickly establish their dominance. The armoured carriers were parked in a herring-bone arrangement at two sites to snare single truckloads of militia and others who still haunted the city in the first few days. The soldiers manning the road block had orders to stop anybody who was armed but not in uniform. They had no idea that Battalion 745 was coming through the night towards them.

Around ten o'clock in the evening, the Brave Ones' motorcycles, riding point on what had grown into a 60-truck convoy, ran up hard against the ASLAV checkpoint. After looting and killing their way across the island from Los Palos, 745 and their Team Alpha cohorts were emotionally unprepared for any resistance. They'd been ordered to chill out back at the Dili barracks, but as the convoy growled and squeaked to a halt in the dark, angry militiamen and soldiers began to shout and wave at the Australians, demanding they move aside. The Brave One's vanguard presented as a sort of B-movie vision of some pirate biker gang from hell, a rat bastard outfit in black tee shirts, camouflage pants, long hair and bandanas, with axes in their eyes and guns at the ready. The Australians—assault pioneers, a couple of rifle platoons and six pairs of snipers—were all kitted out with body armour and night vision equipment, giving them a distinctly threatening, insectile, otherworldly appearance beneath their kevlar helmets. Unbeknownst to the territorials and militia, who were blind in the dark, their every move was being observed in the cool green glow of low-light amplification systems.

The Australian ranking officers, a pair of lieutenants, one of whom spoke Bahasa, informed the motorcycle escort of his orders to detain anyone they came across armed and not in uniform. The riders revved their bikes as their spokesman blustered and demanded passage through the blockade. The voices grew loud and more agitated as it became obvious that 745 might not be allowed through immediately. As more Australian soldiers quietly deployed to support their leader, Indonesians and Timorese dropped from the backs of trucks, unshipping their weapons, crying out, demanding to know the cause of the delay. Some of the hard chargers of Team Alpha and 745 began to shoulder their rifles, unaware they could be seen in the dark.

Under the UN-sanctioned rules of engagement, they were now dead men. But the Australians, outnumbered many times over, did not open up on them. They did not respond in any obvious way. No orders were given, but each man slowly raised his Austeyr F 88 from the hip. Guns on the ASLAVS tracked around smoothly, settling on the trucks full of Indonesian soldiers. Photon streams poured out of laser designators, painting bright dots— visible only through the diggers' night vision goggles—on the foreheads and chests of those men fated to die first.

As INTERFET commander Major General Peter Cosgrove said later, it is no exaggeration to say that the future of Australia's relationship with Indonesia hung in the balance for the next few minutes. So tenuous was the situation in Dili, and so poisonous was the relationship between the two countries at that moment, that everything then turned on the actions of the young lieutenants and the men standing behind them.

Sources

The hard work of tracing Battalion 745's exit from East Timor was not mine but the *Christian Science Monitor*'s Cameron Barr. Supplementary colour was provided by Norman Lewis, as indicated in the text, and the writers of Lonely Planet, whose guide to Indonesia provided useful background information. The events listed as occurring on September 9 were all taken from the ABC's chronology of the East Timor crisis, available on the broadcaster's website. Other media reports quoted in the text, such as Keith Richburg's *Washington Post* article, were accessed through the website of the East Timor Action Network [etan.org]. Details of militia activity were taken from reports by Amnesty International [amnesty.org] and the Carter Foundation [cartercenter.org].

James Dunn's report on the complicity of the TNI in militia violence was provided by the *Sydney Morning Herald* at their website [smh.com.au]. The report of the Indonesian Human Rights Commission (KPP HAM) is available at various sites online. I took mine from etan.org.

The specifications of the ASLAV are given on the Australian Army's home page [army.gov.au], as are some details of the confrontation between 2 Cav and the Brave Ones on September 21. These latter can be found in a speech given by Peter Cosgrove, archived on his home page within the Army site. Bob Breene also described that event and he, along with Cosgrove, is my major source for the encounter.

Jolt Cola

'NOW CONSIDER THE NET, WHICH IN MANY WAYS RESEMBLES NOTHING MORE THAN A WORLDWIDE FELLOWSHIP OF DRUNKEN COLLEGE BOYS.'

DUMB [3]

The town where I grew up, you had to make your own fun. Hunting cane toads with home-made explosives, drunken drive-by shootings of the Assembly of God meeting hall from the back of a ute, smashing Merv the Perv's bedroom windows with ice cubes. Stuff like that. You know, dumb stuff. That's why I love the net. It's just like going home. The dark secret of the net, you see, is that most of it is really stupid and useless. Sure, you could use it to grab a copy of Oxford University's *Complete Works of William Shakespeare* and about a gigabyte of scholarly criticism of those works. But, if you were like me, you'd probably use it to fill your hard disk with dubious factoids about bagpipes, ferrets and alien abductions instead. The thing is, the net can extend human possibilities in any direction. Its power can be harnessed for Good or Dumbness.

We were always kind of limited back home. Consider a drive-by on the Assembly of God. You're looking at some serious man hours to pull this one off, the equivalent of a whole day's work for five or six guys. There's the driving around getting all the guys together, the trek to the autobank for beer money, the drive to the bottle shop for beer, the four or five hours of drinking, the confused and dangerous scramble for firearms and ammunition, the drive to the Assembly of God prayer hall and the shooting up thereof, the arrest, the statements, the court appearances and so on. A lot of effort for what is, let's face it, a fairly marginal if undeniably dumb result.

Now consider the net, which in many ways resembles nothing more than a worldwide fellowship of drunken college boys. While sites archiving the works of Shakespeare do get a decent working out, they've got a long way to go to match the popularity of, say, the web site devoted to Rectal Foreign Bodies; i.e. things people have put in their bottoms. Last time I checked 120 834 people had visited this site, which boasts clippings from *Surgery Magazine*, case reports, a comprehensive list of confirmed foreign body extractions (including a snuff box and a frozen pig's tail) and a suspicious hotlink to the Barbie Doll page. Okay. So some of you are thinking that a rectal foreign bodies web site could perhaps be justified in medical terms, which I doubt, but I like to be fair. And the Butt Page, as it is known to its many fans, is but one of thousands of stupid detours on the infobahn.

As an experiment I have set out to visit as many dumb sites as possible in a given period, say one hour; roughly the same time it takes to gather five drunken cretins with guns from the bottle shop at the One Mile Hotel and drive them to the nearest Assembly of God meeting hall. First stop, the Ferret page, the one page info-shop for all your ferreting needs, including serious answers to the following questions: Where can I find pictures of ferrets online? My ferret trembles a lot. Is that normal? Help! My ferret is going bald! And: What's this I hear about ferrets attacking babies?

Four minutes later, we say a heartfelt 'Hasta la vista' to our furry little friends and hustle over to The Excuse Generator, which pumps out ironclad justifications under the following headings: Didn't mean to kill your pet; Chronically Late; and Didn't mean to sleep with your wife. No time to tarry here though. And no time to download any video from the hundreds of Handycams pointed at coffee pots, refrigerators or closed closet doors all over the planet.

But time enough to quickly scan the messages in aus.sex. I rummaged around in there over a couple of whiskies, hoping to find some droll tale of suburban perversion when instead I found this message which read: Live Nude Video Conferencing. I nearly choked on my ice cubes. Man, this was it! The killer app. The internet tool the world had been waiting for. The message promised that this wasn't just some hokey digitised video recording which would take about three hours to download before stuttering along in a postage stamp-sized window. This was full colour, full motion, real time video of live nude models zapped right onto my screen and just waiting to obey My Every Command. Oh baby. I closed off the newsreader, fired up my web browser and hammered out the address for the site. But I never did get to make those poor, oppressed women dance to my tune. As I waited for a connection to the Hong-Kong based porn server the connection dropped out and I couldn't face getting back into line with the two hundred thousand other net geeks who were obviously milling around the gateway to the site.

Still, the link I'd tagged to the Catalogue of Deceased Porn Stars was pretty cool. Or at least cooler than the List of Instruments Dave has played Smoke on the Water with (including accordion, glockenspiel and tuba). And the Lesbian Barbie Doll Page has my personal stamp of recommendation. While there, you are strongly advised to click the button marked 'Where's Ken?'

After a few minutes of Naughty Naughty Ken it was time to chill out with The *X-Files* Drinking Game. It goes something like this. Mulder rescues Scully: 1 drink. Scully rescues Mulder: 2 drinks. Evidence destroyed: 1 drink. Evidence confiscated: 1 drink. Someone in the pre-title sequence dies: 1 drink. Someone in the pre-title sequence dies in The Generic Forest: 2 drinks. Scully has a bandaid on her forehead: 1 drink. Every time you notice that Scully's breasts are noticeably larger than before she was abducted: 2 drinks. You get the idea.

Start laying in those video tapes and cartons of beer now, before finally crashing into one of the dumbest sites of all: The Really Big Button that Doesn't Do Anything, with accompanying research documents, and the visitors' book, which carried the following comments:

Tiffany: 'They just don't get the button. They can't deal

with its pain so they file it off somewhere as a useless bit of junk. Pigs. All of them.'

And Paul: 'I think there's something wrong with the Big Button. It doesn't seem to do anything.'

Like I said.

Duh.

PATENT FARMING

It's really kind of sad to see a heavy hitter like British Telecom reduced to trying it on with such a third-rate shakedown. Their foray into skanksville with a highly dubious multibillion dollar scam to charge deep-pocketed American ISPs for using hyperlinks, which BT insists it patented way back in 1989, reminds me of some tired old hooker shaking her moneymaker on the frayed edge of a Tijuana whorehouse district while her pimp waits in the shadows to cosh anyone fool enough to be drawn in. Or maybe it just reminds me of Unisys and Amazon.com. Whatever. It's sick and wrong and completely beneath a legitimate operator, but you just know that some poor schmuck is doomed to a good coshing by BT's pimp-lawyer standover team.

Every time this happens we all throw our hands in the air and run around twirling our soiled undies over our heads screeching about how awful it is that these corporate shills could be so darned mean. Remember Compton's

New Media way back in the net's Jurassic period, circa 1993? Remember Compton's ruling junta turning up to Comdex that year and smugly declaring that they had a patent over multimedia? Like McDonald's had a patent over hamburgers, or the nation of France had somehow patented snotty, galling and ill-founded arrogance—thereby locking Compton's president Stanley Frank out of the market.

The neophyte multimedia industry went ballistic, generating enough heat and light to burn Compton's in the mainstream press. Luckily so, for it was the *San Jose Mercury News* which informed US patent chief Lehman that something had gone badly pear-shaped in his office. Lehman had the Compton's patent reviewed and then withdrawn after some bright spark pointed out that *The Complete HyperCard Handbook*, published by Danny Goodman in 1987, provided a blueprint for the same system Compton's was trying to patent for itself.

The issue has bubbled along ever since, only occasionally seeping into mass market consciousness when some dimwitted greedheads like Amazon or Unisys decide to chance their arm. The Unisys racket was, in one sense, an artifact of the old economy. Unisys woke up one morning and realised that many years ago they'd shared a bit of code with CompuServe which made GIF picture files a happening thing. With billions of these suckers now scattered over millions of web sites, the bean counters at Unisys spied the main chance their worn-out old firm had missed so often in the past. They could muscle in for a piece of action, a licensing fee, from everyone using that small piece of code, everywhere in the world, for the previous decade. You could hear the board members' woodies rapping against the big mahogany meeting table from way across town. It was a classic case of the old patent system's inability to comprehend the non-mechanical, non-patentable nature of software.

Amazon's attempt to lock up a one-click ordering system, however, while seemingly an identical form of avaricious folly, really demonstrates a deeper systemic failure which could end up being a much greater threat to digital commerce than any virus, hacker or millennium bug analogue. Jeff Bezos' patent over an obvious method of doing business would never have survived a review under the 'old' patent system. For a start it was 'obvious' and thus not patentable. And secondly it was a 'business method' and ditto. But a series of ill-considered patent applications and legal cases arising from those applications have undermined the future of e-commerce to a point where it presents as a colossal edifice growing atop a thin crust of honeycomb.

We're not talking about one or two cases here. Amazon, Unisys and Compton are merely symptomatic. The underlying cancer has metastasised. In the past decade hundreds, maybe thousands, of firms and individuals have registered completely bogus patents over nearly every aspect of online business. Some, such as Walker Digital, a Connecticut-based 'intellectual property incubator', have moved into patent farming as a massively profitable new enterprise. *Wired* recently reported that 30 of Walker's 150 worker drones are beavering away in the legal department, either dreaming up new business methods like priceline.com, with its 'reverse auction' patent, or sooling the dogs onto other companies who try to emulate them. Everybody wants to be the new Microsoft. (Although it is kind of satisfying in a Schadenfreude way that Bill Gates' evil empire was one of the first to get a blowtorch on the belly from Walker's patent team.)

The web, of course, was supposed to release a tsunami of creativity and we were all supposed to ride that wave into a prosperous, CGI-generated sunset. Unless there is a global response to patent farming, however, I suspect the wave metaphor we're all going to be using is 'wipeout'.

GIVE ME THE REMOTE
NOW, SENATOR

A while back one of those magnificently silly surveys popped up in the media as a sort of surfing dog story of the day. 'Researchers', probably in England, had discovered that if forced to choose between relinquishing their television's remote control or going without sex, most men would prefer to hang onto the magic stick. Our Minister for Communications, Richard Alston, often puts me in mind of such things with his gothic mien of repression, denial, cold showers and birch bark floggings.

The confused tangle of regulation which he has drawn up for the conversion to digital television betrays a reflexive disposition to constraint over autonomy, although given the howling pack of new and old media moguls snapping at his heels throughout the deliberation process, I guess it's a shame he didn't just let them get down to their leather undies and flick knives in the carpark at Parliament House; last man standing gets as many megahertz of free spectrum as he can fill up with cheesy/creepy 1960s TV comedies and relentless home shopping shows hosted by living dead celebrity leftovers. (Usually from the aforesaid sitcoms.)

It's a big ask to settle on exactly who has disgraced themselves the most during this particular teddy bears' picnic. A personal fave would have to be Rupert Murdoch arguing in the US that his free-to-air Fox network should be allocated spectrum gratis, before jetting down under to loudly decry local free-to-air demands for exactly the same shameful indulgence as, well, a shameful indulgence. However, the established broadcasters whining for compensation for the five hundred million they'd have to blow on conversion costs, after the pay TV operators dropped eight billion on their set-up, would rate a punt too.

And into this den of thieves walks our man Alston, with a report from his science guys, full of data and test findings which the pointyheads from the American Advanced Television Systems Committee found 'supported different conclusions than those reached'. Your average Senator might find such a position at least a little uncomfortable. But Alston has had plenty of opportunities to habituate, as the shrinks say. His own government's Productivity Commission, normally a much favoured cabal of free market nutters, has had short shrift for suggesting that the Government's policy might be overly complex, hideously expensive and most likely doomed to failure. (It's not certain you'll see the Opposition crowing about it any time soon, however, seeing as they voted with the Government's legislation in a classic piece of metooism to try to placate the wrath of Kerry before the last election.)

The Howard Government's other trips through the looking glass of new media regulation give rise to a suspicion that they may not actually have anything even resembling a clue. Tooling up the Broadcasting Authority to come the heavy with ISPs for channelling 'potentially prohibited' material from overseas web sites or mailing lists or newsgroups conjures up an image of a thousand monkeys chained to a thousand typewriters in the basement of the ABA cranking out standard access-prevention notices as fast their hairy little paws will go, and still failing to keep up with demand. The legislative contradiction of banning material such as that contained within Kerry Packer's lowbrow stick-book *Picture* from online access, while allowing it to be sold freely across the counter, doesn't seem to have occurred to anyone. But then neither did the inherently unconstitutional restriction on distributing X-rated vids across the net, when distribution through the post from the ACT and Darwin is a multibillion dollar industry.

Meanwhile, at the end of May, the feds' net gambling policy of squeezing their eyes shut real tight and muttering at online casinos to just go away, died screaming at the hands of a couple of state gaming ministers with a woody for taking down indolent losers who can't even work up the energy to catch a bus across town to blow their mortgage repayments. I mean, really Senator, if these idiots insist on sitting around in their skanky bathrobes to hazard the family silver on a few rounds of digital blackjack, can't we at least keep the money in this country to pay for their counselling and rehab? Does the Mob really need it that much?

Perhaps, Senator, given how things have turned out, you might want to think about walking away before Game Over flashes up. Do you really want to be around when a couple of million ticked-off couch potatoes realise just how much this new era of televisual excellence is going to cost them for set top boxes or full conversion to wide screen HDTV? Give it up big guy. Have some dignity. Put down the remote and step away from the box.

THE ELECTRIC FRINGE

Bill Gates didn't get anywhere near the year's coolest infotech conference when he blew into town a couple of weeks back. I'm guessing the Maximum Geek didn't even know it was on. But a couple of big-hearted dope dealers did, and they made sure the festivities at Newcastle's electrofringe festival were, well, really really festive.

Electrofringe mashed dozens of e-zine editors, web monkeys, code cutters and media junkies into a hydra-headed party monster for a couple of days over a hot weekend down the dead end of the steel city's Hunter Street. The presence of a couple of hundred drink and drug addled youngsters at four parallel gigs—indy radio, student media, electronic music labels and the national young writers conference—proved a blue sky opportunity for the entrepreneurial hippies, who refinanced their food co-op through sales of hash cookies, chocolate space cake and $3.30 joints. (GST inclusive, I guess, although they weren't taking ABNs.)

The collision of raw talent at the Newcastle gathering, now in its third year, was a little intimidating for those creaky old duffers like me who were invited along as curious museum pieces or who simply sniffed the air and came to investigate. While the decaying boneyard of BHP's steel division shimmered in a heat haze across the Hunter River, the barbarian hordes of the new economy, in all their tatty, dreadlocked glory, chased down beer after beer and brainstormed perceptual engineering, non-linear videocasting, electronic collectives, VR fiction, the indy-media movement, hacktivism, high bandwidth art, the technological imagination, 'better living through circuitry' and the configurable city.

Sure, you might question the relevance of all this to your business future if you turned up at the Festival Club late Sunday night to be confronted by an angry knife-wielding poet, the cacophonous roar of rap artists and the sight of obscure comic book super-hero Pterodactyl Man in his bright red flying lizard costume chugging a beer through his big, anatomically correct dinosaur beak while a mullet-haired rural type dispensed hallucinogenic Anzac biscuits to the masses. But before you dived back into your rented Fairlane and laid rubber for St Leonard's you might want to dwell on that graphic of the Microsoft founders at the dawn of the disco era, all big hair, thick glasses and gormless toothiness, with a caption asking whether you'd back their fledgling business.

The strident anti-commercial tone of your average e-zine originator masks a frighteningly Calvinistic production ethic overlaying the sort of creative talent top shelf ad agencies hope they're getting from their million dollar a year pony-tailed ego-monsters. Scattered in amongst the dozens of wilfully bolshie conference topics were a few giveaway nuggets: panel discussions like 'Video Performance for Business' and 'Making Usable Websites', and a whole slew of copyright, niche marketing, legal and finance discussion groups.

Taking place within sight of an old economy graveyard like BHP's former steel foundry, the five-day binge gave lie to the image of Australia as a dumbed down, steam driven entity . . . sort of. May my tongue turn black, swell up and fall out of my head but for once I found myself agreeing with Peter Costello. When he argued that it was use of new technology rather than its mere construction which denoted an advanced economic infrastructure, he was much less wrong than usual.

It's a typical Treasury or Industry Commission cop-out to claim we don't need to build WAP phones or plasma screens here because we can just sell a few more of our very competitive sheep and import the gizmos we need from the profits. Down that path lies desolation. But Costello was not being entirely boneheaded when he pointed to Australia's rapid take-up and exploitation of new technology to try to shore up the dollar, which had fallen, according to the chicken entrail readers, because hot global capital was drawn to the great rewards of America's new economy.

They may not have looked it, and they probably don't want to know about it, but those unwashed and occasionally dope-addled teens and wannabe teens who gathered in

Newcastle in early October will be the economic salvation of Australia and her plucky little dollar. You want to know how the new technology is really going to change the world so you can leverage a bit of the action? Get up to Newcastle next year and ask Pterodactyl guy. Or maybe that drunken poet with the knife.

STEPHEN KING: HERE'S YOUR BUCK YOU LOUSY BUM

I'll probably send Stephen King his lousy buck. Or buck ninety-five after correcting for the poor old Aussie dollar. He doesn't need it, I'm not sure I approve of this whole net publishing gig, and I suspect it'll probably cost him more than that to convert the money order anyway. But what the hell? He's Big Publishing's biggest nightmare and we just gotta support the little guy, don't we? Even if he is being kind of disingenuous about the big publishing thing.

King, of course, is the last guy who should be railing against Big Publishing. Big Publishing made him the multi-millionaire he is today. Even he admits that. His name is an immensely valuable brand largely because a succession of multinational publishing houses have assigned hundreds of staffers and tons o' cash over the last twenty years to the task of commodifying it.

King is undeniably, even fanatically, loved by a fan base so large it qualifies as its own mass market. But the front-of-store dump bins, life-size cardboard author cutouts, electronic and print advertising campaigns (Words Are His Power!), movie and TV spin-offs, national and international book tours, trade fairs and, basically, the whole hot and funky hands-on full body market massage which was the foundation of that success was the work of Big Publishing, not the author. King himself has mused on the arbitrary nature of his success, having released a number of books under the pseudonym Richard Bachman which proved to be very ordinary performers at the sales desk, until the identity of their true composer finally leaked out; no doubt at the behest of some hunchbacked, three-toed number-crunching troll toiling away in the darkened basement of Big Publishing with his quill dipped in baby's blood and an abacus made of knuckle bones.

The likes of Random House, HarperCollins and Penguin shouldn't worry that their lists are about to be hollowed out by a mass migration of writers to the net. Stephen King and perhaps Bryce Courtenay locally might have the mercantile cojones to make a go of publishing through their own web sites, but the vast majority of authors will be fronting the publishers' reception desks with heart in mouth and disk in hand for a while yet. And I've still got my doubts as to whether the King of Horror can make his experiment pay over the long haul.

The Plant, King's second foray into e-publishing, has resorted to a variation of the old shareware formula as a revenue model after his initial venture, *Riding the Bullet*, proved to be a lucrative but extremely short-lived formula. *Bullet* sucked in elephant bucks for a couple of hours, until the copy was pirated and posted all over the web, at which point the money gusher trickled out and died. King is promising to finish his latest cliffhanger only if at least three quarters of the downloads are paid for—by the grossly archaic method of everbody snail mailing him a buck per view.

For your dollar you get about 100 kb of text, HTML or PDF on your hard drive, and the story itself is up to King's usual high standard of cheeseburger gothic. But it's a pain to read onscreen and printed out you miss the frisson of guilty pleasure to be had from purchasing such high concept lowbrow brain candy in its trad format. It works as a novelty but whether millions of people are going to pony up the cash time and again is way moot. And yes, these are technical quibbles to some extent. Perhaps a generation or two down the track, printer and screen technology will have advanced enough to provide a truly enjoyable reading experience. But just because a lot of moth-eaten Luddites belittle the aesthetic experience of digital books, we shouldn't underestimate the power of aesthetics in determining market choice. If content were the only factor nobody would ever build bookshelves and stock them with texts they have no intention of reading or returning to.

Digital formatting will obviously have a huge impact on some niche publishing products which lend themselves to that style of delivery. The migration of academic and technical journals to the net is an obvious example. The airport novel is probably here for a while longer though. The web was once compared to the world's biggest library, where every single book had been pulled from the shelves and thrown at random into a huge, incomprehensible pile. While guys like King might have the clout to stand above the pile, most authors are going to rely on Big Publishing to grab them an audience.

And as a self-confessed avid consumer of pulpy mass market fiction he might want to ponder on what happens to all the baby writers if his scheme actually comes off and those awful publishers no longer have an income stream from major earners like him to help subsidise long shot punts on untried writers and weird, left field books. Books like Stephen King's *Carrie*, circa 1974.

NAPSTER

No kid ever picked up a guitar and dreamed of taking a meeting with his accountants and intellectual property lawyer. A hundred thousand garage bands have been conceived to feed fantasies of unlimited free drugs and morally flexible babes, but none ever came together with a business plan and a viable revenue model. The Monkees? Yes, sure, they did. And those batch-cloned, anonymous, boy bands infesting the charts at the moment? Yep, them too, most likely. But the true heart of rock and roll remains a bunch of know-nothing losers with second-hand amps thrashing away in a garage, a bedroom or a warehouse while dreaming of conquering the world. Or at least a couple of groupies.

On such dreams are empires built and wars fought.

It's a tad difficult, however, to have any sympathy for the major record companies in the war they have launched on sites like MP3.com and Napster. While the legalities of song swapping across the net are problematic at best, there's more than a little enjoyment to be had at the prospect of pseudo-brutes Metallica and the preening wannabe street punk Dr Dre fronting for a cabal of corporate goons like Warners, EMI, Sony, and Universal as they fight out a turf war with the digital newcomers.

The recording industry's standard tactic in spin doctoring a legal assault on any emerging threat is to have popular artists rather than oily, well-fed lawyers fronting the campaign. But the image of a couple of hard done by millionaire rock pigs bemoaning the theft of their music belies the true nature of the business, which resembles nothing so much as a sort of remnant feudal system, where a handful of robber barons lord it over a captive population of indentured serfs.

Those poor, deluded little guys, thrashing away in the garage, dreaming of signing up to a major, have no idea of the sort of Dark Ages slave system they're actually trying to sell themselves into. Beau Brashares, a former industry insider (i.e. band member, producer, mixer and serf) who wised up and enrolled in law, explained to a Harvard University conference on the future of internet music that the keyword is 'recoupables'. Our furious little garage band plays like mad bastards all over their home town, garners an intense tribal following, hits the road, gets noticed and all of a sudden some smiling A&R guy from the majors is standing at the back of the gig waving a contract at them. Visions of spa tubs full of champagne and dumb blondes swimming before their eyes, they sign.

The company promises to put a hundred large into the band, recording time, promos, novelty baseball caps, whatever. But that's a hundred grand of the band's money. Of their generous ten per cent royalty. You see, the big studios don't really spend anything. As soon as the release makes any money the record company's number crunchers swoop in and tell the startled, possibly drug-addled band members that although the CD might have sold three hundred thousand units, the band actually owes the company for all of the production, promotion and distribution costs. Oh, and while we're on the topic, fellas, that cocaine ain't free either.

Acts like Metallica which find themselves a few links further up the food chain—vassals rather than serfs—can demand a better deal. But the vast majority of artists signed to the majors lose all control over their copyright and end up deeply indebted to their feudal masters. Most will see out their days delivering pizza.

You can see then why tens of thousands of desperate indie musicians are praying that Napster or any of a dozen other internet distributors will live up to their promise and slay the industry beast. Chances are, however, this dream will prove to be as illusory as all those before it. The business plans of rebel dotcoms like Napster, when they even exist, tend towards vague, wispy notions of earning money through advertising, the tin god of all start-ups. And those neophyte bands which lodge their catchy little pop song online with the new outlaw distributors more often than not discover that they're required to sign away their copyright in agreements just as draconian as anything the hired legal muscle of one of the big studios could draw up.

MP3 will rock the world of the majors over the next five

to ten years. But if you want to lay bets on where the money ends up, back an evil genius with a truckload of venture bucks and a radically new revenue model, or even the old dinosaur record companies if they buy in good advice and adapt in time. The one place you don't want to lay down your hard earned is on a punt that the artists themselves will finally win big.

GIVE ME FAT PIPES
OR GIVE ME DEATH

Oh God, no. Please don't make me wait for this too. It'll be like the fiasco with WWW access again. I remember, a million years ago, trying to convince the hopeless, lentil-chewing morons who ran my very first ISP that their steam-driven VT 100 interface sucked like a vacuum and if they didn't immediately get me hooked up for a little Mosaic action I was going to sneak into their stinking commune, grind up their scabrous, dysenteric camp dogs and adulterate their inedible chickpea-based imitation hamburger patties with honest to God puppy mince. They gave me a lot of snotty, superior net hippy attitude about how WWW was a stupid and possibly fascist fad which would never replace good ol' ASCII text terminals.

Those hippies came up short a few slow movin' doggies the next day.

Are you listening to this, Telstra? Where is my cheap, universal broadband access? Give me fat pipes or give me death. Preferably yours.

About the only noteworthy thing the Microsloth Übergeek did when he was down under for the Olympics and S11 was to blade the government and the telco's for the pathetic state of local broadband. Gates seemed to think the supervillain was Telstra's anticompetitive culture, and I guess we gotta tip Bill the old propeller beanie on that score. If anybody would know about anticompetitive culture it'd be him.

For once, and only once, however, perhaps we could cut those greedhead bastards at Telstra a minimum amount of slack. Compared with British Telecom, the local phone bandits are only comparatively hopeless jokes. The Brits are weeping and wailing and gnashing their poorly cared for teeth over the roll-out of broadband services. A report by the Institute of Economic Affairs cites a litany of 'extreme delays' in the roll-out, poor availability and data speed. Homes in the US and France were found to be six times more likely to be plugged into the big pipes. The price of British broadband was the highest in Europe, but the speed was just about the slowest, up to twenty times more sluggish than in Sweden and Denmark, for instance. 'Indeed,' claimed the Institute, 'the UK's failure has been so acute that the very question of whether we even have broadband at all has been raised.'

But even in the US, waiting for DSL service is akin to loitering in the vicinity of a near-death experience. The number of households jacked into the big Kahuna is growing at a great clip but well over half the country will still be standing around holding its joint in three years' time waiting for a connection due to the collapse of the independent DSL provider market and the general apathy and slothful butt-monkey attitude of the trad telco's like Bell South. So woeful have been the efforts of some providers that rugged individualists in a couple of smaller communities have set up their own high-speed non-profit community wireless internet outfits.

It sounds like a good idea at first, until you remember that's where we came in, with a bunch of know-nothin' know-it-all hippies offering internet services that should rightly have been the province of rapacious multinational conglomerates. Why would you even consider buying your communications product from some woolly, unwashed anarchist with no functioning underpants when you had an alternative. Trouble is, of course, alternatives are thin on the ground round these parts. With the barbarian horde that passes for Telstra's broadband division charging whole-sale competitors more for ADSL connection than it charges its own retail customers, you could be forgiven for thinking that the evil empire is less interested in getting the country wired up than it is in protecting its revenue streams from ISDN and second phone lines. With ADSL outperforming Telstra's hideously expensive ISDN service on price and completely negating the requirement for a second phone line it'd shoot big holes in Telstra's bulging money bag if too many punters put their hands up for the service.

But of course that would never influence the generous souls at our friendly phone company, would it?

TELEMALL OF THE UNDEAD

There was a time when a man with a deadline at dawn could fill a schooner with cracked ice and cheap whiskey, grab a bowl full of beer nuts or corn chips, fire up the old word processor, walk away from the old word processor, and catch six hours of high class televisual spakfilla instead. Five star après midnight stuff like Chuck Conner's *Great Western Theatre*, or *The Thunderbirds* or old war movies. These days, however, after the late news and *Star Trek* have wrapped up you're on a fast ride to TV hell. Home shopping shows have sprouted like poison toadstools across all the commercial networks' dead zone schedules, gradually eating up air time which should rightfully be filled by *Starsky and Hutch* reruns.

In a country of eighteen million people, there's always gonna be a few viewers up for an all-nighter. Not an identifiable demographic but a cheaply accessed lumpen market of shift workers, nightclubbers, students and the sloughed off, broken bits of audience drifting down from prime time to nourish bottom feeders like National Media Systems, the giant American multinat behind telemall shopping.

Telemall shows are the noxious weeds of insomniac TV, spreading everywhere, strangling even the dubious pleasures of late night ads for Canberra-based porn wholesalers. Telemall's proto-programs run straight through. I watched three hours of these suckers the other night, eyeballs a-bleeding and brains a-leaking out through my ears by the end. First off came *Vantage Point* with Kevin Trudeau, a head to head in some prefab studio between Trudeau, his BIG microphone and some sorry-arse potato-headed motherfucker who could speed read the *Encyclopaedia Britannica* over his lunch break. To bleary, sleep deprived eyes it could have passed at first for a satellite feed of some US public affairs show kicking out the jams on subsidies to public schools. Something your desperate undergrad type might be inclined to watch after a couple of cones if they had an Intro Politics paper to plagiarise before breakfast. But it was actually a 30-minute advert for Mr Potato Head's speed reading course.

That's the really evil thing about these shows. They're like those fork-tongued space aliens from *Invasion of the Body Snatchers*. They take the outward form of normality, but underneath? Giant carnivorous space lizards. *The Danny Bonaduce Show*, which ran after *Vantage Point*, put itself about as the 'hottest talk show on TV', hosted by 'our favourite member of the Partridge Family'—i.e. the one who made a small name for himself coming out of rehab a few years back and vomiting the details of his slide into the celebrity abyss all over real talkback shows. And who was the drug addled former child star's Very Special Guest? Memory expert Kevin Trudeau, the same guy who'd pulled talking head duty for the previous half hour's advertorial.

Danny Bonaduce came on as a sort of David Letterman of the Living Dead. All of the talk show elements were there, it's just they were shambling about with bits of rotting flesh hanging off them. The live audience—an evolutionary step down from the show biz offal and fad diet victims bussed in for Sally Jess—filled a little less than a quarter of the available seats and the camera guys had to be careful not to linger on the fringes too long lest eagle-eyed viewers noticed the hundreds of empty chairs climbing away into darkness. Bonaduce's house band, The Critics, were a bunch of no talent, overweight air guitar specialists. The set looked like it had been stolen from a Tijuana second-hand furniture barn and everybody's favourite Partridge presented like a red-headed pit bull terrier with a small amount of brain damage. It was the appearance of Trudeau which really put the zap on me though. At that time of night (or morning I guess) having the 'journalist' from the previous 'special' suddenly materialise on a different counterfeit talk show touting his own garbage was a little like indulging in a seven-hour porno vid binge where all the wet bits blend into each other. So to speak.

Short of cutting off Trudeau's head, filling the mouth with salt and burying the body under a crossroads at midnight, I don't see how we can kill off these shows. NMS already operates in 62 countries, broadcasting their crap again and again until you give up and hand over your credit card number. Optus and Foxtel are praying that home shopping will be a Pay TV killer app. And even if it's not, free to air stations aren't going to have anything but advertorial to broadcast in five years anyway.

BOTTOM FEEDING

Perhaps Westfield are just a bunch of bottom feeders. Last year the guys who perfected the model for shopping as retro-futurism—think THX 1138 meets Brave New World at the mall—were obscenely aroused at the prospect of ponying up five million big ones to build a virtual mall. Then, just as they've got maybe a hundred potential retailers ready to lie back and give it up for the band, they come over all English and coy and suddenly there ain't no more five large. Just a black, smoking hole where Frank Lowy's e-tailing strategy used to be. Or at least that's what it looks like anyway.

But friends, I'll lay money on the barrel that five years from now Westfield will still be bringing the world retail therapy as a Skinner Box encounter; with all the joyless, stamp pressed ambience and feedlot psychology that have made them the market leader today. And they'll be doing it online. Westfield knows it doesn't have to waste its own hard-earned readies proving a new paradigm. There's dozens of haplessly enthusiastic e-tail newbies who'll do the hard yards for them, developing business models, beta testing fulfilment systems and burning their cash like drunken communists. And at some point before they spontaneously combust Frank will be there, chequebook in hand, with an offer they can't refuse. No matter how much they'd like to.

Westfield's withdrawal from the bull ring is tactical, not strategic. It's akin to Woolworths taking a position somewhere in the rear of and menacingly close to Greengrocer.com. The short-term dance move seems to be spinning in the opposite direction to Westfield, but they are both headed the same way. It's happening all over, to plucky little winners like Greengrocer and bloated freak shows like K*Grind and Fashionmall.com—which had itself only just snacked down on the bones of Boo.com for small change and a stale cracker.

While the consumption of sinking, sloughed off bits of flesh at the bottom of the dotcom deadpool is a naturally occurring phenomenon, and thus nothing to be afraid of or squeamish about, there are inevitably going to be some ugly moments. Sometimes these will be amusing, in a scatological sort of way. Overstock.com's bargain-basement-from-hell site is like purgatory for all of the unsold stock and office furniture of failed e-commerce outfits. Cheesy, garish and quite magnificent in its awfulness, it's not a bad joint for a bankruptcy chopshop and is one of the positive effects of the commercial net beginning to eat itself. All it lacks is an MP3 of a grating cockney spruiker imploring the world to 'cum orn in an' 'ave a shoofty at the b-a-a-a-a-r-g-a-i-n-s'.

On the other hand the annexation of the entire Usenet archive by Google, the cannibaliser of deja.com, is a standout example of the downside. Without warning, one of greatest free resources remaining from the net's garage band days has been totally cornholed in one of the grossest, most unnatural violations the online community has ever witnessed. Usenet was not just an endearingly clunky piece of VT 100 era technology. It was a vast and important historical document, a record of the conversation of the human race as it realised it had created a new world. If you want to be a little less vegan about it, it was also a powerful business tool, with thousands of companies using it to keep track of consumer sentiment. When Apple's Australian operations turned all mouldy and stiff a couple of years ago because of the appalling performance of their reseller network, the litany of complaints in aus.computers.mac played a part in alerting Steve Vamos to the problem.

Well, those days are over, it seems. Google's half-arsed re-engineering of the Usenet log has meant that only the last six months' worth of posts are available, it's impossible to delineate searches by date or hierarchy and users can no longer follow threads. Calling their efforts amateurish would be a rank insult to the thousands of amateurs who built the thing in the first place. If some monomaniacal James Bond supervillain was scratching around for a plan to destroy Usenet, he could do no better than to send a couple of goons over to Mountain View to borrow Google's template.

If there's anything to be salvaged from this fiasco,

perhaps it's the heads-up call it makes for the rest of the really cool stuff which might get flushed down the crapper during the looming shakeout. During its deathrattle deja.com was even contemplating deleting the entire 500 million message archive. Perhaps overstock.com could pick it up for a song. Or maybe Westfield could send it on a permanent tour of its real world malls, with the kids from *Young Talent Time* incorporating free public searches into a rocking little song and dance routine. It'd have to be better than what we've got now.

[Since the initial publication of this column Google have heeded JB's stern admonitions—or, uhm, maybe the barrage of abuse from thousands of hardcore Usenet fans—and greatly improved their service.]

UNCOOL

During the 1960s it was a truism of the Main Hippy that when *Time* magazine finally stumbled across some counter-cultural artifact, it had most likely been dead, or at least inert and devoid of any significance, for three years. In millennial Australia that role is fulfilled by Mike Munro. A few months back the Nine network's *A Current Affair* ran a puff piece on the internet grocer Shopfast. The producers sitting around at Willoughby taking calls direct from their watch-me-play-banjo-with-mah-toes demographic received more than one enquiry asking just where this 'internet' was. The callers would like to go shopping.

The faux-revelatory tone of such mainstream media Kodak moments—'Imagine shopping from the comfort of your recliner rocker!'—set me to wondering on just when it was that the net stopped being cool; when it was that the number of truly woeful promo pamphlet corporate web sites exceeded the number of Exploding Head style personal sites. And when it was that, like the victims of the Borg, all of the millions of creative and anarchic personalities who seemed to populate the earliest bulletin boards, MUD and Usenet were assimilated.

Most cultural revolutions go the same way, of course. There is an eerie similarity in the efficient manner by which the free world dealt with the threat of the Sex Pistols and the efficient manner in which it responded to the Exploding Head web page era of the net. These evolutionary stages, dumbed down for mass appeal, run from:

- emergence on the fringe—a lot of drunken geeks getting very excited by digitally altered binaries of Shannen Doherty, and by the jihad launched by the guys from alt.flame against alt.pet.cats
- mainstream discovery—surfing dog news items at the end of the six o'clock news are temporarily displaced by chatty little pieces opened by the network anchor grinning inanely and saying, 'They call it the internet and scientists say it will change your life . . .'
- fear and backlash—every newspaper in the country begins to run 1200 word features on wired-up paedophiles and the Anarchist Cookbook Online. Bob Carr and NSW Attorney-General Jeff Shaw respond to the *Herald*'s grave warnings about the danger to Our Kids with some of Australia's first net censorship laws.
- greed and assimilation—Nasdaq, Juice.net and Mike Munro. A symbiotic ménage à trois.

Why then did the internet era of clunky, migraine inducing VT 100 terminals seem so much cooler than T1 lines, streaming, Gnutella and Shopfast? I mean, these are all good things. But are they that cool? Do they, to borrow from Matt Groening, embiggen us?

Because that's what the promise of the net's early days was. That somehow the ability to reach out and connect instantly with anyone anywhere would enlarge the human spirit, not just James Packer's inheritance. Telecom companies show they understand this when they spend elephant bucks on mood advertising, such as Telstra's old 'Memories' ISD commercials, or even One.tel's much less endearing 'tell someone . . .' series. The really cool thing about the net was the way it compressed time and space, an invaluable development for a country like Australia, forever suffering from Blainey's tyranny of distance.

Maybe the explosive growth of connection these last few years has destroyed that sense of closeness which was a defining characteristic of the net's early period, changing it from a village to a global mega-mall forever. But that doesn't mean that people no longer covet the village and its intimacy. People know that cookies, MMF posts, E*trade and Beenz are not cool.

We also know, almost instinctively, that dopey old fishtank cam, coffee pot cam and even vending machine cam, circa 1995, were all infinitely hipper than Dormcam.com at whatever rate per minute it's now charging. We know that most people, when faced with the infinite choice of a billion web pages, will regularly visit only a dozen or so, that they will mostly email the same folks they phone or talk to over a real world coffee. And while it's kind of cool being able to sit in Sydney and hit up Amazon for a Tennessee Williams bio that would otherwise never see the light of day in Australia, it is at best a half-woody proposition, not the full johnson.

The killer app is still out there somewhere. But tracking it down is going to need more than an online site guide to shopping and sex. Is embedded connection, as promised by WAP, likely to be different? Is anyone really going to go insane in the pants because their washing machine can dial up the company home page to download diagnostic software when the whites just aren't as white as they should be? Is digital TV and the home shopping network going to be as good as it gets? I doubt it.

We need ideas greater than that. We need some really cool stuff that will totally embiggen us. And I guarantee one hunnert per cent that whoever thinks it up will be able to buy and sell Bill Gates' worthless monopolising butt.

DAY TRADERS

Maybe we should forget about bear markets and bull markets for a while. Maybe when we're thinking about online day traders we should be thinking about bison markets. Remember? Those huge wandering masses of dopey, cud-chewing herbivores? Their herds would stretch out across the American grasslands, all the way to the horizon. Until some pioneering types hunted them into virtual extinction, of course.

Your average day trader would do well to dwell on the image. They might like to picture themselves as some sort of modern day Daniel Boone, striking out across the e-prairie, hunting down big juicy trades with only their frontier expertise to rely on. But sadly, in the world of real things, they are the prey; isolated, slow-moving, and ill-adapted by evolution to survive in the new environment. For instance, the old steam-driven media made a big hot meal of the Mafia's recently bungled foray into e-commerce, with the FBI taking down dozens of traders, stock brokers, analysts and a whole crooked investment house, a joint venture of two New York crime families.

All five New York families demonstrated their adaptive survival skills by moving from old economy businesses of hijacking, drug running and retailing fanny into the new economic vistas of online stock trading. Like any savvy business, however, they leveraged their real world competitive advantages into the digital realm; bashing the cooperative spirit into those brokers who couldn't see the immediate benefits of working their cold calling routines on behalf of the Mob. The various rackets involved a number of scams but one of the more lucrative was a simple micro-cap hustle. The Mob's tame brokers would cold call thousands of small investors, recommending a buy on some worthless, bottom drawer stock, which Mafia investment houses would then talk up on their web sites and in chat rooms.

But the entrepreneurial verve of the Mob should not have come as a surprise. The legions of small individual investors who have flocked online to try to take a bite out of the big boys have been expertly marked by legions of hotwired grifters for a long time. ASIC has logged dozens of e-scams, and even run a few itself in an attempt to teach the gullible a lesson. The Commission's Millennium Bug Insurance scam 'netted' $4 million from over 200 investors who bought a fake website's claim that blue chip companies would pay heavy premiums to protect themselves from Y2K-related lawsuits. Despite having no information other than the pile of old willies on the website itself, investors clicked away between ten and fifty grand each.

More recently, ASIC posted a warning about an

offshore investment club offering 'international wealth building opportunities normally reserved for the super-rich'. Le Club Prive, which gathered its victims via a spamming campaign, was offering returns of between $500 and $3500 a day. Another scam which has made the jump to spam is the hoary old Nigerian letter rort, now taking the form of an 'Urgent Business Proposal' from a Sir Marthins Ike of Nigeria. Sir Marthins will cut you in for a piece of the action on $50 million worth of missing Nigerian National Petroleum Corporation funds in return for your bank account details.

Of course your average hard-knuckled day trader would dismiss the Nigerian pitch for the load of old cods it is. But would they have seen through the sting in the US which borrowed the MLC's good name to rip off hundreds of thousands of dollars from incautious American investors? They thought they were dealing in legit securities offered by a legit Australian finance company when in fact they were buying vapour stocks from a team of bullshit artists in New Jersey who had no connection with MLC at all.

It wasn't so long ago that the net monsters du jour were paedophiles and bomb throwers. Given the gullibility of most neophyte investors in our rapidly developing 'share owners' democracy, however, it'll probably turn out that the greatest damage to the social fabric is not done by sick pervies or wired-up anarchists but by the old, original sin of greed. Lawful online trading is already a lot riskier than the spruikers for E*trade would have you believe. Punters get caught out by assuming that they are hooked directly into the black engine of the market and that when they click the mouse the deal is done, little realising that their supposedly instant trade is actually made some time after the click, by a licensed broker at the end of the line. Others may get pinged by the technology itself, authorising multiple buy or sell orders by repeatedly clicking because their clunky, overcrowded copper wire connection to a poorly designed online trader doesn't acknowledge their original orders quickly enough.

The old advice still holds—that when your shoeshine boy starts offering stock tips, it's time to get out of the market. Unless you're a Mobbed up dot.con, of course. In which case it's probably time to lay on some hookers and blow.

CYBERBLUDGE

Best damn job I ever had was loading boxes onto trucks in the basement of *Rolling Stone* magazine. Not the best paid of course, and not the easiest. But I loved it because you could disconnect the higher cortex from what you were doing and let it run free while you heaved those heavy bastards onto the flatbed. The guy I worked with back then was one of the last great unskilled survivors of the old economy. Pat, his name was. He'd been a leather worker, a cleaner, a storeman and packer. He'd washed out the brewing vats at Tooheys, loaded trucks with newspapers for a very young Rupert Murdoch, and even tried his hand at a little freelance break and enter—for which he'd received a corrective flogging, he claimed, from the legendary detective Roger Rogerson.

What Pat remembered most fondly about the salad days of his young working life was the sweet and complete impotence of management in the era of full employment. 'If you didn't like the bastard's attitude,' he told me, 'you'd just tell the boss to piss off and you'd find another job. Just like that.'

Of course, those days are over. Even with acute skills shortages in hundreds of emerging job categories, the digital economy doesn't really provide the sort of margin a footloose journeyman can dance around in anymore. Most folks with keyboard jobs are keeping one eye on Nasdaq, praying the whole circus doesn't pack up and split town. The other eye? Well, that's apparently scoping out Ultima Online or doing a little e-shopping at D-store while the bossman's not watching.

Still, I don't see there's much worth getting all hot and bothered over in the recent Red Sheriff report on cyberbludging for software company Lanvision. The Sheriff mashed ABS figures into a couple of surveys of businesses and individuals to generate an average figure of 72 hours a year wasted by each worker drone on the net while the Man was busy elsewhere. The *Sydney Morning Herald*, which reported the findings, served them up with lashings of stern stuff from some bizoid mouthpiece in the Victorian Chamber of Commerce and Industry who made a big hot meal of the instant issue. It's 'a growing problem', apparently, this 72 hours a year.

Dude, get a life. I'd call 72 hours a goddamn triumph of productivity.

What I'd like Red Sheriff to tell me is why millions of put-upon wage slaves aren't blowing off eons more time than that cruising nude celebrity web sites or tourneying to the max on Bungie.net. Because despite quantum leaps in business technology, most folks are still trapped in mindless, soul destroying employment hell from the era of my buddy Pat's heyday. Indeed, globalisation and the quest for the grail of productivity at all costs has made the working lives of millions even more tedious, robotic, insecure and thankless than Pat's time in the vats at Tooheys. At least there they worked with the interesting and ever-present possibility that somebody might tumble into the caustic soda and come out all melted and angry, like that guy in *Robocop*.

Rather than restricting web time, culling email lists and imposing a sort of corporate Net Nanny scheme on their connected staff maybe the anti-fun types from the Victorian Chamber of Commerce and Industry might want to ask themselves why their employees are driven to find a little virtual solace each day. Perhaps they're bored and pissed off. Perhaps their imaginations stretch to more than scratching out an existentially futile subsistence enriching the lives and portfolios of shareholders and upper management. Perhaps, rather than launching an office jihad against those stolen 72 hours, the enlightened employer might even build them into the standard working conditions. A happy drone is a productive drone.

Before the web provided employees with a chance to stick it to the Man online, they were stealing time from him playing Doom across the intranet. Before that it was Solitaire or Asteroids on standalone PCs. Before that they were photocopying their arses and faxing them across town. And before that they were standing around the water cooler wasting time talking about the Fonz and Ritchie's latest adventure. Employees who've never opened a comic book in their lives, let alone trawled through Das Kapital, can still have an instinctive feel for the sharp end of the stick which gets jabbed in their butt when the boss extorts another whole heap of surplus value from their working day. They will always find a way to sneak a little back for themselves.

Deal with it, use it, and get over it.

Bong water

'YOU GUYS AREN'T REALLY COPS, ARE YOU?' HE ASKED. 'SURE,' I SHRUGGED, 'OF COURSE WE ARE.' I PULLED OUT A JOINT TO TOKE UP AND BLOW HIM OFF. 'BAD COPS,' ADDED MCALLISTER, NODDING SAGELY. 'WANNA BUY SOME DOPE?'

THE BUCKET BONG

First, understand the technology. A joint is simple. Just like the rollies Grandad smoked while seeing off Rommel, sort of. Some marijuana chopped up, rolled in between two fag papers and smoked like a cigarette. Note: you must inhale.

A bong is more complicated, usually a home-made device, most often constructed from a plastic fruit-juice bottle, a small length of garden hose and metallic or aluminium-foil-based cone.

A bucket bong is something else again. It is to the simple bong as the cruise missile is to the snide remark. Smoke is collected inside a bottomless plastic bottle, which is then pushed down into a bucket of water, forcing the smoke up through the top of the bottle into the user's mouth.

Now, understand the context. Research by the National Campaign Against Drug Abuse indicates that five million Australians have smoked marijuana. One million regulars smoke 120 000 kilograms a year. If all of this were rolled into one joint it would be so much bigger than the biggest joint you have ever seen that you would need to smoke two really big joints just to deal with the concept of its incredible bigness. Only a small percentage of the marijuana for this megajoint would be imported. Marijuana is the country's second largest cash crop. It is an Australian success story.

Laws vary greatly across the country. In South Australia and the ACT, possession of small amounts for personal use is not a crime. In Queensland, possession of an Orchy bottle can be.

Finally, understand the subject. Marijuana has as many different grades and effects as it has names. The poorest smoke will encourage you to watch daytime TV and wish that your flatmate would walk to the corner shop for another packet of Tim Tams. The best smoke will peel your head like a fat Bondi orange, pour rainbows through your eyes, punch out the seven veils of conciousness separating this world from the next and make you wish your flatmate would walk to the corner shop for another packet of Tim Tams.

Across the nation, marijuana is one of our largest subcultures. The term 'subculture' may strike a false note, but while smoking the gear remains punishable by imprisonment it must remain a subculture, even if a huge, popular and readily accessible one.

Elements of the culture, the language, the implements and the product itself are readily transferable. But at the level of attitude and ritual, differences are becoming manifest and resistant to transfer. These differences are finding material expression in the technology.

Consider the bucket bong. It appears to have originated in the early to mid-1980s on campuses in Queensland. It is now very popular in the north, but much less so south of the Tweed. The bucket bong is a complicated arrangement, not lending itself to quiet reflective smoking, not easily dismantled in times of crisis—*Open up, Birmingham, we have a warrant*—and not very dignified. Punters sit on the floor and take turns at plunging their heads into a bucket of water while sucking on a very large plastic bottle. It is a sharing experience.

The bucket bong encourages excess. This is called putting the boot in.

Because smoke can be held in the cooling chamber of the bottle indefinitely, there is none of the discomfort associated with sucking straight from the burning leaves of a joint or a simple bong. (In the latter, smoke does pass through water to cool it down, but it is a fleeting visit.) While the smoke cools, the lungs can be emptied of air at leisure. As much more smoke can then be pushed in and held for so much longer, the bucket has a reputation for turning the most bogus leaf into killer weed.

There is a wealth of ritual attendant upon the bucket bong. In Queensland it is not enough to sit around all night going down on a bucket. There is good form and bad. At a party a 'green room' will be set aside; not the lounge room, for that is usually near the front of the house and accessible to the wallopers when they call in about the shopping trolley races and the 6000-watt stereo. Bedrooms or enclosed sleepouts at the rear of the house are preferred. Punters sit in a circle, usually on the floor. Anybody can join by sitting down but it is considered bad form to drop right in front of the bucket and wrap your slobbering chops around the bottle neck. A punter of refinement will sit where the bucket has just passed and await their turn. Turns run counter-clockwise. The host of the party packs the cone and instructs any neophyte punters on the finer points of bucket use, gently guiding them through if need be. The supplier of the weed sits to the left of the host, the position of honour, as it ensures they get first suck.

It is okay to foul up. It is not okay to laugh at those who foul up. It is okay to become a stupid giggling puddle on the floor so long as you don't ruin anyone's concentration. It is okay to comment on the quality of the stone. Indeed if it is an outstanding stone it is good manners to say so.

On my first encounter with the bucket, I had eight goes by mistake. I fell into a plastic wading pool and remained there until late in the evening. Soon after this I became involved with a plot to procure a very large amount of smoke for a Bucketfest. A minibus full of people clutching money and drugs arrived in the afternoon to pick me up. It went around Brisbane collecting supplies and punters. Brisbane, of course, is the worse place in Australia to do this.

But this was regarded as an excellent adventure and a very cool way to waste one's youth.

Perth and Brisbane took to the bucket bong as though the want of it had lain within them like a disease. Sydney and

Melbourne did not. The tyranny of distance cannot explain the failure of buckets to take hold in Sydney and Melbourne, for they have leapt directly across the continent to Perth.

Why would such a difficult technology, one not at all amenable to stealth, subterfuge and a fast getaway, find ready acceptance in the repressive environment of Queensland but not with their bohemian cousins south of the Rio Grande? Why should Queenslanders be clutched by the Fear when they cross the border, yet fire up a cone beyond the reach of anti-drug paranoia in their home state? Why do Adelaide punters enjoy smoking more in Sydney than in their liberal home town? Why don't Melburnians giggle?

Interviewed for this article, Harry Stringer, who was raised in Brisbane, moved to Melbourne and has made a film about a fridge which eats people, said this: 'The difference between Melbourne and Brisbane smokers is that Melburnians have cruise control. Brisbane dopers often crash the bus.'

Crashing the bus is the metaphorical equivalent of pulling eight buckets, falling into a wading pool and being unable to escape for a whole day.

'In Brisbane, crashing the bus is fairly common,' said Mr Stringer. 'The town has a loser mentality. In Brisbane, we really don't believe that we're up to much, therefore crashing the bus is something we can accept in ourselves. A lot of Brisbane's humour is self-deprecating, something I have never heard of in Melbourne.

'The important thing is not to be seen to be stoned.

It robs you of your cred, and cred is the only thing Melbourne, and Sydney for that matter, understand.'

This may explain why my attempts to introduce Sydney to the benefits of the bucket have been greeted with polite bemusement.

A vast body of scientific and pop-psych literature has grown up around the drug culture. A tag has been penned for research purposes: ethnopharmacology. And ethno-pharmacologists agree that the context or the setting of a drug experience is more important than the drug itself. To support and make safe the use of any drug in any society, a body of ritual grows to control the experience.

Generally, the more powerful a drug is, the more complex and demanding are the rituals around it. Alcohol requires company and context. The most powerful drugs, the hallucinogens, are marked everywhere by a high degree of ritualisation. The first time someone uses acid they are usually guided into and through the trip by someone else who has much more experience with the drug, much as the Navajo are led by the medicine man who sings them into the peyote trance and interprets the visions afterwards.

Dope, which is not all that scary in its effects, does not generally require ritual where it is freely available. But where it is made powerful and scary by illegality and hysteria, it is surrounded by strong ritual. In Queensland the tribal nature of the bucket, the rules and etiquette, shape the experience and reduce the fear, making it fun.

Outside of that context the poor Queenslander stands naked and alone, facing a lifetime of learned paranoia and fear. The southerner approaches the joint like a vodka martini or imported beer, an opportunity to swan about and show off one's incredible James Bond veneer. By the time we get to Adelaide, the marijuana experience has all the rakish appeal of a warm can of KB lite.

Lesson ended.

Now, whose turn is it to get the Tim Tams?

LEMMING STAMPEDE

Armageddon is coming! Bring your surfboard!

It was all supposed to go down in September of '99. The end of the world, the Tribulation, the Great Water Baptism, the unveiling of the Antichrist. They were all pencilled for September by legions of web-enabled prophets, nutjobs and fundamentalist tax evaders. Somewhat awkwardly for millions of anxious, glassy-eyed apocalypse buffs, however, the month slipped by without so much as a minor planetary collision. Even the much anticipated mini-millenium bug, the glitch associated with the date 9/9/99, passed without any airline, stock market or power grid crashes. The only big news was the slaughter in East Timor, but unfortunately none of the A-List doomsayers like Jack Van Impe, Marilyn Agee, Nancy the Zeta Emissary or Australia's own Little Pebble had thought to work that cataclysm into their predictions, despite ample forewarning that rivers of blood would flow in the province. The latter day Nostradami, it seems, were no better prepared than the Foreign Affairs Department in Canberra.

Still, thousands of years of kooky, wrong-headed predications of doom have not even marginally dampened our enthusiasm for kooky, wrong-headed predictions of doom. Most of the hundreds of web sites predicting heavy 'end-time' scenarios for September were kicking out new and revised agendas within a few days of the Antichrist's inconsiderate piking out. While the details vary according to the delusions of the individual visionary, there are a few bedrock presumptions underlying almost all millenarian doomsayers.

Firstly, the end of the millennium will mark the end of the world as we know it. For the righteous Christian this is not to be feared but anticipated with glee. An event known as the Rapture will see millions of the worthy teleported off the planet in the wink of an eye. God, who has apparently become increasingly ticked off with his wayward flock, will finally throw up his hands in disgust, beam up the pious, and leave the rest of us to sort out our own mess. Naturally, chaos will ensue. Clean living, God-fearing airline pilots will simply vanish from the cockpits while their fully laden passenger jets are cruising at thirty-one thousand feet. Trays full of food carried by prayerful waitresses will clatter wastefully to restaurant floors all over the world. The guitars of Christian rock bands will suddenly clatter onto the stage in a whine of feedback a split second after their sanctimonious owners disappear—although, of course, the audience won't get to applaud, having been snatched up themselves at the same time. Fires will break out as millions of the toasters of the faithful are left unattended. Fred Nile's phone will just ring and ring and ring. And traffic will pile up in massive, catastrophic snarls as the devout occupants of those cars with stylised Christian 'fish' stickers on the bumper wink out of existence while their vehicles hurtle along the freeway at a hundred kilometres an hour.

Some thoughtful Christians have taken to displaying bumper stickers warning fellow motorists that their car will suddenly become uncontrolled during the Rapture. Less Godly types have replied with stickers saying: When the Rapture comes, can I have your stuff?

But don't imagine that those of us left behind are going to be allowed to party like it's 1999 when we suddenly realise that every unctuous, pointyheaded anti-fun type on the planet has suddenly gone missing, because after the Rapture comes the Tribulation. Once again details vary, but you are basically looking at seven years of heavy tunes: plague, pestilence, famine, war and nuclear confrontation in the Middle East, all reigned over by the Antichrist— either Bill Clinton or Prince Charles. At the end of the seven years, Jesus is scheduled to return to Earth and establish a thousand-year reign.

That's pretty much it as far as general principles go amongst the end-of-the-world crowd. Beyond the Rapture and the Tribulation, both prescribed in the Bible, details become a little hazy. It is, of course, a Christian apocalypse, with billions of Muslims, Buddhists and Hindus resolutely refusing to get on board. There may be a shortage of cheap tofu burgers and saffron-clad bald men around, however, as Sree Vishiva Karma Veera Narayana Murthy, an avatar of Krishna, is a righteous certainty for a soon to be established 108-year reign of dharma, after the required period of chaos, of course: 'a rain of blood in towns and villages, circulation of poor quality coins, [and] the appearance of male goats and oxen with mammary glands that can be milked.'

Fans of Nostradamus, a heavy hitter in the apocalypse stakes, read in his work a prophecy of death from the skies around about now. With the recent popularity of comet impact movies like Bruce Willis' *Armageddon*, it's no surprise that the preferred form of terror from above is usually a rogue asteroid, although more adventurous types have also opted for planetary alignments resulting in massive distortions to the space–time continuum.

Futurologist Edgar Cayce believes 'a cosmic storm . . . with winds of 1000 miles per hour and tremendous swings in temperature' will hit the Earth some time soon. Archaeologist Richard W. Noone's book, *5/5/2000*: *Ice, the Ultimate Disaster*, predicts that the imminent alignment of Mercury, Venus, Earth, Mars, Jupiter and Saturn 'will cause total devastation. Ice build-up at the South Pole will upset the world's axis, sending trillions of tons of ice and water sweeping over the planet.'

Russian 'scientist' Vladimir Sobolyov thinks the planet will simply keel over on its axis, tilting about thirty degrees and drowning Great Britain. Luckily, Sobolyov says aliens will save the rest of us. They are already here, but in hiding. Writes Vladimir, 'If we completely believed in them, we would get lazy. So they are clever. They stay hidden in the fourth dimension and only show themselves from time to time.'

The alien motif recurs through a great deal of current apocalyptic thought. Orville T. Gordon, alias Nodrog, is the leader of the Texas-based Outer Dimensional Forces, which are waiting to hitch a ride with some UFOs just before they destroy the US with a biblical flood. The Nuwaubians of the Holy Tabernacle Ministries or Ancient Mystical Order of Melchizedek fully expect Noone's planetary alignment to cause a 'star holocaust', dragging all of the planets into the sun. First prize, however, goes to Nancy, Earthly Emissary of the Zetas, who warns of an approaching comet, last seen around these parts 3657 years ago. When the Earth passes through the comet's tail it will stop turning for a few days. The upper atmosphere will be rent by 'gigantic lightning bolts' and massively violent winds. Petrochemicals will form in the air over Europe, ignite, and rain down as a firestorm. As the Earth's magnetic core begins to align itself with the comet's, there follows 'a pole shift with continental rip and sinking and rising land.' Kilometre-high tsunamis will roar ashore as tectonic plates shift and the Atlantic floor sinks.

Sounds cool.

The good news is that Australia, or at least the eastern seaboard, is one of the best places to ride out this catastrophe. Nancy the Emissary's well-organised web site, with many helpful hints for avoiding personal annihilation, assures us that most of the western half of the continent 'will go suddenly under water' as the plate it shares with India slides under the Himalayas. But the rest of the land mass will actually rise a little. Around Perth, writes Nancy, it will seem, 'as though a tidal wave were steadily moving inland, and where the crest of the wave will not at first be high, the waters will just keep rising until all not afloat are drowned. Those in boats may survive, though there is risk of capsizing, and they will find themselves out at sea and in the washing about that will occur afterwards.' Far-sighted surfers who can pick the right spot in the line-up have a shot at a world record 1400 kilometre-long ride. There is no information yet on whether this wave will break left or right.

It is difficult to gauge just how widespread is millennial nuttiness. It has a vast audience in the United States, and a spiritual home on the web, where anybody with a cheap internet account can put themselves about as the new Nostradamus to a global audience. The complete disconnection from reality suffered by many of these fevered sages is demonstrated by the fact that they aren't even seeking donations, simply offering advice on how to avoid material and spiritual extinction.

The mainstream Christian churches, especially the Catholic Church, are all slightly embarrassed by the frenzy, much of which has its roots in early Christian eschatology, or the doctrine of 'end-times'. The books of Daniel and Ezekiel in the Old Testament, and the book of Revelation in the New, provide the bedrock canon for most of the apocalyptic cults. However, Nancy, Doc Sobolyov and Orville T. Gordon's Outer Dimensional Forces are not without some mainstream support. Some Seventh Day Adventists and a fair swag of Mormons are quietly hunkering down to await the Second Coming. And of course one Adventist splinter group, David Koresh's Branch Davidians, has already perished in the fires of its own end-time.

Koresh thought himself a figure from Revelation, the Seventh Angel, come to announce the Kingdom of God. For people like the Davidians, who feel themselves oppressed, who think that time is running out, Revelation has an irresistible magnetic force. Vivid, confused and garishly violent, it is perfect for identifying friend and foe, good and evil. Its powerful hold over the imagination of millions of true believers is providing an exciting subplot for public order officials already struggling to manage the millennium bug and the biggest party in the history of humanity. Israel has expelled a number of US Concerned Christians accused of planning to bring on the Second Coming with a series of massacres in the Holy Land before 1 January 2000. The main psychiatric hospital in Jerusalem has a whole new wing ready for an influx of intensely distressed and potentially violent fundamentalist Christians who wake up on New Year's Day to discover that God has not beamed them up to the starship Rapture. And Richard Landes, from Boston University's eminently respectable, completely non-nutty Centre for Millennial Studies, is warning of thousands of groups simply exploding under the pressure.

Besides the Davidians, a number of high-profile end-timers have already checked out. In 1997 the Heaven's Gate cultists in California took poison and teleported up to a space ship they knew was hiding behind the Hale-Bopp comet, leaving their corporeal bodies behind to rot in a sterile mansion. Japan's Aum Shinri Kyo preferred to let others lead the way, unleashing sarin gas in the Tokyo subway system in 1995. Ugandan police have broken up a millennial cult which went on a rampage of theft and rape, presumably because with the end so near there was no reason not to misbehave. And one Russian prophet is threatening to unleash a deadly virus if the world refuses to sign up for his vision of a 'City in the Sun' in Siberia.

Most of these guys will either implode when the end turns out not to be nigh, or will simply redraw their calendars, pushing the millennium back to 2001 or 2033, the anniversary of the Crucifixion. Failed prophecy has a long and noble history. At any point in time there are plenty of doom traders offering tickets to time's imminent end. Perhaps the example of Margaret Rowan might reassure the nervous reader.

In February 1925, Margaret announced the Angel Gabriel had appeared to her in Los Angeles to warn that the end was nigh—due on Friday the 13th, to be precise. Robert Reidt, a house painter from Long Island, took both Gabriel and Margaret at their word and spent his life savings purchasing billboard space to advertise a hilltop vigil to see out the Apocalypse. Come the 13th the hill was swarming with believers, many of them dressed in vaguely biblical bed sheets. As the clock struck twelve they fell to their knees, raised their arms to heaven and cried to God. Five or ten minutes passed without so much as a rain of toads. The crowd grew restless, until assured that since Gabriel had appeared in LA, his prophecy must have been logged in for midnight 'Pacific time'. Mollified, the throng waited until three in the morning. Again, nothing. The disappointed believers went home. When reporters mischievously asked Reidt what had happened he could only shout at them that they had 'scared Gabriel away with their Satanic flashbulbs'.

THE BIG SMOKE

It was about 11 o'clock in the morning, late April, with the sun not shining and a look of hard cold rain in the darkness of the hills around Nimbin. I was wearing Blundstones, black jeans, an old flanno shirt and an army jacket. I was tired, dirty, unshaven and wired and I did not care who knew it. I was calling on a million dollar cannabis harvest.

The vaguely-credentialled McAllister occupied the driver's seat of our cast-iron Lada. A fantastic rippling world of valleys and peaks swept by as he ripped the little Russian farm vehicle through kilometres of narrow, deadly pot-holed curves. Until recently this landscape had held, folded within its vastness, cannabis plantations of all sorts and sizes; huge commercial crops planted by syndicate interests from the metro centres alongside hundreds of smaller concerns, scattered all the way through the Tweed Valley and up into the ranges of northern NSW. Some were personal stashes, as small as two or three plants.

Others were big enough to return an average wage for the year. *If* the weather held good and the black rot did not set in. *If* thieves did not rip the lot off. And *if* the police choppers did not come roaring over the ridge one day, all hot guns and muscle. One raid this year they even painted a big skull and crossbones on their bird, which dropped out of the sky like Robert Duvall in *Apocalypse Now*.

This is the sort of thing which guarantees that fear runs through the ground around Nimbin at a constant low wattage, making everyone testy and suspicious and liable to jump at shadows. Especially during the harvest festival. A dope conference, mardi gras, growers' cup and annual harvest ball are a lay-down to bring the freaks out of the hills for kilometres around. And on their heels the media, the cops and the curious.

We drove into the paranoia as the Lada hauled around the final bend and an old butter factory, now a Nimbin village meeting place, swung into view. A hundred people sat outside, colourful and weird even from a distance. Hippies and crusties and the occasional misplaced suburban spider-person drifted about on rich clouds of ganja smoke. None of the timid forest friends approached us, however. Most careened off at right angles when they saw us coming.

Before driving down, I had asked Jiggens, a Brisbane HEMP (Help End Marijuana Prohibition) rep if the locals would mind us blowing in and covering their festival. Jiggens did not know. He said Nimbin was a place where total acceptance and total paranoia meshed easily together. The Aquarian generation still clung to the shreds of their cherished freedoms, but were unable to cope with their kids dealing smack from the dunnies near the hotel. The vision of two seedy-looking thugs loaded down with surveillance and communications gear tipped the balance in favour of free-falling anxiety.

'This is serious, Pete,' I muttered. 'We got to establish some cred here or people are going to be taking us for cops.'

'You guys aren't cops or something, are you?' a sluggish voice asked from behind us.

We turned to confront a middle-aged man with long, stringy hair, no shoes and a pot belly poking out of an old army shirt. 'There's cops everywhere,' he said.

'We're journalists,' I answered, which only cranked him up. We discovered later that the drug squad or the DEA or some other state sponsored desperados had been in town a month earlier to spy on a law-reform demo outside the police station. At the time, the local police were having no part of it. They buttoned up the station and refused to come out and deal with the protesters, who waved stalks of marijuana in their faces. The undercover types were less coy. They spooked around the fringes of the action with camcorders and rifle mikes. When David Heilpern, a local solicitor, asked them what they were doing, they said: *We're journalists*; and when he asked where from, they said: *Pacific Productions*; and when he asked who the hell's that, they said: *Fuck off*. We now stood confronted with the outcome of their handiwork; a barefoot hippy loon about to go suborbital on fear.

The scene was short circuited by the appearance of a

conference organiser who took us to the press desk. Here at last was someone who understood the media. Taped to the back of our little red press passes were a couple of big fat spliffs packed tight with the season's finest. In the interests of fitting in, we pocketed the joints and asked for more.

The courtesy spliffs came as harbingers of a basic shift in the cannabis debate. While Nimbin was overrun with a primitive cabal of freaks and hippies, the real action was being run by straight and connected players from politics, medicine and academia. Major luminaries included Paul Wilson, the ubiquitous criminologist professor; Dr Alex Wodak, director of alcohol and drug services at St Vincent's Hospital in Sydney; and Tina Van Raay, secretary of the Australian parliamentary group for drug law reform.

Wilson, long an advocate of decriminalisation, had a road-to-Damascus experience during the conference and haltingly came out as a proponent of legalisation. 'The current prohibition has backfired,' he told a hall full of cheering stone-heads. 'I think it's just bloody madness, putting it bluntly, to have these laws which are utterly failing and which are in fact creating more crime . . . I'm still debating this in myself but there may be an argument for controlled availability.'

Wodak agreed that decriminalisation is inherently unstable but said it is at least a starting point. 'Having a system that is illogical and knowing it is going to collapse is better than having [the existing] system which is indefensible from every point of view,' he said before lecturing the hall full of perplexed stone-heads on the Protestant ethic and law reform.

'If you want something, you've got to work for it and cannabis drug law reform is no different,' he said. 'You've got to get allies from all quarters of the community. It's no good just looking at atypical areas like northern NSW. We have got to put arguments to different groups in the community just as niche marketers sell toothpaste to different kinds of consumers.'

It was music for the audience, even if they had trouble with the more involved arguments, what with their short-term memories being shot to hell by that stage of the afternoon. It was also news. The cannabis debate in Australia has been left, for the most part, to the sort of people who made up the audience rather than the panel on that day. It has usually revolved around the more politically-saleable notion of decriminalisation rather than legalisation. The change of both fronts is, as Wilson described it, a clear break with past models. But when the discussion was thrown open to the floor, the disconnection between the new marijuana movement and the old became obvious. The panel sat nonplussed through the first question:

I heard about a guy in Melbourne that . . . I think it was Melbourne . . . but you know . . . uhm . . . if we said we were Rastafarians could we . . . you know it would be a religion then and could we smoke it . . . religiously?

They grimaced through the second, delivered by a dope-addled Christian whose eyes ran in separate orbits and who rambled on about Jesus in the herb before focussing on the obscure dangers of prohibition:

This, uhm, guy who . . . came to my house . . . he was going to kill me . . . yeah had a gun too . . . and he was . . . so I thought whooooah! . . . and we had a smoke . . . I blew him out and after . . . well you know I said like you don't have to kill me now man . . . and he didn't . . . uhm . . . but that guy he was the backpacker killer! . . . at least . . . uhm . . .

Or something like that. David Heilpern ushered him gently away from the mike. A local woman asked how much it cost to run a helicopter. She said the police could not possibly be making enough money from raiding people's stashes to keep flying their choppers. Somebody announced there were cops in the audience posing as journalists and all eyes turned on us. As the meeting broke up, the same barefoot man who had fronted us that morning appeared at my elbow again.

'You guys aren't really cops, are you?' he asked.

'Sure,' I shrugged, 'of course we are.' I pulled out a joint to toke up and blow him off.

'Bad cops,' added McAllister, nodding sagely. 'Wanna buy some dope?'

We had a plan for the afternoon, but it disappeared in a ball of flame and smoke. The organisers had promised to connect us with some big-time growers—one of whom had largely bankrolled the conference. There were hints of late-night meetings in mountain-top retreats where we would glide about in dinner jackets, sipping dry martinis and swapping even drier *bons mots* with the captains of the industry. Sadly, in winning over the suspicious freaks and hippies, we ended up about eight joints into the wind, missed the connection and spent the rest of the night looking for Mr Spliffs, the organiser rumoured to have a one-kilo courtesy stash in the boot of his car. With night-fall, a freezing mist descended, throwing a fantastic shroud over the village. Hundreds of bizarre, mediaeval creatures shuffled through soft coruscated globes of light cast by the street lamps. They were only vaguely illuminated but easily traced by the glowing embers of joints and cigarettes which attended them like tiny burning angels. A crowd thickened up around the town hall, the venue of the Harvest Ball. We moved easily through the pink feather wigs, the jester caps, the bearded witch-hatted flute players and their children— third-generation hippy hill people, kids in cast-offs and headbands of leaves and twigs. Apache girls toted peace pipes and Zulu spears, with rings through their faces, heavy Celtic runes smudged around their eyes like masks, and pigeon feathers in their hair.

Inside there was little room to move until local rappers took to the stage and the audience erupted in a weird fusion of modern dance and hippy shuffling. Here and there, crop circles of open space stood out and we moved gratefully toward them, only to find children sleeping under piles of blankets on the floor while their parents boogie-stomped around them. A HEMP activist told me a lot of these kids dream of becoming Westpac clerks in Lismore.

Finding no sign of Mr Spliffs, his car or our connection to the growers, we finally retreated to the motel. It was left-handed luck in its own way. Through missing the growers that night, we were forced to attend a small but historic moment in the morning, the first press conference run by the marijuana industry.

We never actually saw them, although their voices were recognisable. (Just before the conference, one said to me: 'I've got to go to the growers' press conference now . . . oh, whoops!') A dozen or so journalists crowded into the stair-well of a recording studio at the back of the butter factory while Bob and Carol and Co. were hidden away in a booth.

Between the four of them, they have been growing for 64 years but each still has a day job. The fickle nature of the industry demands an alternative income. Bob, for instance, has had 70 per cent of his crop ripped off this year, Ted has lost none. All four became growers because as smokers they could not afford the prices being asked. Now they sell mainly through friendship networks. The price varies from nothing—you give away a lot, says Bob—to about $300 to $400 for 25 grams.

The big consumers of the Nimbin crop are friends of the growers from Brisbane and Sydney. 'They make the pilgrimage each year and I might add they are absolutely delighted that they know someone they can get it from,' said Ted. A lot of the crop is also traded locally for work or, indeed, for anything that can be bartered. 'It works because not everyone can grow their own,' said Carol. 'It's a great benefit for a small community to be able to do that.'

Ted, who came from an agricultural background, dis-covered that tending the weed was a lot more interesting and challenging than standard cash crops. 'Most other farming is boring compared to marijuana,' he said. 'It's a very complex plant.'

Carol described it as engrossing. 'I got into growing dope through a love of the drug and I continued because I love the plant,' she said. 'I no longer smoke but I love to grow. For a weed, marijuana is really involved. Each plant is different. Even if you have the same seed strain, they all put out different heads in the long run and they all have different smells and taste depending on what they've been crossed with. Smelling a fresh head in the morning is as good as flowers. If you could bottle it you'd have a million dollar perfume.'

Even so, there will be years when you make nothing. 'You can get ripped off or busted at any point in this enterprise,' said Carol. 'You're never safe. You don't want to be too successful. In a small community like this, there is jealousy. If you make a lot of money you are going to get busted. You're going to be a target for the thieves who make a better living than most growers. They tend to concentrate around the communes. I met two guys in Melbourne a couple of years ago, that's all they did for a living.'

Alice also intimated that the hassles are not worth a million bucks. On a slope not far from her place, there is only one woman to look after a 'ravaging pack of teenagers' because every father from the communal group is in jail. 'This happens around here,' she said. 'I would love it to be legal because I would still be able to grow for my own pleasure and we would not have our children growing up with the paranoia. When I first came here a really long time ago, I really believed it would be legal in ten years at the outside. It's still ten years away and I just can't wait for that day. I believe the vast majority of growers just want that day because there will finally be peace and security in our lives.'

Yet they know that if the plant was legalised they would be quickly squeezed out of the market by the cigarette companies. 'They'd have the capital and they'll get the licenses,' said Carol. 'On a purely pragmatic level, I don't think we'd get a look in. I'd love to see it as a cottage industry but my criminal record would wipe me out.'

An extensive black-industry structure already exists: an organisation in Amsterdam collects strains from Afghanistan, Siberia, Hawaii, all over. 'You can buy a catalogue from Amsterdam with about 25 different strains,' said Bob. 'They actually market them over there. You go over, bring them back and cross them with the local varieties.'

Such a hybrid won the growers' cup this year. For the connoisseurs, it was a Thai-Afghan cross from western NSW, producing a tightly packed 30 centimetre bud about the size of a twenty-cent piece across. It had a light-green colour, strong aroma and was sticky to the touch. The stone was described as intense, uplifting and funny.

'Some people are such craftspeople,' said Alice. 'They just grow really excellent dope.'

SCIENTOLOGY

Grow hair. Meet Tom. Battle evil from across the stars. What The Church of Scientology can do for you!

The colours. That's what I noticed first. The striking bright blue carpet. The violent slashes of orange and yellow on the covers of hundreds of books. The photograph of Tom Cruise posed against a bright red backdrop. Then I noticed the volcanoes. Volcanoes everywhere. Exploding on the boxes of do-it-yourself mental health kits. Erupting on the cover of *Dianetics*, the bible of Scientology. They'd even built a giant electric volcano just down from Planet Hollywood in Sydney, perhaps hoping to nab a stray movie star emerging from a premiere or out for a quiet nosh-up. After the lonely-hearted and the deranged, media superstars are the Church of Scientology's favourite targets. John Travolta, Tom Cruise and Charles Manson. They've all been there. Although only Manson has had the good sense to let his membership lapse.

Superstars are generally recruited by other stars. Rank punters are more often dragged in off the street for a free 'personality test' after being bailed up by some loser with a clipboard, usually near a pedestrian crossing. Anxious Matthew, a thin, pimpled teenager, was my clipboard guy. He asked what I most wanted in the world. Scientology street sweepers ask thousands of people the same thing every day, and most folks very wisely reply, 'To avoid entanglement with loonies like you.'

But I rambled softly to myself, 'Oh you know, to lose some weight, regain some hair, overcome my morbid fear of enemas . . .'

Matthew was a little rattled. Probably still recovering from Steve Le Marquand, an actor I'd hired as wingman on this caper. Matthew had asked him, 'If you could be anything in the world what would that be?' And Steve— an intense character with knives in his eyes and a deeply menacing air—had twitched a lot, stared threateningly into Matthew's left pupil and said he wanted to be successful 'at being the most famous person ever'.

When I followed him in a few minutes later it was like walking into a room full of Daleks trying to cope with Daffy Duck on amphetamines. They weren't squawking 'Exterminate!' and firing their death rays yet but you could see the odds were shortening. Steve was fidgeting, flicking his pencil away, glaring at everyone, asking how many famous actors were in the Church. Was Kate Ceberano coming in today? Could he talk to her? Was there a place in the States he could meet Tom and Nicole? Was there any chance they'd be dropping by later?

They gave him a cigarette and a personality test just to shut him up.

We did our tests at the same time. Two hundred questions like: Do you often sing or whistle just for the fun of it? Are you a slow eater? Do some noises set your teeth on edge? Forget the answers. The result never varies. You need help. Lots of it. Costing hundreds of thousands of dollars. I was a cold, snappy loner who couldn't commit to relationships. A sad overweight blonde girl who came in just before us was . . . well, ripe for the picking I guess.

'I want you to buy this book, John. *Dianetics* can really help you,' said Greta, my 'analyst', who managed the neat trick of appearing completely self-assured and completely vacant, all at the same time. *Dianetics*, I noted as she thrust it at me, comes wrapped in plastic, just like Laura Palmer in *Twin Peaks*. In both cases the wrapping serves to hide a horrible secret. A murder in the TV series. A load of old willies in the book. As a marketing ploy, however, it works. *Dianetics* has sold squillions of copies. Pretty good for six hundred pages of demented gibberish, the sort of thing a thousand monkeys sitting at a thousand typewriters are much more likely to knock up than *Hamlet*, especially if you spike their bananas with terrible drugs. Unfortunately the plastic wrapping stops you from discovering this fact until you've handed over the folding stuff.

I was so busy getting hammered about my many faults that I forgot to ask about the ubiquitous volcano. But if you stay with Scientology, they eventually explain that about 75 million years ago some villain called Xenu, who ruled a bunch of planets, flew the entire population to Earth and dropped them into volcanoes, which were then blown up with hydrogen bombs. Problem was, these guys had indestructible souls, or 'thetans', which had to be rounded up, a bit like in *Ghostbusters*. But the thetans got out, just like in the movie. They took over our bodies, just like Sigourney Weaver's, and now you have to rid yourself of unseemly thetans with a strict course of *Dianetics* and about half a million dollars. Cash, cheque or credit.

Unless you're Steve, of course. When they tapped his results into the computer it started to smoke and spray sparks everywhere. They didn't even try to make him buy the book, just hustled him out of there before he carved X's on their foreheads. I guess even *Dianetics* can't help some people.

A CHRISTMAS TALE

Peter Reith's phonecard wasn't lifted by some sticky-fingered hotel receptionist. Or dangled in front of a winsome Adelaide gel by some dumpy oaf looking to leverage a bit of raunchy business. It wasn't trousered by a golfing buddy of Prime Minister Mahathir Mohammed. Or farmed out across the internet to every impecunious Asian student in Australia.

No.

I know exactly what happened to that card and can account for nearly every dollar of that bill because just before Christmas of 1997 a guy named Loody, a half-blind, one-legged pimp dressed as Santa, stole Peter Reith's telecard off me. I had taken it in lieu of a drug debt from a bunch of North Shore private school kids who were living large on Reithy's tick at Schoolies Week. And they had simply lifted it during a tour of Parliament House the month before.

He's a generous soul, old Reithy, you know. Benevolent

and selfless to a fault. And what was he supposed to do when fronted by one of these snotty, blazer-clad Charlies outside the Parliamentary Dining Hall, sniffling and tugging at a forelock, mumbling, 'God bless, kind sir, but I've lost me lunch money. Could you spare a few coppers for an 'ungry urchin. Me old dad was ruined by Mistah Keatin', 'e was, and I've been turned out of doors to support me only survivin' muvver.'

Well, old Reithy's eyes fair welled up, they did, and before you could blink away the tears he's whipped out his roll and peeled off a generous wad of redbacks. So shaken was he by the young rogue's fabricated predicament he didn't notice his pristine telecard fall to the floor. Phone card, PIN, everything still in the shrinkwrap. Nor did he attend to the sharp-eyed villain's placing one Bata Scout over the card while deftly dropping a pencil, thereby to retrieve it. To be sure, if there was an innocent victim in all of this it was poor old Peter Reith. I'd just like to make that clear.

And how did I come to involve myself in the imbroglio? Well, as sometimes happens I found myself embarrassed by a funding shortfall at exactly the moment a hard-hearted financial institution decided to restructure my debt burden in a gruesomely onerous fashion. I tell you, farmers and small business aren't the only ones doing it tough out there. If you think the banks are a bunch of vicious, Devil-worshipping greedheads . . . well, you're right. But they're pussycats compared to Anxious Stan, my fat Russian bookie. So the second week of December, at the fag end of Schoolies, I was reduced to retailing bags of parsley to idiot teenagers in Cavill Mall, Surfers Paradise.

And I wasn't the only one.

My old confrere 'Fingers' was trawling the Casino for gullible, cashed-up youngsters to invest a little beer money in a crash course from his 'University-accredited' card counting school.

'Son, in a globalised economy you can't just plan for your future. You got to seize it every day,' he'd say, slipping an arm around some hopelessly plastered spotty oik while fanning an original pack of 1967 Playboy Playmate Cards in front of him. 'And nothing guarantees a man's future like an intimate familiarity with fifty-two of my closest friends here . . . Plus, chicks really go for a smart shuffling dude.'

Fingers never did explain exactly why a woman would go for a balding con man with a chronic urinary tract infection, sustained after he refused to leave a table at Crown for eighteen hours because the deck was surely just about to run hot. But that's the beauty of Schoolies Week. The young and the restless attend in their thousands for plucking by the old and disgraceful.

Loody, for instance. Couple of years back he scaled the peaks of a personal big rock candy mountain by mugging a David Jones store Santa. Loody cold-cocked our man Kringle with his detachable wooden leg and made off with a sackful of toys previously destined for a kiddies hospital, legging it, so to speak, with Santa's jolly red outfit for good measure. He figured that even a horrible one-eyed hop-along Loody Claus was less likely to draw the rozzers' attention if tricked out in a genuine Santa suit with his ugly cyclopean visage partly hidden by a false beard and his bloodstained peg leg conveniently tucked away in a big black boot. Bizarrely enough, it worked, and Loody celebrated with a four-day bender, waking up a thousand miles north, in the midst of a roaring, bacchanalian pool party where a lot of teenaged girls pressed wine coolers and flu tablets on him instead of just running away, screaming, like normal.

So by the good grace of the Great Pumpkin, Loody too had found himself at Schoolies Week, where the pickings were rich enough to keep him out of fast food dumpsters right through the festive season. (Testimony to just how easy those picking are, given that Loody was reduced to one leg during a bank robbery where he first lost his glass eyeball when smacked upside the head by an angry lesbian who thought he was staring at her. He was then slammed against the roof by a security screen, activated while he was standing on the counter, distracted from the business of robbery by demanding an armed, plain clothes police officer fetch his eyeball from where it had rolled under a nearby desk.)

I guess I wouldn't have come across him, and Peter Reith would still have a shot at the Lodge if it weren't for Fingers. I'd only just laid hands on the Ministerial telecard, purloined in Canberra. This kid had offered to trade it for a $300 bag of worthless herbs and lawn clippings, explaining that it was as good as cash to those in the know. To confirm his story, we found a pay phone and I called up my friend Sputnik, resident as always at the Crazy Horse gentleman's club in Adelaide. The call went through no problemo. I pocketed the card and the kid placed within his possession a couple of ounces of dessicated prickles and oregano.

I had planned to negotiate a handover to Anxious Stan, who was sure to take it in lieu, or at least as part payment for my debts. But I ran into Fingers outside Jupiters and when he heard about the score he insisted we celebrate. Everything sort of turned pear-shaped from there. We found a bar and bought a couple of rounds and then Fingers waved over the bartender, an English back-packer.

'Ever see one of these things mate?' he asked, placing a hand on my arm before I could protest.

The barkeeper turned Reithy's telecard over a few times and shrugged. Of course he had.

'So if we were to tell you the PIN here, and let you have the card number, you'd be able to call up the Old Dart for free just about any time you wanted, wouldn't you?' said Fingers.

He clued in immediately. 'Would you gents like another drink?'

'A couple of bourbons,' said Fingers.

'And how would you like to pay for that?'

We both looked at each other.

'Plastic,' we smiled.

Neither of us paid any attention to the dishevelled Santa who eyed the transaction from the other side of the bar. And we paid him no heed over the next few hours as he sat nursing a single beer, watching us fall into alcoholic disrepair courtesy of Peter Reith and the lax accounting procedures of the Department of Finance.

Fingers did mutter, 'Piss off Loody', when jostled on the way back from calling his mother in Florida, but it was another two hours before we realised the telecard and that gruesomely deformed Santa Claus were gone. By then the card details had been handed over to all the bar staff, Fingers' mum (who subsequently put it to good use in her lucrative mail fraud business) and some old chick at the end of the bar who showed us how she could fit a whole stubbie into her mouth.

I did get that card back, after some trouble. We caught up with Loody in Coffs Harbour, when he fell asleep in a McDonalds drive-thru, in a stetch-limo full of home brew and prescription drugs. But I guess we don't have time to go into that now. Fingers, for anyone who's interested, eventually took a consultancy shuffling voter enrolment cards for my distant cousin, Lee, in Queensland. And the last I heard of Loody he'd stolen a high-tech aluminium running leg from a Spanish Paralympian who didn't really need it.

Oh well. Sorry about that Reithy.

OLD FLATMATES AND
SKANKY HO'S

I wish now that I had kept the letter. It was such a fine example of the genre: exotic, startling, and more than a little scary. I received it care of the *Independent Monthly*, a long-dead magazine where I was holed up a few months after *Felafel* had been published. At first I thought it was just one of those things which come your way when you're out there in print, giving it up for the punters on a regular basis. I'd received my fair share over the years and until that point my favourite had come in response to a *Penthouse* feature I'd written about a former politician who'd been convicted of going the fiddle with underaged girls. That letter began: 'Dear Grub. Oh my, what a waste of talent you are!'

This new letter did not begin on such a promising note. In the first few lines the young woman who wrote it assured me that she was not in the habit of doing anything so lame as writing fan letters to a favoured author. But a fan letter this was, she confessed. So much had she enjoyed

He Died with a Felafel in His Hand that she'd been photocopying enormous chunks of the text to show her friends. At this point I'm thinking with some chagrin, thanks for nothin', you skanky ho. But things improved rapidly from the second paragraph. Here she revealed that this was not just a fan letter and that she was indeed a skanky ho. For this was an invitation. To have sex with her.

I've had sex with a quite a few chaps, she wrote. (I'm quoting from memory here but believe me, it's a clear memory.) I had sex with a chap once because I really liked his shoes. I had sex with another chap because he had a nice chest. Anyway, I don't know whether you have great shoes or a nice chest, but I'd like to have sex with you. If you're ever in Surfers Paradise and have a spare fifteen minutes feel free to give me a call.

She then listed her phone number and address. There were any number of points at which this whole business could unbalance a young chap. The strange use of the arcane term 'chap', for instance. Was I dealing with some sort of mental case from an Adelaide private girls school? And this frankly ridiculous guff about fifteen minutes? I don't want to blow my own horn, so to speak, but 'Hells Bells!' I muttered darkly, I'd half a mind to make this wanton trollop boogie oogie oogie till she just couldn't boogie no more. Alternatively, I figured we could give away the letter as a subscriber prize for the magazine. Sign up for twelve months' home delivery and you could win a chance to be JB for fifteen minutes.

Steve Congerton, the publisher, was very keen, but there were a few other highly placed anti-fun types who put the zap on my scheme. Something about being prosecuted for false and misleading conduct. But we weren't misleading the punters, I argued. Just some whackjob in Queensland with a shoe fetish and a spare quarter hour. Whatever. Nothing came of it and the *Independent* folded shortly afterwards. Needlessly, in my opinion.

For me it was an early introduction to the power of that weird little book. I'd written it for the advance, four grand, and although I thought it would sell well enough in the inner city and perhaps in Brisbane, my old stomping ground, I never once imagined that it would mutate into the monstrous, self-supporting life form it has become. The early signs were entirely discouraging. I was bitch-slapped at my own book launch by the fearsome wife of a prominent novelist. And that was pretty much the extent of the excitement until the appearance of one witheringly negative review in *Black + White* magazine, the spiritual home of humourless self-importance. I've been searching for the author of that piece ever since, intending to lay my vengeance on him. But he seems to have slipped into a vacuum even colder and darker than the one for which he suggested my poor little book was headed. So contemptuous and certain of its total lack of any redeeming features was he that I later developed a comedy routine which consisted of simply deadpanning the review with an occasional raised eyebrow to a room full of *Felafel* fans. After seeing me do it once, Luke Davies said he was so taken with the audience response that he dug out the worst reviews of *Candy* and started bagging himself out on stage too.

In the beginning, however, it seemed that *Black + White*'s

know-nothing know-it all might well have been right on the money. *Felafel* trickled into a few bookstores and promptly died a nasty, twitching, quiet little death. None of the chains would touch the ghastly yellow thing and the small number of brave independents who did take it complained about the odd shape. The first print run was square, like a pizza box. It was my idea of doffin' me lid to Douglas Coupland's *Generation X*, which partly inspired *Felafel*. Poor Michael Duffy, the publisher, was reduced to driving around Sydney in a beat-up old station wagon, flogging copies of this dead dog from the back like stolen car stereos, while squads of my friends and flatmates were dragooned into phone calls to a long list of bookshops demanding to know why they weren't stocking The Masterpiece. When sales assistants foolishly offered to order it in, my crew would claim they needed at least a hundred copies. Michael had printed 8000, an enormous run for a first book in Australia. He arrived at that figure because that's how many he could afford to print before it bankrupted him. Standing before a mountain of unsold *Felafels* in the distributor's warehouse, he nearly wept while some grizzled old storeman patted him on the back and muttered something like, 'Aye, it's a tough game is publishin', son.'

To this day I have no idea why that mountain of books began to run out the door. Given the lack of media attention, both Michael and I can only ascribe it to the almost mythical power of word of mouth. We gave away a couple of hundred copies to cafes and hairdressers where we thought potential readers might be found with a bit of time on their hands, and this was successful in a left-handed sort of way. The freebies were all quickly stolen. At one point I was reduced to shamefully sneaking around Darlinghurst in the wee hours, sliding copies under the front doors of obvious share houses where I thought it might get a good reception. Maybe it helped. Maybe it was just sad and a little pathetic.

There was no point at which we suddenly realised *Felafel* had come to life, crawled off the slab and gone shambling out of the laboratory to terrorise the simple village folk. But if pop-cultural mavens were looking for a convenient moment of acceleration I think they could do worse than examine the day a bunch of unemployed theatrical scam artists fronted me in the Tropicana Cafe in Kings Cross and asked whether they could have the stage rights to *Felafel*. They'd managed to finagle themselves onto some dubious make-work scheme in the dying months of the Keating government, about twenty of them pooling their dole cheques to set up a theatre company. The training component of this outrageous fraud on the taxpayer consisted in part of adapting a book to live performance. It was supposed to run to a minimal audience of long-suffering friends and relatives in the week before Christmas. After catching the first gig in a largely empty pub I wondered whether they'd see out the week and congratulated myself on the hard-headed business sense which had seen me charge them an up-front licensing fee of one hundred dollars. Five years later they tell me it's the longest running play in Australian history. At one point last year it was showing in three cities simultaneously. My busy little welfare monkeys had set up a franchise operation and reanimated the corpse of lowbrow pub theatre into the bargain.

There are some actors who found full-time employment through the latter half of the nineties pretending to be old flatmates of mine. There are some punters who've been sucked so deeply into the vortex of the play that they've been to see it over a dozen times. And there are a few dozen actual flatmates who've had the unsettling experience of seeing their worst moments portrayed on stage. At best their reactions are rueful. I suspect that Steve le Marquand, the character cum character actor who has somehow ended up with all the theatrical rights to the book—the contract which was originally written on the back of a beer mat says something about from this day to the heat death of the universe—will end up making a lot more money than me out of all this. Not that I really care. The idea that more than fifty actors have so far turned a quid off my dissolute couch-dwelling period is deeply satisfying in its own right. (As is the knowledge that they occasionally spike Le Marquand's onstage bucket bong with a tightly packed cone of the finest purple heads. When you've been playing the same role for so long I guess you have to make your own fun.)

As for the flatmates themselves—the fridgepissers, bong pullers, scam artists and whackjobs—what of them? Mostly, we're still friends. There are one or two who didn't get the joke. But then again, they never did. Curiously enough they're some of the characters who made the transition to film with the least difficulty or mutation. Remembering Dirk and Nina's violent showdown over the

Tiny Teddies, I shudder to think what they'll make of their big screen debut. The rest of them? Well, there was a deal of unseemly revelling in their nano-celebrity. There were even some poor, sad cases who claimed to be characters in the book, whom I've never actually met, let alone shared a house with. For some reason Adelaide seems to have more of these nutters than anywhere else.

After thirteen or fourteen editions, however, I find the nutters are thick on the ground all over. It's surprising the number of people who think it's endearing, rather than deeply disturbing, to approach you in a bookstore and commence a word perfect recitation of whole chapters of *Felafel*. Like Monty Python freaks, doing their favourite sketch. Usually with a messianic glimmer to their eye and just a hint of terrible consequences should you question them or begin to back slowly towards the exit. And I still occasionally receive offers like the one from my friend in Surfers Paradise, fifteen minutes of rumpy pumpy to brush up against my fifteen minutes of highly marginal fame. Sometimes folks will just sidle up after a reading or one of my very rare cameos in the stage play, offering a joint or a tab. And I don't really mind that. I'd like to encourage it actually, except that my good lady wife she done cured me of my wicked ways. And I don't even mind listening to people's flatmate stories, because there's always the chance they might surprise me. But ladies, before you waste your time slipping those phone numbers into my pocket, or blocking out a spare quarter hour in your busy schedule, just ask yourselves the same thing I do. Where the hell were you when I was actually living that life the first time around?

THE MAN WHO FELAFEL
TO EARTH

I guess I sort of imagined they'd cast Keanu as me. Or at least Adam Sandler. You know, at a pinch. And Winona as the sensitive but spunky gothic chick. Who I'd make out with. And maybe Bridget Fonda as the psycho flatmate. Who I'd make out with too, even though it would be Wrong and Dangerous. Bridget Fonda would have been kind of cool, I thought. Like an inverted cross-reference to *Single White Female*. And my mate Big Bob, who came home to find the new guy sniffing everyone's underwear, well, I figured Arnie was a shoo-in for Bob. And Bobcat Goldthwaite as Taylor the taxi driver. At first I thought either Cheech or Chong would have done sterling service as The Decoy. It wouldn't matter which because I get them confused all the time anyway. But then I thought it'd be really cool if Smelly Todd from *Big Brother* took on that role. And Michael Stipe from REM was a lay-down for Gay Dirk. The resemblance is amazing, believe me. And Nick Cave as Nick Cave. And perhaps Sophie Lee as Crazy Nina.

Oh well. At least they did get Soph. And she nailed that whackjob flatmate to the wall too.

The soundtrack would have been really cool too. You know. If they'd let me have a say in that. I'd have laid down lots of Bachman Turner Overdrive for starters. Well, lots of 'Takin' Care of Business' anyway. I figure you can put down eight or nine versions of that baby and you're only just starting to explore the possibilities. Sure, your Mobys and your Spiderbaits are fine for a B-side. But if you owned a popular music shop I don't reckon you could stock enough copies of an entire CD stuffed with extended remixes of 'Takin' Care of Business'. The kids today, they just love that lumbering, guitar-driven rock'n'roll. It's like a symbol of their individuality and rebellion.

But I can see from your frozen grin and a hint of panic around the eyes that you're beginning to empathise with Richard Lowenstein. I seem to recall the same look in Richard's eye too, as he backed slowly towards the door after foolishly inviting me to help out in the early stages of the *Felafel* film. Reminds me of the note of extreme caution in the voice of his agent, as she explained that we'd only write me into the contract as a script guy for the first draft or two 'because it might turn out you hate script writing'.

Or it might turn out that I'm totally crap at it too. As, in fact, it did.

The terrible saga of the meat patty is a good example. The patty is still in the film. A scary but strangely alluring goth chick—Winona, in my version, Romane Bohringer in Richard's—tries to move into a skanky all male house in Brisvegas. While she's interrogating the lads about whether the fridge has ever had any meat in it, they're all trying to ignore the greying mincemeat patty hanging from the ceiling directly above her like the Sword of Damocles. In my film Winona looks up and the patty takes a kamikaze dive right into her pretty moosh. I've still got the scar lines from where they had to operate on me because I hurt myself laughing so much when I first imagined that scene. But Richard remained unmoved by its comedic brilliance.

And there was the rub, from the very first days of our very brief collaboration. My sense of humour was entirely lowbrow and undergraduate. Richard's was more sort of upper–middlebrow and postgraduate. He would become quite excited at the prospect of referencing the films of Hal Hartley, while I'm like, 'No way dude! Lets reference *Porky's 7* and *Police Academy 6*. And while we're on the topic, we could really do with some more Bachman Turner Overdrive on the soundtrack, too.'

It seemed to me that I was cranking out jokes about farts and lesbians like a goddamn sausage machine but my poor little sausages were just hitting the floor and dying in the dust. It was not long before we moved into tantrum territory. When Richard floated the idea of Noah Taylor taking the lead I quietly brain-spasmed. To my way of thinking Noah would bring way too much sensitivity and intelligence to the role. And more importantly, he was a little guy. We'd probably kill him, force-feeding him all the T-bones and banana thickshakes he'd need to bulk up enough to play me.

The epic hissy fit came the day I laid hands on the fifth or sixth draft of the screenplay and discovered an ensemble cast of characters, none of whom I could recall appearing in the book. I began to fear another *Welcome to Woop Woop* was in the offing and in a fit of pique and panic rang Richard to give him what for. Unfortunately I was so twisted out of shape by then that I managed to unwittingly negotiate away two-thirds of my payment for the film rights in return for taking my name off the credits. Later, when my own agent tersely pointed out what I'd done, I think we could say I'd hit bottom. The page to screen experience didn't get any more dire than that. I had thought when I signed the original deal that I was standing at the foot of my personal Big Rock Candy Mountain. But in fact I was about to hitch a lift down to the seventh level of hell.

And whose fault was this? The producers'? The director's? The agent's?

No, I think we all know who's responsible. I doubt that if you searched from this day to the ending of the world you would find a more naïve and ignorant moo cow of an author than I was when I stepped through the looking glass into Movieland. I honestly believed that I would get absolutely everything I wanted and a big sack o' cash to lay my weary head on at the end of the day.

I think the solitary nature of book writing leads a lot of us to underestimate the difficulties of working with a hundred different people, each with their own agenda—as you must in film. I recently emailed Linda Jaivin, whose book *Eat Me* was optioned soon after it came out in 1995, to compare war stories. *Eat Me* had 'only just got script funding from the AFC,' she said. 'I knew movie-making was a slow business, but I never imagined it'd be THIS slow.

My agent tells me that this time frame is actually considered "quite fast". Imagine that. The process is a bit like watching one of those ponderous Swedish films—frame by frame—but without any aesthetic compensation whatsoever.'

So I did poor old Richard a grave disservice over the five years he struggled to get his work to the screen. I was one of those terrible bastards who stands just behind your shoulder while you're working on something, bitching and moaning that you don't like the way it's turning out before the work has even moved off the back of a napkin. I know now that both Lowenstein and Taylor suffered heroically to get their film in front of an audience, that if it hadn't been for years of sacrifice on both their parts there would be no film today. They did a lot of work for free in the final stages, when the cupboard was bare, and even now a good deal of the promotional material is being funded out of their own pockets. Given that I wrote the book in just five weeks with a lot of help from friends and flatmates, it's really kind of shameful now to think that I was down on those guys for so long.

And, in the end, I was pleasantly surprised when I viewed the final cut to discover just how much I liked their take on my book. There will be plenty of *Felafel* fans who don't like it, who say it isn't true to the text. But that book has no story line, almost no dialogue and no characters who hang around for more than a page or two. Given those constraints, and the fact that Richard ended up using quite a few of my jokes, I had to admit he done good. But I still think it would have been a lot cooler if he'd used 'Takin' Care of Business' as the opener.

BEACH BLANKET MASSACRE

You might remember my friend the Decoy. The Decoy was this guy I knew, a lightning rod for bad vibes and harassment. It was mostly from guys with badges and guns and an attitude surplus, but pretty much anyone who felt like it was free to kick in. You'd be walking down the street with the Decoy when he'd suddenly jackknife over and fall to the ground because some lunatic had slammed a fist into him as they passed. This madman would be all over him, dancing a frenzied hobnailed cha-cha on his ribs and screeching like some weird space alien with Tourette's Syndrome about how the Decoy might have thought he could get away with it but this guy knew all about him. And his plans. Oh yes, he knew! He fucking knew! And the loon would continue until he got tired or distracted, or just plain forgot what he was doing there, and wander off without ever having laid a finger on you.

You shouldn't get the idea that the Decoy would go around looking for trouble though. It's more that trouble came looking for him with sniffer dogs and a death warrant. The Decoy, you see, is this fully preserved *Flintstones*-era hippy. Got himself a greying ponytail and this little pot-shaped lentil belly and, unlike most of the boomer scum he grew up with, the Decoy never actually got with the Program. Never wised up. Never came on board for the big win, as they say. Worse still, he speaks in this soft Canadian accent and presents with a sort of wounded Bambi demeanour which affects cops and psycho-killers in pretty much the same way, like a bucket of fresh chum thrown into a tank full of hungry mako sharks.

The Decoy and I crossed paths during one of my slacker periods when I was just spooking round the campus video game room and kicking back on the verandah at the Student's Club for nine, maybe ten hours a day. I had this cruisey summer job back then, reading newspapers for a clipping agency. I'd browse all the metro dailies and put little X's next to the stories which were interesting enough to warrant filing. They had a list of topics we were supposed to follow, mostly politics and war and stuff like that, but I liked to throw them a curve ball every now and then, mark up something like the obituary of this totally bogus Irish soothsayer who invented the practice of Mammarism, also known as 'chest clairvoyance'. He figured to read a female client's future by painting her boobs and pressing them against a sheet of paper to get an imprint which he could then study. My personal unclassifiable fave, though, was this little piece about a factory which cranked out generic brand prefab frozen pizzas until the local council realised it had clogged the sewage system with about 18 000 tonnes of pizza sludge. They couldn't even bury the stuff in case it 'moved' in the ground and, say, swallowed up a whole housing development or something.

That job was the sweetest set-up. It really let me explore the whole 'man of leisure' scenario. There was a drawback in that I had to get there about five in the morning, but they always put on gallons of thick, tar-like, scalding hot coffee and a jumbo feast of sticky buns and sugar hits. I'd come roaring out of that place about ten or eleven in the morning, completely wired on Colombian Roast and jelly donuts, a free man looking for trouble. Mostly I'd have a swim then head to the Club for a couple of beers and a burger with the works, some hot greasy meat and a soothing ale to smooth the jagged edges of my massive predawn stimulant binge. And that, by way of a long and winding road, is how I came to meet the Decoy. He was my boss at the clip joint, and a finer boss I could not have wished for. The man was an anarchist, did not believe in hierarchical structures at all, and would take the most egregious slackness and back chat from his self-centred, ungrateful, Gen X workforce.

Sadly for us drones, however, the Decoy kept poor company. He lived in a decaying, eighteen-room house with an outlaw cabal of public broadcasters, drug addicts, losers, drunks and political activists. Make a long story short, he had to flee after the drug squad or Special Branch or the Premier's Own Praetorian Guard or something came through the windows before dawn one morning and threatened to execute every fucking one of them who didn't get a haircut and start driving trucks for their country. So the Decoy takes the hint—sort of—loads up his Combi and makes a midnight run for the coast. Plans to hang with some aging hipsters he knows down there. Got themselves this commune going in the Gold Coast hinterland. A very low profile affair up in the rainforest. Great views of the sea and all approach roads.

The Decoy got word to me back at the clipping room that he'd legged it out of Dodge and asked if I could bring down some stuff he'd left at the office; his string bag, spare sandals, and a half a box of Jamaican cigars. (His one vice. He liked to toke up with a black coffee after his lunch.) On the one hand, I'm thinking: Bummer, now they're gonna put some fascist dickwad in charge of this place. On the other hand I'm thinking: Excellent! A new place to crash for Schoolies Week or a casino run.

The Decoy's friends had this old, highset house in the rainforest, way up on stilts, with a tree growing up through the middle of it. What had happened was that some old guy had originally slung this canvas arrangement about two or three foot off the ground under the house. It was much more complicated than a hammock, more like a hanging tent with separate rooms and everything. He'd also planted a palm tree at some stage so he could stick his head out and pluck dates. But of course the tree wouldn't grow under the house. So the hippies had cut this big square out of the lounge room floor, then another one out of the ceiling, and then the roof. This whole house had been opened all the way through so this joker could grow his sticky dates. When you walked into the lounge there was a four-foot-wide path around this big hole. You'd sit around the edge of the wall and watch the top of this little tree trying to make it to freedom. First time I went round, to take the Decoy his stuff from the office, I saw this big canvas thing hanging from the underside of the floor. I'm standing there scratching my head, thinking, what madness is this, when this old guy swings out on a rope, completely starkers. Nuts hanging free and everything.

'Hi there!' he goes. 'Beautiful day.'

You got used to it though. You'd often go round for a visit and find the place full of naked hippies. And you'd have to be very cool about it too. Instead of gawking and running off at the mouth you'd have to sit there, pretending to chill while the breasts of some totally nude forest nymph smacked you in the head as she bent over to top up your peppermint tea or eco-cino.

I'm only telling you all of this so you can put the Decoy in context. The basic thing you've got to understand is that the Decoy is a very gentle, very non-confrontational sort of guy. A live and let live, to each his own, whale watching, soybean eating, tuned into the cosmic concert sort of guy. I said before he had only one vice that I know of, the cigars? In fact he had two. The Decoy's other deadly sin was cards. The man was a demon for blackjack. He loved the game, and that love almost finished him. But not in any way you're likely to imagine.

Jupiters at Surfers Paradise was, as far as I can recall, my first legit Casino, and I've seen some desperate fucking action at their tables. I'm not one for the cards myself, you understand, but I've known some in my time. The Decoy for one. And 'Fingers' for two. Fingers is in Thailand now, hiding from a bunch of Lebanese builders who were compounding fifty points on the dollar for short-term loans to hapless card counting losers who couldn't keep track of their sums. But one of the last times I saw him he'd been down at Jupiters, doing okay, when he hit his groove and shot two grand up in about half an hour. Man, we shoulda took that money and run. But we didn't, and in not doing so we set out on a journey of nearly three thousand miles, to madness, deliverance and back.

Now, as I said, I'm not much of a gambler. Haven't got the nerve for it. But Fingers had been buying drinks all night that night, and when he flipped me a hundred dollar note and told me to go wild, I was drunk enough to shrug and figure what the hell. I threw that grey nurse at the dealer. Three quick hands. The house bust on two of them and I made blackjack on the last. The tiny crowd which had gathered to watch exhaled in excitement. Damn! I figured. I'm walking with the King. I must have been up five or six hundred by then, all in the space of a few minutes. The quiet but annoying voice of reason—kind of a whining little Johnny Howard at the back of my mind— kept nagging at me to take the money and run, to be comfortable and relaxed with what I already had. But the roaring drunken Visigoth of my greed smacked him down, yelled to a waitress for another hogshead of ale and told me to keep my arse where it was until I broke the house and had a pit full of casino goons at my feet, squealing like stuck pigs and howling for mercy.

Fingers had quit the table by then, a slight tingling at the tips of his fingers warning him to back off. He couldn't stand hanging around and not playing though, so he decided to ghost me, started pushing out bets on my bets. I chipped up and went for the max. I got a split and a double down. Bam! Another four hundred unearned dollars. All right! I'm thinking, This is meant to be! This is where we make the big league. Where we become rolled gold Masters of the Universe. Where the horny casino babes appear at my elbow and ask breathily, Is zis zee only game you like to play Mistah Bond?

And then our luck turned rancid. Instantly. We started going down in flames on these excruciatingly big bets, gave them back every cent we'd won in the space of three heart-beats. We walked out into a hot close night, both of us completely busted, both cursing the Casino and ourselves and saying it's a mugs game, never again, you know. It was 4.30 in the morning. We kissed off the idea of a consola-tion six-pack down in the dunes. Just jumped into Fingers' car and drove off. I'm laughing at him. He's laughing at me. We're like, Never Again. We spent the entire drive shit-canning gambling and gamblers. Then, when we made the tollway on the outskirts of Brisbane I discovered ten bucks in a shirt pocket. I couldn't believe it. It was so late. I was half blind. I felt like shit. But Fingers' face just lit up. He put that car into a screeching, smoking powerslide, howled through degrees one hunnert and eighty and thundered back towards the coast, into the rising sun, chasing our lost three thousand with this ten dollar note. We marched in, laid it down, and two minutes later we're back in the car park having the same conversation. Never Again.

We just could not face another drive to Brisbane and we were shit out of luck on the Strip so I say to Fingers that we should hit on the Decoy for bed and breakfast. He's like, 'Excellent idea JB.' So half an hour later we're bouncing over a rutted dirt track, past the handpainted sign which points the way out to hippy valley. The Decoy's Combi wasn't around, but blue smoke curled out of the kitchen chimney so I figured he might be making an early run into town for some leaf and twig bread or maybe some soy milk.

'Don't sweat it, Fingers,' I said, catching the flicker of concern which flashed across his face as he came to terms with top of the tree which emerged from somewhere within the middle of the old Queenslander.

'Yo! Tree Guy!' I shouted into the unnaturally well-lit house. 'What's cookin'?'

I moved through to the rear of the place, skirting the parapet in the living room. I heard Fingers mutter something like 'Sweet Jesus' as he stumbled, literally, across the renovations. Tree Guy was out the back with a sleepy-eyed nymph stoking an old wood-fired stove.

'Decoy around?' I asked, entering the room.

'Nope.'

Tree Guy, normally generous with his hail fellow well met routine, just shook his head then and pointed at their battered answering machine. The wood nymph keyed the play function and Decoy's voice—disjointed and panicked—filled the kitchen.

'What's goin' on?' asked Fingers, who wandered in at the end of the message.

'Fingers,' I said. 'A brother is hurtin'.'

'Huh?'

'To the batmobile. There's not a minute to lose.'

'But . . . uhm,' said Fingers, sort of nailed to the floor and heedless of the small tendril of drool dropping slowly from his lips. Unexpected naked wood nymphs before breakfast will do that to a guy.

Stray morning mists held soft against the land as we boomed down through the Tweed Valley. Not much traffic at that time of day so Fingers pushed his beloved, black HQ Holden through a fantastic rippling world which climbed steadily up into the ranges of northern NSW. We were both tired, dirty, unshaven and wired. We had not had time to change from our formal casino rig, but they're used to a little weirdness around these parts and the drive-thru crew at McDonalds did not so much as blink at the two crazed and vaguely criminal types in black tie ordering up six egg McMuffins, a dozen black and super-sugary coffees and half their back room stock of McDonaldland Cookies.

'How's the Decoy fund holding out?' asked Fingers around a mouthful of McMuffin.

I flicked through the big, creased envelope we'd picked up from his room. Inside were an unemployment benefit claim, a piece of note paper with an address and phone number, about two hundred and seventy bucks in notes and a top-up from the phone change jar. We'd tipped that in as we were leaving. Said it was an emergency and Tree Guy agreed.

'I think we got enough,' I said. 'You ever been to St Kilda?'

'Nah,' said Fingers. 'But I figure if we keep the ocean on the left-hand side of the car we got to hit it eventually.'

'Sound thinking.'

I loosened my bow tie and cummerbund and settled into my meal on wheels. I'd catch flashes of the morning sun on the Pacific as we ripped through the scenery. I wondered if we'd get there in time. Wondered how the Decoy gets himself into these things. But I already knew the basics of that, and although the details really came later I figure you may as well know too.

The Decoy had met this girl, Jesse, on the rebound, and after they'd been going out for a week or so she suggested they go to Melbourne for a holiday. Said they could stay with friends of hers who had this big old place on the beach at St Kilda, just across from Luna Park. This huge white Victorian terrace with about a million bay windows, she said. They could hang out in Acland Street, get drunk at the Espy, and perhaps drop down on the sand after dark for a little waterfront nookie. Now, the Decoy hadn't been to Melbourne before so he carefully answered yes, wary of the sort of trouble he could get into such a long way from home, but thinking that anything which took him out of Queensland had to be good and thinking, but not saying, that he might even be able to get away for a little blackjack action at the Crown tables. Nothing serious, you understand, just a little low-rolling diversion for a couple of hours. A chance to smoke a big cigar and lay his accent on just a little bit thicker.

Well, it started on the bus trip down. Jesse was drinking from a small bottle of brandy. She'd insisted they sit down the back of the bus, of course, because that's where your born-to-run badass road warrior types prefer to hang out when they have to take a Greyhound instead of a chopped hog. Somebody snitched, or maybe the driver had psychic powers or a really strong nose for cheap hospital spirits because they pulled over about three in the morning and he powered up the intercom to wake all the passengers with a booming announcement.

'Somebody's drinking.'

Well, forty or fifty of them turned as one and stared at the Decoy. Jesse wouldn't fess up of course. She just sat there, quite happy to let the driver tell the whole bus what a bad influence the Decoy was and how he should be ashamed of himself and how he'd be walking the rest of the way if it weren't ten below outside and he, the driver, would probably be charged with negligent homicide or something for turning him out. And the only thing for the Decoy to do is nod and mumble and 'yessir' at the driver because he's a path of least resistance guy and he knows that if he ventures from that path he'll be spending the night in a ditch by the side of the road because that's just the way the universe is.

Anyway, they get to Sydney, where there's a two-hour delay. They get off the bus and wander around and it only takes a few minutes before the Decoy realises he's left most of his money back on the Gold Coast along with his unemployment form and a covering letter from his local dole fascists allowing him to temporarily sign on down south. He'd given them some frantic bullshit about going to Melbourne to look for work and they'd shrugged and signed and stamped and thought 'fucking hippy' as they handed the paperwork to him with the blank, dead stare of the deeply indifferent. He told Jesse he needed to get to a phone to deal with this hassle, otherwise he'd run out of money before they even got there.

The coach had pulled into the Darlinghurst depot and they'd walked out into the grittier end of Oxford Street, the end where the sex shops and Yeeros bars have got it all over the fashion boutiques. Jesse, who seemed to have plenty of money, said she'd wait in a coffee shop while he went in search of a phone. There was supposed to be a bank of them in the terminal but they were all out of action because of building work. The Decoy meandered around, wary of getting lost with no money in a new city, finally spotting an old blue phone in the foyer of this gaudy little cinema. The guy in the booth looked like Jack Kerouac's demented older brother. He was tricked out in a tweed jacket that had every known form of human grease and snot wiped over it. A wet cigarette hung out of his mouth and a matted curl of pepper-grey hair obscured one eye. The Decoy smiled at him, said 'Just here to use the phone', but he didn't even move. He could have been a wax model with a real cigarette stuck in his mouth for effect.

So the Decoy gets on the phone to the dole fascists, makes his way through their defences, sneaks past the dopey receptionists, the couldn't-give-a-shit clerks, the clay-mores, the trip flares, the man traps and razor wire. He argues and begs and whines and cajoles and he finally gets on to somebody with the authority to help him out. But as he's babbling on to her about leaving his money and papers back in the Deep North this terrible moaning and groaning starts up, then this shouting, 'Oh yeah, do it to me. Do it to me. Harder baby. Harder. Do me like a horse.' He cringes and tries to cover the mouth piece. He ploughs ahead regardless, hoping it would die off. But it didn't. It kept going. Louder and louder and more perverse than before. The dole fascist is going, 'I beg you a pardon. I beg you a pardon.' To this day he remembers the odd way she said it. 'I beg you a pardon.'

She hung up when the horse fucker reached a crescendo. Left the Decoy with a dead phone in his hand and about eight cents to his name. He stared at the phone. Just leaned against the wall with his eyes bulging and a thin greasy sheen of sweat on his face, stared at the scarred and battered body of the phone, stared at the burns and slashes, the deep wounds and gouge marks. After a few minutes of staring and breathing and feeling his sanity drain out through the soles of his feet like ice water, the Decoy pushed himself off the wall and shuffled numbly out into the day. Grandpa Kerouac hadn't moved once.

The Decoy found Jesse, told her what had gone down. She shrugged, said it was a drag and all but at least she had some cash. She suggested they just head on down to Melbourne, crash for a few hours, get over the trip and then charge into the valley of DSS death again. The Decoy thought that was an outstanding suggestion. Jesse bought him a health food bar, they hopped back on the bus and pretty much dozed through the rest of the trip.

So they get to Melbourne. They do some walking, catch some trams (which the Decoy really digs), do some more walking and arrive at a seedy but sort of charming seaside strip less than an hour later. There's a big mad grinning Luna Park face just across the way. Some place called Greasy Joe's just around the corner. Trams everywhere. Seagulls. Food smells. The water and a sunset. Okay, thinks the Decoy, cool.

They stood out front of this big old dump which had been turned into a boarding house about twenty years ago. All the Decoy had been told was that it was a housing co-op and in the world he came from, anything with co-op stamped on it had to be good because co-ops were going to Smash The State. Okay, good, thought the Decoy. A co-op. Sounds fab. Jesse told him they'd be staying on the ground floor with a friend. Great, he said, your friend in the co-op.

They knocked on the door until it became obvious nobody was home. They walked around the back. Nobody home there either. So they broke in after Jesse assured him it would be okay. Been there, done this, been told it was cool, or something to that effect.

We'll cut to the good bit.

It had been a long bus ride, a day and a night. The Decoy was on the rebound. Hadn't had sex for six months or more. There was a mattress on the floor in the co-op. This girl was keen. So he was quickly talked into a shag on the floor of somebody's room in this strange house at the beach in St Kilda. Long as they changed the sheets afterwards it'd be fine, she said. So they are naked on the floor.

The floor of the co-op. Naked as the day they were born. They're doing the wild thing. They're getting right into it. There's bumping, grinding, biting and scratching. There's moaning, groaning, grabbing and jabbing. And then there's a scream.

'Jesus fucking Christ!'

And the Decoy knows it's not Jesse. He goes right up into the air, spins around like a cartoon character, comes down, lands next to her with a thump and sees the intruder, an intensely angry-looking bald woman in boots, dark purple leggings and a leather jacket.

'Hi. It's only me,' pipes up Jesse.

'And me,' adds the Decoy. 'We're friends.'

The woman barks that he's no friend of hers and if he doesn't get his filthy hairy hippy carcass up off her mattress she'll be wearing his balls for earrings. Gee, thinks the Decoy, that's a bit excessive. But he's reassured as the two woman, who are friends it turns out, embrace and greet each other warmly. The woman, whose name seems to be Ingrid, gives Jesse a sarong to wrap herself in while they touch and talk and excitedly catch up on each other's lives. The Decoy wasn't offered a sarong and after standing around being ignored for a few minutes he quietly covered himself with a cheap faux Persian door mat before skulking off into the other room where he'd left his back pack. He hurriedly put on some clothes and returned, a little red-faced but being as brave and English about everything as possible. 'So this is your place eh?' he ventured during a lull in the chatter. But Ingrid just glared at him, said she didn't know Jesse was going to be bringing somebody with her. They would have to talk it through to see if it was okay. Fantastic, thinks Decoy. What happens now? He goes back to Brisbane with his eight cents in his pocket?

Well, it took a while but Jesse did smooth things over. They agreed that yes, the Decoy was a jerk, and yes, it was a horrible, impossible imposition, but if he kept his mouth shut and his dick stowed he'd be allowed to stay. He could send them a rent contribution when he fixed up his dole back in Surfers. Okay. Fine. He was keen for a shower and figured nobody could object to him cleaning himself up so he asked for directions to the bathroom. They were collective facilities, of course, and they were on the second floor. He had to walk around to the front of the house to get access. So he grabbed his gear and made the trek and was starting to relax under a strong, hot shower when there was a really loud knock at the door, actually more of a thump, and someone yelled 'Would you get the fuck out of there! Other people have got to go.' He cursed softly under his breath, but it wasn't his place and he didn't want trouble so he got out and dressed quickly and emerged from the bathroom to be greeted with another, 'Jesus fucking Christ!'

Another large woman stood blocking his way, yelling at him, demanding to know what the fuck he thought he was doing. He hastily explained the situation. That he'd been on a bus for two days, and he left his money behind and . . . and . . . and . . . But she cut him off with a backhander to the solar plexus. Said she didn't give a fuck. Said to get the fuck out. Said if she caught him in there again she was going to cut his balls off and so on and so forth. The

Decoy hammered down the stairs with this information ringing in his ears. Wondering what is it with these women and his balls. They were nothing like the gentle beach people he'd been expecting. No friendly forest nymphs around these parts, it seemed. The Decoy scarpered around to Ingrid's room again, running out the front door, onto the street and around the back of the house, mortified at the stares of passers-by and terrified lest some ravenous seagull swoop down to tear off his vulnerable, freshly-scrubbed genitalia. It seemed to be all the rage around here. He came in all breathless and flushed, asked if there was a large, angry woman resident upstairs. Ingrid turned aggressively, 'Yeah, lots of them. What's the problem? What have you done?' The Decoy thinks, Oh shit, lots of them, so it's not just this dragon. There's a whole house full of these ugly angry women with their bad vibes and short hair and I'll probably have to . . .

. . . Oh! . . .

And then all became clear. This wasn't any old co-op. His girlfriend had brought him to St Kilda to spend the weekend in a lesbian separatist co-op. A place which had an absolute rule of no men under any circumstances. So, in fact, it was explained to him it was probably best if he didn't go to the toilet or the bathroom at all during his very short and uncomfortable stay here. He'd have to urinate out in the back alley for a couple of days. And number two's would have to wait until he found a public toilet. Perhaps at the Esplanade Hotel up the road.

The Decoy had to have a long sit down after that. He sat, swallowed up in his own private world for a good half

hour or so, until Jesse suggested they go out and find something to eat. And he didn't have to worry about having no
money. She'd lend him some. She was gentle with him,
didn't want to dump any more surprises on him. Said he'd
really enjoy eating out in Melbourne. It was a world class
city. Not like Brisbane. You could get anything you wanted
here. Pasta, vegetarian, Albanian, Chinese, Cajun, African,
anything. He slowly regained his composure. It wasn't so
bad. He could avoid the lesbians, keep out of their way,
avoid the house altogether in waking hours. Jesse could
lend him some money. He didn't need much. He was used
to being poor. And he was hungry. His tummy was actually
growling. Yes. A big hot feed was all that he needed. He
started to cheer up. He darkened briefly when Jesse mentioned that some of the wymyn might be tagging along, but
as she explained, they knew the area and it was their van
they'd be riding in. Okay, he mumbled. He would sit down
the back and practice becoming invisible, a skill he planned
to call on a lot during the next few days.

Half a dozen of them piled into the van a bit later and
drove around to Fitzroy Street looking for some new place
which Ingrid had just read about in *Brother Sister*. Riding
up and down the restaurant strip was torture for the Decoy,
who'd had nothing more than a couple of Tic Tacs and a
health food bar since leaving Brisbane. He could smell what
seemed like thousands of spices and exotic bouquets
wafting out of dozens of different ethnic eateries. His
mouth watered so much he could have gargled with his
own spit but when the van drew up outside some rustic cafe
and the doors slid open to allow everyone out, he found his

path blocked by some shaven-headed Suzie who asked him, predictably, where the fuck he thought he was going. He said, without too much hope, 'To fill my tum?' But she shook her head and told him she wouldn't step out if she was him. This was a Wymyn's Restaurant. So the Decoy sat in the car for a couple of hours, a bit too scared to get out and walk around. After all, he might be in the middle of a whole separatist neighbourhood. Best to lay low.

They came back after a while, climbed into the van smelling of garlic and red wine, announced they were off to a party. He pretty much knew what sort of party, but hope springs eternal. There's often food at parties. Maybe Jesse would bring some out to the van. Sure enough they rolled up to an old warehouse with boarded-up windows but lots of noise and light coming from inside. It had some name like The Place painted on a sign out the front. This 'Place' was jumping with people and lots of aggro sounding music. The Decoy was sure he could smell food. So sure he forgot himself and made to climb out.

'The fuck you think you're going?'

'That's horrible,' said Fingers, shaking his head after I gave him the shareware lite version of the Decoy's travails. 'Just horrible.'

'A trail of tears, my friend.'

'You really think we can get 'im?' he asked.

'Got the address in here,' I said, flicking the Decoy's forgotten envelope.

'Right,' muttered Fingers, hunching over the wheel and pouring on speed. 'Lets roll.'

The HQ's fat tyres bit deeper into the road as it growled, leaned forward and started to chew tarmac. We drove straight through, apart from a few petrol and toilet breaks and one stop at a BP road mart in Coffs Harbour where I bought us a case of Jolt Cola and a handful of speed from some Greek guy hauling five tonnes of frozen chicken up the edge of the continent. Fingers didn't bother with any questions when I offered him first pick from our small but power-packed selection of contraband pharmaceuticals four hours later. Just made a greedy lunge for them.

'Hey, these ain't fuckin' Smarties you know.'

He turned to face me as we barrelled down the road at about a hundred and sixty. Dark black smudges were starting to emerge under his swollen eyes.

'Sorry man,' he said. 'Bad sleep dep. Rack of LEM sleep. It's a killer, you know.'

'Eyes on the road Fingers.'

'Whoops!' he blurted, jerking the wheel to correct for a slight ten degree drift towards the shoulder.

We fish-tailed along for a while then settled back into a comfortable if fairly dangerous cannonball run through to Melbourne. The new dawn found us twenty miles out. We were in a bad way by then. Unshaven, unwashed. Still wearing our filthy black tie gear. Fucked on junk food, sugar, caffeine and drugs. Fingers was worse of course. He'd carried all of the driving (I don't have a licence) and gobbled the lion's share of the speed. Twitches and tics ran wild over his face and neck and words tumbled out in off-tone staccato riffs of increasingly borderline gibberish. Mostly semi-deranged bursts about 'evil bitches' and 'political

correctness' and 'ants crawling around under my skin'. Even
in my own advanced state of decay I worried that amphet-
amine psychosis would rear its ugly head before this day was
done.

Fingers wound it back a little as we hit the city grid.
After a couple of bad moments with the trams we settled
into a clean run through to the beach. The morning peak
hour was still a way off then and most of the traffic was
light commercial, delivery trucks and vans and so on. We
slipped around the Grand Prix circuit at Albert Park and
down onto Fitzroy Street. Port Phillip Bay lay flat and grey
at the end. Half a dozen street people shuffled aimlessly
about in front of Leo's pasta bar. We pulled up beside them
for a minute on a red light. Two fat old rummies were
arguing over a carton of box wine about 'strayan idennity'.
Seagulls fought over a pizza rind in the gutter.

'Down there and a left Mr Sulu,' I said as the light
changed.

'Aye cap'n,' he giggled.

Hmmm, I thought, watching him through narrowed
eyes. This was not a good look.

'How you figure we handle this, Fingers?' I asked carefully.

'A walk up snatch and grab. Straight in, straight out. No
prisoners,' he answered right off.

''Cept the Decoy.'

'Yeah right, 'cept him.'

O-k-a-a-a-y. Seemed reasonable. We pulled up in front
of the address written down in Decoy's jiffy bag. It looked
quiet. Too quiet. The sombre expanse of the Bay was

unsettling, an unnatural affront to Queenslanders brought up on booming swells and long curling surf beaches. It didn't smell salty or refreshing. Just kind of thin and oily. Fingers hopped out and started to button up his jacket, bouncing and rolling around on his loafers as his badly damaged nervous system cruised the jagged edge of meltdown. He threw my bow tie and 'bund at me.

'Better suit up, JB. A job worth doing is worth dressing well for.'

It was a fair enough idea, I thought, perhaps giving away a little of my own loose connection to the world of real things at that point. We smoothed our act out, shot our cuffs, spat in our hands, slicked back our hair.

'How you feeling Fingers?'

'Like a lean, mean avenging machine.'

'Wanna do it?'

'And how!'

We charged up the front path to shoulder the door off its hinges but pulled up just before impact. A note was stuck on next to the knob: 'Jackie. Can't do brekky. Gone down Station Pier to the warships protest. Meet us all there.'

We hammered on the door but no answer came. It was a heavy blow to Fingers' precarious sense of balance. He was twitching and shivering and going 'what the . . .' a lot. But I chilled him out. Said it was okay. Pointed off down the thin curve of St Kilda Beach to a huge grey mass laid up in the distance.

'Gotta be one of them US nukes visiting. They tie 'em up down at that pier where the Tasmania ferry takes off. Seen it on the news. These dykes musta taken off to protest 'em or something. Probably gonna throw a lot of fake blood over them. It'd be fake blood too you know cos these sort of women are always your hard core vegetarians. You can bank on it my friend.'

His shoulders jerked up violently.

'Damn! That makes *my* blood boil.'

We banged on the door one more time but you know that feeling you get when you're rapping at the door of an empty house? Well, we were way too drug-fucked to get that feeling but we were firing on eight cylinders each and ready to rock so we piled back into the big black Holden and made smoke towards the Dykes, the Decoy and a hundred thousand tonnes of nuclear armed American military might.

The beach whipped by in a blurred ribbon on my side of the car as we powered towards our final goal. Fingers' white knuckle wheel grip and crazed, bulging eyes raised the faint but worrying prospect that he might not stop when we reached the pier. Might just plow right into the massed ranks of screaming lefties. But the scene that loomed as we drew closer stopped even him. He jammed the brake pedal and took us into a barely controlled forty-metre-long skid. Madness and frenzied chaos played out in tableaux before us.

The anti-warship coalition had organised a huge demonstration for the early morning docking of the US battle cruiser. Hundreds of protesters had gathered in secret locations around the bay before dawn, receiving their instructions and equipment as Fingers and I had sped through the last hundred miles of our long journey. The equipment was simple. Animal suits, three types. Koalas, possums and cockroaches. Some forest group had lent the coalition two dozen furry critter costumes but that wasn't nearly enough to cover the one hundred activists who had volunteered to climb a temporary chain link fence and charge the cruiser in a weird piece of metaphoric protest theatre—you know, the marsupials of Australia don't want your weapons of mass destruction here. That sort of thing?

The press figured most of the details pretty quickly. The news that night explained that a sympathetic theatre worker from Sydney had access to a whole bunch of cockroach suits left over from a rugby league State of Origin promo and had sent them south on loan. At seven in the morning thirteen battered combi vans and minibuses had screeched to a stop outside the dock and with a call of 'Possums Ho!' the first wave of demonstrators stormed out of their improvised troop carrier and charged towards a couple of sleepy security guards.

Tactically it was a fine set of moves. The initial attack came from the centre vehicle and each subsequent wave from the next ones out, spreading the field of engagement beyond the small security detail's ability to cope. A couple of International Socialist possums, the shock troops of any well-planned protest, made straight for the guards while their comrades went for the fence. Then with a cry of 'Go bears go!' another series of doors rumbled back to disgorge another squad of determined native fauna. The koalas charged away as fast as their little legs and poorly fitting costumes allowed, which wasn't too well and quite a few tripped over each other.

Fingers and I climbed out of our car, jaws hanging slack, just staring as the rest of the convoy came to life with a rallying cry of 'Roaches Ho!' and dozens of giant insects swarmed towards the fence, which was already shaking and buckling under the weight of fifteen, maybe sixteen possums and koalas who were scaling it and dropping into the arms of the military police on the other side. We started to walk into the melee as the first of the roaches made the fence and sirens began to wail in the distance.

'Sweet mother of God,' muttered Fingers as the tide of roaches hit the fence and stopped dead. A quiet, curiously suspended bubble of time seemed to envelop the whole scene for a second, just before chaos broke out again and the roaches suddenly started running back and forth at the fence, bouncing off each other and the chain link barrier. It was like the unseen hand of God had sprayed them with a giant can of Baygon. You see, nobody had thought to cut arm holes into the costumes and the roaches' own limbs—sewn-on strips of plastic tubing—were useless when it came to scaling obstacles like a six-foot-high barricade. All they could do was to run back and forth, impotently crashing into each other and getting entangled while the first police units arrived to sweep them away.

'Over there, JB,' shouted Fingers, grabbing my arm and digging in painfully. A group of roaches which had emerged from a van a hundred metres away was standing around in obvious confusion. One stood a short distance apart from the others with its hood pulled back to reveal a greying pony tail and a preternaturally sour scowl.

'Decoy!' yelled Fingers and set off at full tilt, nearly

yanking me off my feet. I ran to catch up. Cockroaches turned to gape at the sight of two dinner-suited lunatics accelerating through the chaos. The Decoy gave a little start when he recognised us and tried to wave. Best he could manage, of course, was to shake his floppy roach tubing from side to side. A couple of hefty lesbians foolishly tried to block Fingers from his friend but, mad with sleep deprivation, food poisoning, dirty speed and moral outrage, he simply lowered his shoulders, charged and bellowed: 'Out of the way ladies, or feel the mighty prick of my pork sword!'

Two or three roaches went flying as he crashed in amongst them, grabbed the Decoy in a fireman's lift and came charging back. I turned and headed for the car. Last I saw of the Decoy's failed seaside holiday was a bunch of angry lesbian roaches knocked flat on their arses and struggling to get up again, little hairy brown legs peddling furiously away in the air.

We sat in the sand just up from the Kerford Road Pier nursing a six-pack and snacking down on the last of the McDonaldland cookies. The Decoy, happily engorged with cold junk food leftovers, stretched out in the sun, smoked a cigar and sighed heavily and often. I rifled through the envelope which he had left behind him in Queensland. There was about twenty-three bucks left. Not nearly enough to get us back home.

'Gentlemen,' I said. 'Next stop, the Casino.'

But that's another story.